More Advance Praise for
Great American Outpost

"An important addition to the literature of the US shale revolution—too often underestimated and misunderstood—*Great American Outpost* reminds us that the revolution is not just a story of frack fluid and oil production but a story of the human experience. Through Didionesque scenes of the North Dakota boom, Maya Rao evokes America in extremis with glimpses of lives and decisions that are sometimes frightening, sometimes inspiring, and sometimes just nuts."

—Gary Sernovitz, author of *The Green and the Black: The Complete Story of the Shale Revolution, the Fight over Fracking, and the Future of Energy*

"From the upper reaches of North Dakota, Maya Rao extracts a potent metaphor for modern American capitalism. Her bracing dispatch from the Bakken reveals the toll of fracking on everything it touches—from the soil of the Great Plains, to the precarious lives of roughnecks, to the remote communities that became boomtowns full of hustlers, dreamers, and opportunists. Keenly observed and vividly told, *Great American Outpost* also has an undercurrent of anxiety that seeps from abandoned oilfields into the larger landscape of our culture, in the form of a question few dare to ask: What remains when the profiteers move on?"

—Jessica Bruder, author of *Nomadland: Surviving America in the Twenty-First Century*

"I'm grateful for this stunning work of immersive reportage. Maya Rao tells us a tale from ground zero for modern American capitalism: the North Dakota oil rush, from boom to bust. It's a remarkable book for right now, mixing compelling portraits with smart, big picture analysis. Rao shows us stories that visiting reporters would likely miss, and the result is a rich, nuanced book that's a crucial guide to understanding twenty-first-century America."

—Tracie McMillan, author of *The American Way of Eating: Undercover at Walmart, Applebee's, Farm Fields and the Dinner Table*

"With oil at $100 a barrel, greed in North Dakota was manifest and the characters were right out of the Gold Rush, from some of the craziest get-rich crooks to the recently paroled who could make $90,000 a year hurling big trucks down two-lane roads. Maya Rao's description of one of America's biggest rushes of sheer greed ranks right up there with the great books of the California Gold Rush of 1849 . . . . This is one of the best books in America about working men and women—and life in the oilfields when the lid blows off."

—Humpy Wheeler, retired NASCAR promoter and former president of
Charlotte Motor Speedway

"Maya Rao didn't just write about the boomtown life, she lived it capturing the hope and despair of a nation of citizens looking for a break. A gimlet-eyed look at the oil, dust, and, most importantly, the people living on our country's last frontier. This is essential reading for anyone interested in how the American Dream or the American Nightmare can be made and lost in the blink of a two-week pay period."

—Stephen Rodrick, contributing editor to *Rolling Stone*

GREAT
AMERICAN
OUTPOST

GREAT
AMERICAN
OUTPOST

DREAMERS, MAVERICKS,
AND THE MAKING OF AN
OIL FRONTIER

MAYA RAO

PUBLICAFFAIRS
NEW YORK

PublicAffairs
Hachette Book Group
1290 Avenue of the Americas, New York, NY 10104
www.publicaffairsbooks.com
@Public_Affairs

Printed in the United States of America

First Edition: April 2018

Published by PublicAffairs, an imprint of Perseus Books, LLC, a subsidiary of Hachette Book Group, Inc. The PublicAffairs name and logo is a trademark of the Hachette Book Group.

The Hachette Speakers Bureau provides a wide range of authors for speaking events. To find out more, go to www.hachettespeakersbureau.com or call (866) 376-6591.

The publisher is not responsible for websites (or their content) that are not owned by the publisher.

Print book interior design by Amy Quinn.

Library of Congress Control Number: 2017044028

ISBNs: 978-1-61039-646-2 (hardcover), 978-1-61039-647-9 (ebook)

LSC-C

10 9 8 7 6 5 4 3 2 1

To my parents

Contents

PART I
THE ADVANCEMENT OF MAN

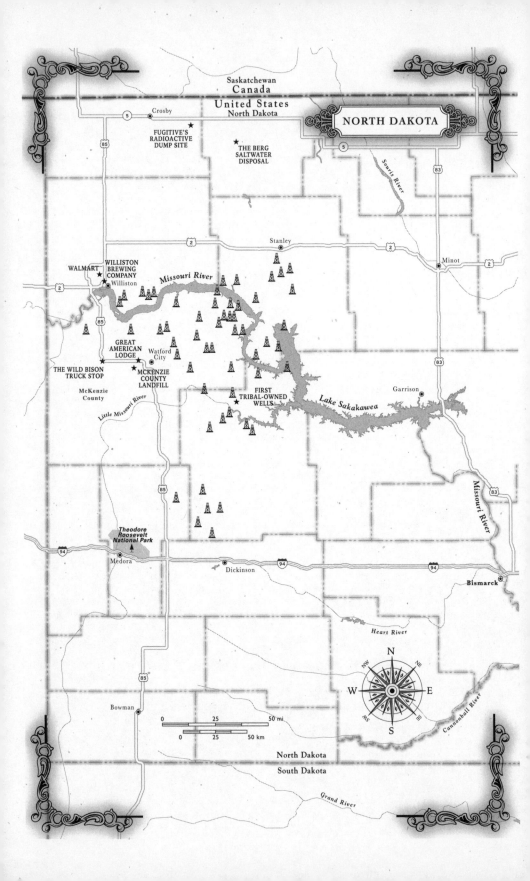

Introduction

*P*ast the abandoned shack that said GREAT FOOD FAST and FOR SALE, rows of trailers lay forsaken in the weeds. Laborers had run out of time to install the doors and windows in several dwellings, and rain seeped through the openings. Cement slabs marked parking spots that had no vehicles. The dining hall was locked; the boot scrubbers on the porch had no mud in their bristles. Federal authorities had evicted the tenants. A banner had begun to drag off the chain-link fence, the red lettering barely decipherable: GREAT AMERICAN LODGE.

Once a symbol of prosperity in the North Dakota oilfield, the lodge had become a gallery of fortune gone to ruin. Investors from Hong Kong to Madrid were reeling from revelations that their money had vanished in a $62 million Ponzi scheme. The British developers had disappeared overseas. Only the squirrels remained, running along the tarp and pallets that lay scattered in the grass. I drove by several times a week for much of 2015, looking, to no avail, for the smallest change; eventually the lodge loomed as just another landmark fringed by weeds along the highway. A Colorado real estate broker who did business with the swindlers told me they could have done well enough without scamming. "But no!" he said. "Greed, greed, greed!"

Artifacts of dreams abandoned have long strewn North Dakota's landscape: old farmsteads, shuttered schools, wood planks rotting in the prairie grass. The Northern Pacific Railway drove settlements along the tracks west of the Missouri River, but residents built too many towns, churches, farms, newspapers, and schools to support a society that never grew as populous as planned. Farmers struggled against blizzards and droughts and meager harvests. Some starved. Many fled. Half of North Dakota's communities were losing people by the 1930s, when the state's population peaked at nearly 681,000. Citizens clustered in the cities of Bismarck, Grand Forks, and Fargo. The western edge of the state faded into earthen bones as the young left for better prospects and the old died off. Loss and despair vexed the buttes and grasslands; it brooded in the savage emptiness and the derelictions of wood and blotched glass.

North Dakota's first oil discovery came in 1951 in the little town of Tioga, but the petroleum was difficult to extract profitably. A burst of oil development came in the 1980s, followed by a bust that stranded local governments with debt. By 2008, advances in hydraulic fracturing and horizontal drilling confirmed the largest domestic oil deposit since the discovery of the reserves under Prudhoe Bay, Alaska, four decades earlier. Billions of barrels of oil lay in the Bakken shale formation. Western North Dakota became an astonishing laboratory for the Darwinian, breakneck capitalism that one imagined was no longer possible in modern America, as outsiders engulfed the state to get rich, hide out, or start over. The state's population grew for the first time in the lives of even its most elderly residents.

Observers often compared it to the California Gold Rush, when hordes of people flocked to an untrammeled terrain to make their fortune and, unwittingly, redefine the American dream from a steady grind of work and thrift to a gamble that favored the bold. The journey to the West Coast by ox- or mule-drawn wagon was long and arduous in the 1840s, as gold-seekers fought cholera, hostile Indians, and starvation. Voyages by sea could be perilous. In modern times, the way to prosperity was unimpeded. Adventurers drove, hitchhiked, or rode the train to the great land north. There was little of the speculative nature of past booms. Nobody wildcatted anymore—companies knew where the oil was and had the technology to extract it. Newcomers were almost guaranteed to find a job as long as they could pass a drug test, and if they couldn't, those were easy enough to fake. North Dakota was again at the whims of exploitative outsiders, a half century after historian Elwyn Robinson claimed that the state's remoteness had established it as a colonial hinterland dependent upon faraway markets.

Journalists from around the world came to North Dakota, often for just a few days. I was one of them, traveling from Minneapolis to the oilfield for a week in 2012. Yet most news stories could never capture the reality of it—the Bakken defied mainstream explanations. That place was an outpost of outcasts and dreamers and geniuses, an unending paradox in what it meant to be American, a phenomenon that called for nuanced reporting that captured the hopeful and the dark and the absurd. North Dakota! What a wild frontier. Who were all these people rushing in, and why? I tried to imagine the civilization they would build and its trajectory when the frenzy went away, the things the pioneers would leave behind. How might the natives regulate mass industrialization when they were so resistant to government intrusions, so protective of their own liberties? Observers always said this would be studied in history classes a century from now, and history demands a book.

I began going to North Dakota to pursue these inquiries more seriously in May 2014, stopping for gas near Fargo off Interstate 94, where there would invariably be some shifty-eyed man at the next pump over—probably just out on parole—and I would know, without either of us saying a word, that he was bound for the oilfield six hours across the state. *That look*. Freedom, desperation, adventure, meth, money . . . it was perhaps the only time I would harbor a vague respect for a gas station ruffian. There was something so brave about heading out there that who one was mattered far less than that he was headed to the Bakken at all, and this was the truism that bound everyone.

It was such a novel place, so inscrutable to those who'd never been, that the oilfield remained a secondhand story even to inhabitants of the more populous eastern edge of the state. Farmers and barflies I met on the way out warned against going out there—not that they had ever been, but they'd heard all about it. Seen it in other ways. Take Casselton, the little town where an oil train derailed in 2013 causing an inferno so tremendous that people could feel the heat through their windshields a half mile away. The following year, oil began displacing the farmers' crops on the tracks, delaying their transport of grain. "Warren Buffett can go screw himself," several farmers told me, alluding to the billionaire's ownership of the Burlington North–Santa Fe railroad. They already had a dim impression upon hearing of oil workers who'd make $17,000 in a month or two, fly to Las Vegas, then come home broke and eat ramen noodles. And another fellow from Casselton speaking of the supposed violence: "You wanted to go to a bar and have a beer—physical assault charges are up . . . and someone's going to beat you up? You can go get a six-pack and sit home and watch *Wheel of Fortune*."

One could travel there by taking the interstate all the way across North Dakota, then going up Highway 85, which formed the backbone of the oilfield and ran 1,479 miles from El Paso to the Canadian border. But to really understand the place, a traveler ought to make a series of northern and westerly turns from Jamestown and its iconic buffalo sculpture, into long and green hollows of feral quiet that ran hundreds of miles. Get out in some smudge of a town like Harvey to fill the tank again—shiver in the eyes of stillness that beamed over that endless expanse—retreat to the car as if to escape forces that would pull a human interloper into the fissures of the earth. Remember this upon arriving at the western flank of the state, where trucks and rigs and men ran roughshod and nature was the trespasser.

I spent seven weeks in the oilfield during 2014, including a stint cashiering at a truck stop for all of June, a month that would make world history for being the final peak of oil's historic run trading at more than $100 a barrel. I lived in western North Dakota from April 2015 to January 2016 to conduct more in-depth research, finding that it was then, as the oilfield matured, that the missteps sown during the boom came to the fore. It was a story that would last for at least a generation, and over time I shifted my interest to investors and longtime residents of North Dakota, knowing they would live with the legacy far longer than the mass of transients who left after the easy profits dwindled.

North Dakota was always a trusting place, where a handshake was as good as a contract and nobody was a stranger—and yet this is a book threaded by mistrust and shaken faith. Even the most naïve among them became hardened to unscrupulous outsiders, as they discovered people were not who they seemed and grand promises danced away like mirages on the prairie. Landowners became leery that regulators would protect their interests against Big Oil, and migrants knew they could not count on the structures of mainstream society—from corporations to the government— to advance their lot. They had only themselves.

Many didn't foresee the boom lasting much longer and hustled for a profit as fast as they could get it. *Now* was what mattered; *later*, an afterthought. Made-in-America exuberance abounded— and with it, a great deal of waste: illegally dumped oilfield brine, pipeline spills, trash scattered along the highway, the excesses of a boom revealed after the fall. Critics decried the transformation of their home into an industrial wasteland. Even the migrants were spoken about as refuse: oilfield trash, white trash, society's cast-outs, the broken and disposable. This sense of things thrown away came into sharper relief after oil prices saw the worst rout since the eighties and empty oil trailers and tanks scattered like the old farmsteads, relics of different eras but the same American way.

This is not a tome on fracking. Nor should this be taken as a comprehensive account of the Bakken oilfield, a topic too vast and multifaceted for one book. This is a narrative, on-the-ground account of capitalism, industrialization, and rugged individual-ism in twenty-first-century America. This book is about what that Ponzi scheme symbolizes: the ways in which the largest oil rush in modern US history wrestled with ephemeral and lasting interests, scam and legitimacy, and the power and failings of free enterprise.

I Should Be Dead

*I*t was winter when Danny Witt left the Outer Banks islands of North Carolina in a Toyota Tundra driven by a friend who opened a can of beer on the interstate every afternoon at three o'clock and wasn't on time for much else. They drank too much at the bars in Charlotte, meandered awhile on the highways, and got waylaid for three days at the casino in Milwaukee, even as Danny kept telling him they'd better hurry and get to the oilfield. The plan had begun while Danny was painting white trim on a beach house somewhere in the dunes, working a job he had no intention of keeping for long. An old biker friend drove up blustering that he was making five grand a week driving a freshwater truck in North Dakota.

"You should do it, man," the biker said.

"How'd you get your commercial driver's license?"

"Just BS'ed my way through."

It was a curious proposition, given that Danny had never cared a whit about Peterbilts and spent most of his life riding a surfboard. He was a disciple of the Atlantic Ocean and a dabbler of the Pacific, a man of erudition and adventure who at one time or another had worked as a bartender and carpenter, cleaned swimming pools and driven a cab, gotten married and divorced, bummed around Panama, found love with a beautiful but difficult woman and lost it again, taught himself Spanish, built decks in the jungle, found Jesus Christ, made a little money along the way and spent it all. But a man has to attempt a high-paid career at some point, so Danny enrolled in a month-long trucking course. The students drove a ten-speed in circles in the parking lot and practiced how to downshift and back up slowly. He struggled to maneuver the truck and could only reverse once during each test run if he was lucky—that was, thankfully, all he needed to graduate and earn his license.

Recruiters came to hire students to do long hauls on the interstate, but those jobs paid a pittance, and Danny was set on being an oilfield trucker. A lot of people from the Carolinas were traveling to North Dakota at the time because the oil jobs there paid more than the ones in Texas and Oklahoma. Danny's acquaintance with the Toyota Tundra was game to join him—the fellow was going through a divorce and had a lot of money to blow before his ex-wife took her share.

As they rambled north and west, past the Appalachian hills and Midwest cornfields and Chicago skyscrapers, Danny felt the whimsy of their lackadaisical days and hard-drinking nights fade. He hadn't lined up a job and knew his qualifications were suspect—he wanted to know as quickly as he could if he was going to make it in the oilfield, or else he might as well return to the beach to remodel houses and serve tourists heavy platters of snow crab legs and hush puppies.

They made their way to Interstate 94, journeying west through the Twin Cities and over the flatness of Fargo and the Red River Valley, past the squat buildings of Bismarck, across the Missouri River, and on toward the badlands, where the terrain turned hilly and stark. The men turned north less than an hour before the state line. They passed small Main Streets with grain elevators and Jack & Jill grocery stores, relics of humble livings anchoring a countryside now overrun with the accouterments of a massive industry: tankers, trailers, garages, pipes.

The dark and cold hung as heavy as a tarp, and wind blew the snow from the pastures into finger-shaped mirages that swirled an inch or so above the road, as if the asphalt itself were oozing. Night fogs rolled over the plains, barring sight more than a few feet ahead. In the dark, the natural gas flares reflected purple beams, like UFOs, from behind the hills. Buttes colored in burnt orange, ocher, and sepia whorled in bizarre and terrifying shapes. The wind blew so hard that drivers clung to the steering wheel as though trying to right a capsizing ship. The vermilion hues of scoria clay over the oil well tracts and roads bled through the gray and white of winter.

Hotel rooms . . . truck stops . . . nights at a bar called TJ's, where the Outer Banks biker spun tales about all the times he'd nearly frozen himself senseless. Danny and the Toyota Tundra driver stayed in a truck behind somebody's oil services shop for a few days. The owner finally agreed to hire Danny if he could pass a driving test. But Danny forgot whatever scant lessons he had learned from trucking school as he tried to maneuver a thirteen-speed loaded to a hundred thousand pounds, water sloshing inside the tanker as the northern winds bellowed. He looked down when shifting gears during their test run. "I hate to do this," the interviewer said, "but if you have to look down to shift, you can't be driving a water truck. It's dangerous up here."

Some of the truckers went to a bar later.

"Hey y'all, what's going on?" they asked a table of women.

One of the women smirked as Danny went on about trying to find a water-hauling job. She said he had the hands of a pretty boy—wouldn't last a day in the oilfield. But the woman took pity, offering to have her husband put him to work on their property full of train cars, trucks, bulldozers, tractors, cranes, and tires. Danny moved some equipment on the site for a few hundred dollars and quit three days later, determined to make it as an oilfield trucker. The driver of the Toyota Tundra absconded, and Danny never heard from him since.

So the biker gave Danny the keys to his semi, telling him to impersonate the biker to the dispatcher over the phone while running loads of water with another rookie driver. The deal was that Danny and the other man would get to practice hauling while the biker paid them $700 a week out of his inflated paycheck—exactly what the biker was doing while they worked this ruse was neither entirely clear nor of much concern. The men drove a seven-mile stretch on Highway 85 that was an ideal training course to practice downshifting, accelerating, and turning. Danny took over the driver's side at night because there were fewer vehicles to hit if he lost control of the semi. They drew water from a pond to take to the frack, as it was called, where a crew mixed the water with sand and chemicals and sent it two miles into the earth to blast oil out of the Bakken shale formation.

The newspapers regularly featured front-page displays of overturned eighteen-wheelers, but soon the accidents became too routine to warrant a photo. The locals learned to be resourceful. One holiday season high school students butchered six elk mowed down by a semi and donated nine hundred pounds of meat to charity. Highway 85 was the most dangerous route in the oilfield, and everyone seemed to know at least one motorist who had died in a wreck there. A truck driver started backing up after missing his turn on the highway, and a Hummer struck the semi from behind; the trailer caught fire, killing the Hummer driver. The driver of a Chevy Silverado swerved to avoid a deer while heading north and spun clockwise on the icy shoulder; a truck struck the passenger side. Two teenagers died and a third was hurt after their Subaru Forester hit a patch of slush, spun out, and was split in half by a semi driven by a Texan on the same stretch where Danny practiced driving. The mayor of Watford City decried the state's transportation regulators, saying they should take the blame for the thousands of oil trucks passing through his tiny town. "It makes me sick to think of children dying on our roads," he said. "It's a nightmare."

The drivers and victims of Highway 85's trucking collisions came from around the country. A semi hit a Ford truck that ran a stop sign coming onto the highway, killing the driver, from New Mexico, and the passenger, from Nevada. A man from Wisconsin was killed after a truck hauling pipe slammed into him in a three-vehicle collision. One icy evening, a pickup driven by a Louisiana man spun into traffic and a second pickup struck the passenger's side; then another truck slammed into them and killed the Louisianan and his two passengers, from Alabama.

Locals resented Danny's kind—they often complained that some foolhardy southerner would be the death of them, all these rednecks who didn't know how to drive a big rig in North Dakota or anywhere else. Danny's justifications lurched from desperation to some great shade of invincibility. After the other driver nodded off one night as they delivered water, Danny found himself steering through a wild stretch of badlands. It was midnight as the snow fell and the asphalt froze over. He began climbing a sharp hill, fearful of stalling out, and remembered what the biker had told him earlier that day: "Take your seatbelt off, unlock the door, and get ready to jump if the truck starts to roll." Danny downshifted all the way up and reached the top in low gear, shaking, praying, startled that he was still upright. Years later he would say that was his real graduation, all those months after attending a trucking school that had garnered several angry online accusations that it was a CDL mill. *I should be dead*, he thought sometimes. *Should be dead.*

Danny later set up a cone on a mound and moved the semi back and forth a hundred times until he felt confident that he could reverse. He taught himself well enough to find work hauling sporadic loads of water with a ragtag outfit. He and some of the other truckers played Texas Hold'em at a driver's trailer a lot of nights, cooking and drinking rum. Whenever he landed in a ditch or ran out of fuel, his poker friends bailed him out. But Danny was low on the dispatch list and often found himself sitting at a Cenex gas station, where he noticed an obnoxious man who was always running his mouth. Danny knew the type from his days as a bartender.

"You wanna drive oil?" the loudmouth asked him after a while. "Tell you what—I'll train you."

Tales at the Water Depot

T en semis idled around a median thick with weeds, waiting to load freshwater. Dirt and dead bugs shielded the license plates, as though the drivers were hatching a robbery and these were their getaway trucks. Brown-white tankers were scattered over the embankment ahead, where a McDonald's billboard rose through the fog of diesel exhaust. The interstate lay just beyond— east to Bismarck, west to Montana. Dispatch, as usual, had sent too many trucks, and if someone was going to wait, the operators would rather it be the deliverymen instead of the high-paid frack crews. The oilfield moved so fast that for some workers, everything slowed to a stop.

Danny pulled into the depot in a semi with a navy blue tractor. Dainty swirls of light blue gave it a misplaced touch of elegance. A smokestack had fallen off, and sundry fluids were leaking. He was eleventh in line, and each truck ahead would take twenty minutes to load. That would entail three hours of dead boredom, staring through the cracked windshield at the fast-food billboard and wondering if the truck tankers lying in the grass were naturally brown and fading or if they used to be white and had lapped up the filth of their surroundings. It was that same achromatic sprawl across the oilfield. For many laborers, the days blurred as dully as the palette of their surroundings. Danny had been telling me his story to pass the time—I was his passenger for the day—his legs relaxed as he leaned against the intersection of the door and his rickety blue seat. Danny wore a fluorescent orange vest over gray flame-resistant (FR) coveralls that spilled over his steel-toed boots. He was trim and boyish in the way of a man who had spent most of his life on the beach, with wide brown eyes and an earnest face.

"And you hauled oil with that obnoxious man?" I asked.

Yes, he said—that had been two years earlier. Danny had gotten his hazmat endorsement back in North Carolina, though he didn't know anything about hauling hazardous materials. Transporting oil from the wells to the pipelines and railcars was an elite trucking job. Driving was only part of it: a crude hauler had to climb the stairs to the catwalk along tanks twenty feet off the ground and gauge the temperature and gravity of the oil amid vicious fumes.

Danny ran a few dozen loads with the loudmouth, who had a connection with a man who leased trucks from a rodeo buddy. The leasing company agreed to hire Danny if he could pass a test run. The night before the test, Danny played cards with his old poker friends. They were in a trailer whose owner was something like $25,000 in debt to the IRS, but there was always money to party. The workers passed around an expensive bottle of Honduran rum and listened to that classic seventies trucking song "Willin'," singing about going from Tucson to Tucumcari and Tehachapi to Tonapah. *Driven every kind of rig that's ever been made, now I've driven the back roads so I wouldn't get weighed . . .*

Danny hadn't meant to drink, at least not that much. But he woke up dry-mouthed and sluggish. "I'm reeking of rum, hung over as a dog . . . passed the test without a hitch," Danny told me. The company let him pick out a top-of-the-line Coronado, and he set about hauling crude for five dollars a barrel.

Civilization was so new in those days that many oil wells did not appear on maps or GPS. Danny's directions once led him astray into a farmer's field. As he struggled to turn around, a man came out wielding tin snips, threatening to stab his tires. There were stories of North Dakotans coming out with shotguns and crowbars after drivers trampled over grass or spilled wastewater on their pastures. On the reservation, a semi nearly ran the tribal buffalo ranch manager's SUV off the road while his son was in the car. The manager tracked the driver down and hollered, "I'll knock your damn teeth out if you do that again!" Some truckers were rude right back. When a landowner told a sleeping truck driver to get his vehicle off her property, he retorted, "Lady, you should be thankful! I'm here getting your oil out of the ground!" Danny told the man he was only following directions. He didn't realize they'd all heard too many excuses.

"This isn't for oilfield traffic!" the man yelled. "Last week I had a trucker take out all my mailboxes! Tell me why I shouldn't call the sheriff on you!"

"If you cut my tires," Danny said, "I can't leave."

Camaraderie soon faded among the poker gang. The trailer's owner seduced the trucking dispatcher and she began assigning him the best loads. The other truckers turned on the lothario, graffiting his trailer with lewd insults. Somebody tipped off the man's wife, who stormed up from Texas in a fury. She hooked her husband's trailer up to a pickup and gunned the accelerator, blasting south down the highway as wires snapped and pipes hung off. Danny and the others stood agape, then collapsed in wild laughter. "That's what you get for screwing the dispatcher," he said.

By then it was summer, season of dust. Oil workers hacked it up like cigarette smoke, and people kept their vehicle windows rolled up to avoid coughing fits. The dust floated off unpaved roads in a tall haze that lingered long after the semis went by, hovering like a ghostly apparition. Sometimes it seemed like the whole oil-field was haunted.

During one run, Danny felt an explosion as he filled out his paperwork in the semi. A tank of oil had ignited and a man caught fire. Terrified, he put his truck in low gear and drove off as several workers milled about. The other drivers later told him that the blaze struck when somebody dangled a cigarette too close to the crude. Something always seemed to go wrong on that site. He dozed off around midnight while waiting for the oil to load from an enormous tank, worn down from working twenty-hour days, and awoke to crude shooting out of the vent pipe. A contractor charged him $3,000 to clean up the spill. Oilfield truckers were often exhausted because of federal exemptions allowing them to drive more than the standard limit of eleven hours.

Danny grew intrigued by the rodeo boss's success. In the early days of the oil rush, companies knocked on ranchers' doors and offered outrageous sums for their beat-up trucks. The oilfield depended on a ragged militia of trucks to deliver water and sand to the fracks, pipes to the drilling rigs, and oil from the wells to the railroad stations. Driving a truck was the most common job in the Bakken, and it took twenty-three hundred truckloads to service a well from the time it was drilled until it produced oil. The rodeo man operated two terminals using five hundred drivers and became one of the largest transporters of freshwater, saltwater, and crude in North Dakota. His success soon caught the eye of corporate interests, and he sold the business to the largest chemical bulk tank truck network in North America for $79 million.

The new owners had stricter standards than the old cowboy. They fired Danny after discovering a decades-old felony for growing several marijuana plants in his apartment. He got on with another trucking outfit, but then it was dead winter. The fracks slowed, and Danny found himself sitting back at the Cenex again. Just sitting was all it was, and that gave him time to change his mind about being in North Dakota at all.

Danny traveled to Phoenix upon a friend's vague suggestion, hoping to land a job waiting tables or tending bar, but people kept telling him he was overqualified. So he took up work as a day laborer. People's faces were wan with desperation everywhere he looked; they were all faking disability for government benefits and smoking weed and doing pills. Danny drifted back to the beach in North Carolina and worked an assortment of lousy jobs. He went to Missouri and talked to a friend about hauling zeolite to the oilfield. Nothing came of that, either, so he returned to North Dakota.

Danny resumed hauling freshwater. It took an average of one to five million gallons of water to frack an oil well, and he discovered he liked the rhythm of it when he got a fast assignment of loads. The fracks vibrated like an overamped pulse deep in the plains, or maybe they were a dragon whose maw stretched as wide as a summer sky, always thirsty, insatiable, and just when the workers filled the belly of one frack another rose from the prairie's bowels even more ravenous, so the drivers trampled some of the most distant roads in the Lower 48 from the water depot to the frack, the frack to the depot, their mission—*get the water, get the water, get the water*—swelling in a rhythm harmonized by the engine's roar.

So much of the job was stop and go, idling and stalling, that Danny read a lot of books. His first love was *Shantaram*, the nine-hundred-page epic about an Australian bank robber who escaped prison and joined the underworld of Mumbai. He favored the Florida crime novel oeuvre, from Randy Wayne White to Tim Dorsey. He tore through *Beach Music* and *The Water Is Wide* by South Carolina writer Pat Conroy. He read a six-hundred-page tome about the Federal Reserve, *The Creature from Jekyll Island*. A woman he met on a dating website gave him a copy of the eighties classic *Writing Down the Bones* and he eagerly read the advice about how to be a better writer, though he never wrote before or since. He studied books on stock investing.

Danny couldn't believe he had buffaloed his way into one of the most dangerous jobs in America, and he understood, on some level, that it was because he'd been a surfer all those years. You couldn't take a novice out in a hurricane surf and say, *If you do this, then you'll be all right*. A surfer had to master the melody of the waves on his own, trying and falling, feeling that crush of sand and water, rising again. Surfing, oilfield hauling—both were one-man sports.

·⁙·   ·⁙·   ·⁙·

It was two in the afternoon now, and Danny had been talking for hours. We had reached the front of the line. A coworker called, and Danny began running on about his faulty truck. "We got a frack that's going to last probably a few days and it's real good money." He was set to make $80,000 this year. Danny told me that if I wanted to become a trucker he'd give me test drives in the Walmart parking lot and prep me for the CDL test; perhaps we could even go into business together. He pulled up alongside the white shack that housed the water system, then put on his green work gloves and white hard hat speckled with dirt. Danny unhooked a hose from the bottom of the truck and attached it to an opening at the depot. He stepped inside the shack to punch a code into the screen. Someone had written a note in marker: BE CAREFUL WITH BUTTON. YOU PUSH OR TURN TOO HARD YOU WILL PULL THE VALVES OUT AND BE S.O.L. We watched the numbers on the machine rise:

GALLONS PURCHASED

6,350

THANK YOU

6/24/14

A significant week in oilfield history, though we didn't have an inkling then.

Danny loaded up and turned out of the depot onto Interstate 94. His fan kicked on as the engine heated up and we rumbled uphill. We were going to a frack run by Whiting Petroleum, a Denver company that was the second-largest operator in North Dakota at the time. He complained they were picky about safety. "I'm not really a rules person—I'm a surfer from the East Coast."

I told him I didn't like being told what to do, either—that's why I always felt ambivalent about working for other people.

"You need to have your own business," said Danny. "You should read *Micro-Entrepreneurship for Dummies*. It's incredible!"

He began slowing a mile from Exit 42, the turnoff for Highway 85, and made a few turns before steering onto a narrow dirt road. The horizon was all green and telephone lines. The oil rush had started north of there, a two- or three-hour drive, but it had since sprawled relentlessly in all directions and we were at the southwest edge. Danny stayed on guard for pheasants—"psycho birds," he called them, because of their tendency to skitter in front of traffic with suicidal urgency. He turned into a lot where several dozen blue frack tanks with yellow rails were lined up. He backed up in front of one, stepped out, and hooked his hose to it. Danny opened the valve on the tank, then the one on his semi tanker. It was a simple choreography, but he was careful to do everything in the correct order because the system's high pressure was dangerous. A pipe delivered the water from the tanks to the great corpus over the hills. The frack always seemed a secret beast to him, some unseen master. At last Danny turned the valves off and unscrewed the hose. He climbed back in the truck. "It doesn't have to be $100 a barrel," he said. "It doesn't have to be $4 a gallon . . . there's more oil than they know what to do with."

Several hours north, oil industry leaders were preparing for a grand party the following morning to celebrate the state's new milestone of producing one million barrels of crude a day. Black and gold balloons would dance. Thousands of guests would come to eat barbecue and watch the Texas Flying Legends air show. The governor would talk up the state's lowest-in-the-nation jobless rate. Danny and most of his kind had no plans to go—the fracks were too thirsty. He dropped me off at my car, where a tire was slumping after weeks of driving rough oil roads, and returned to the water depot as I made my way up Highway 85, that great vantage of progress. . . .

Beyond the Eyes of Roosevelt

The first stretch up the highway was a lazy idyll of pastures, scattered homesteads, and industrial shops. The Long X Bridge towered fifty miles north, passing over the Little Missouri River from Mountain to Central Time and into the stark uplands that jagged toward the heart of the oilfield. They had to close the span a few times when eighteen-wheelers smashed into the overhead girders. The river formed the southern border of an enormous jurisdiction that rambled all the way to the confluence of the Yellowstone and Missouri Rivers more than an hour north, where explorer Meriwether Lewis wrote in 1805 that "the whole face of the country was covered with herds of buffalo, elk and antelopes." In the nineteenth century, the rivers cordoned off the area from the growing bustle of commerce and railroad expansion. Thus people called it the Island Empire, though the county was officially named after Alexander McKenzie, an investor and political boss. Ranchers found the land prime grazing for cattle, and whites began homesteading by the turn of the twentieth century.

The early settlers and their descendants were of a hardy ilk, carrying on through the droughts and blizzards, ice and desolation. But farms struggled during the Great Depression, and people had been departing ever since. As the latest oil boom began, McKenzie County still had only 6,360 people over a territory more than twice the size of Rhode Island that stretched from the Montana border to the western edge of Fort Berthold Indian Reservation, from just south of Williston to the national park named for former president Theodore Roosevelt.* The prairies and rugged hills seemed bowed in a torpor from hopes lost—and still something in them held a quiet endurance. Sons and daughters would leave the ranches of their childhoods to settle in Fargo, Minneapolis, or beyond, but city life seemed so soulless that they sought to return to the warmth of family and community and land. It would have been foolish to return for any other reason, as there was little money to be had. Then the Bakken oil discovery revealed a wealth they had never imagined.

Advances in hydraulic fracturing and horizontal drilling, along with a record run of oil prices at $100 a barrel, made production astonishingly lucrative. Land men came to secure drilling rights; then came the rigs and frack crews. Word got out that North Dakota was a place to make money, or at least trouble, and people rushed in from across America. There was so little civilization in McKenzie County that it did not institute a building department or zoning code until several years into the boom, as it became the fastest-growing rural county in America. The population nearly doubled in five years, though officials considered this an underestimate because it didn't account for all the people in RVs scattered about the countryside. Outsiders shoved hundreds of trailer parks, subdivisions, apartments, and man camps wherever they pleased at such great speed and quantity that the authorities—an inapt term, as they had little authority in practice—could not tally what was in their own jurisdiction. "You just built something," an engineer told me. "Nothing met code."

To gauge the transformation, one needed only curve through a tremendous sweep of badlands on the highway soon after the

---

* Williston is a town in Williams County, just north of McKenzie County, and is the most heavily populated town in the Bakken. I've referred to the municipality instead of the county throughout this book because that is how locals mainly define the area. By contrast, I refer to McKenzie County as such because it is an enormous rural jurisdiction, though it also includes Watford City, the second-largest oilfield hub, about fifty miles south of Williston.

Long X Bridge, where the landscape was layered in sandstone, cypress, cedar, clay, shale, and petrified wood, the hills and rifts carved by the Little Missouri during the Ice Age, when glaciers diverted the waters from their northern route to Canada and began the steep erosion of sediments. The burning of lignite coal created patches of red-orange scoria, or clinker, that was used to build oil well pads and roads. The trappings of industry began to emerge . . . TURN HERE—LEASING NOW, rows of beige shipping containers squatting like military barracks across from a trailer park warning SLOW—CHILDREN AT PLAY by a playground near rows of white nitrogen tanks, dead-ending at a congeries of ramshackle RVs. Past an oil waste disposal area, a sign for a trailer park pointed east onto a dirt road, leading to rows of temporary dwellings, piles of tires, beige shops with a string of white campers, and a sign that read LODGING & RV, FURNISHED 2 BEDROOM UNITS, BEST PRICES!!! AND GREAT LOCATION!!! Families paid to park their campers in storage units, which shielded them from the cold and the wind. In the surrounding hillsides, chain-link fences ran alongside stacks of pipes and trailers and overflowing dumpsters.

Weeks before my journey, a tornado descended on that very hillside after a shock of hail, striking rows of beige trailers with white skirting at 120 miles an hour. "Where do we go?" asked a man as the gray colossus spun over the horizon. "We've got nowhere to go!" Few migrants had basements. The twister hurt nine people, including a fifteen-year-old girl, and destroyed more than a dozen mobile homes, flinging tumbleweeds and plywood.

I knew a rancher who lived perhaps a dozen miles' drive past those encampments in the most majestic home I had seen in all of western North Dakota, and she told me that as she rode horses there she was closer to God than inside the family's old Lutheran church. But with the trailers and tanker trucks and machines, all I saw, in every direction, was the relentless advancement of man.

RV parks with names like Prairie View and Low Down emerged. A shopping mall had risen from a blank field, with a Taco John's, FedEx, Home of Economy, Cash Wise, Jiffy Lube, American Smoke Wagon BBQ, and China Express. Hotels, a sushi restaurant, and a gym clustered along the highway. Institutions remained from the days before the boom, like Outlaws' Bar & Grill, which displayed a chalkboard listing the price of oil and natural gas. The Long X Trading Post, with a museum and liquor store, had been built a decade before in hopes of bringing traffic to this corner—these days officials were pleading for the traffic to stop.

Down the way was the Little Missouri Grille, a Comfort Inn, an old grain elevator, a bank, and the future home of a Mexican restaurant where customers would also be able to cash checks, get cellphones repaired, and send MoneyGrams. A thirty-foot white bust of Theodore Roosevelt dressed in a suit and tie stared onto the highway, looking out from the parking lot of a hotel named in his honor. His mustache drooped; his hair was cropped closely. "We must keep steadfastly in mind that no people were ever yet benefited by riches if their prosperity corrupted their virtue," he said at a famous Independence Day address in 1886 near the water depot that Danny and I had just visited. "Here we are not ruled by others, as in Europe; here we rule ourselves."

Today, the countenance of North Dakota's great frontiersman betrayed no judgment upon the rush of commerce before him. The narrow eyes rimmed by spectacles seemed almost jaded, as though he had seen too much and was looking past it all. Trucks rumbled back and forth to deliver construction materials for the mass of new developments that conjured some distant idyll: Bison Run, Pheasant Ridge. Trailers loomed on the hillside like gargantuan tombstones.

They hadn't built the highway to accommodate the twelve thousand vehicles that passed each day between Williston and Watford City, a sixfold increase from before the oil boom. Farmers who lived a half mile back from the road stopped hanging their clothes out to dry because the fabric would be soiled by flying dust from the traffic that snarled and spat like the New Jersey Turnpike during rush hour. I was late to several appointments on account of the delays. The highway was only two lanes, and laborers were widening it to four as part of the largest road construction project in state history. Drive north another half hour and the side roads took on oilfield names . . . Roughneck Road . . . Roustabout Road . . . Shale Shaker Street . . . Monkey Board Lane . . . Thousand Dollar Way . . .

Ahead was the truck stop where I'd met Danny several days before. He had stopped in to buy hydraulic fluid and coffee; indeed, thousands of oil workers had passed through at some time or another.

WILD BISON

TRAVEL CENTER

UNL: 3.76

DSL: 4.19

By then I had driven all over the country, and wherever I found myself, in the Great Plains or the Deep South, the Eastern Seaboard or the Northwest, I felt little more comfort than when the lights of a truck stop were shining far ahead like a lodestar. Transience turns so many of the old routines into open questions—where to sleep? to eat? to shower? to think?—and the American truck stop bundles all the answers to life into one massive building. Comfort is in the generic: a sad-sack song from the eighties playing over the speaker, pizza and chicken fingers from the freezer, coffee machines and packets of French vanilla creamer.

Inside the Wild Bison, the counters displayed barbecue lighters in the shape of bolt-action rifles and CDs with song titles like "Oilfield Trash with Oilfield Cash." Red bottles of 5-Hour Energy Shots advertised NO CRASH LATER. SUGAR FREE. FOUR CALORIES. FEEL IT IN MINUTES. The workers arrived in trucks loaded with sand and scoria, oil and water, their boots brown with dust and hands black with filth. Everybody was in a hurry; the oilfield demanded it. Run the pipes. Run the water. Run the tools. "People think New York's fast-paced . . . get in line," said one customer. "You want fast, it's fast around here." North Dakota produced more oil than any state except Texas, but it was second to none in hustle and spirit. The workers filed in at every hour to load up on candy bars, cheeseburgers, beef jerky, and frozen meals ("I ain't got nobody to cook for me," as one derrick man explained). Platter of chili cheese fries, $6.99—*beep*. Monster twenty-four-ounce energy drink, $4.09—*beep*. Five-gallon diesel can, $20.99—*beep*. They bought tins of Copenhagen straight (red), wintergreen (green), and southern blends (gold); tobacco was essential.

It was routine for truckers to hand over their corporate credit cards and charge $900 in diesel fuel. The cashiers complained that the customers' hands were always stained and reeking of chemicals. Standing there in their Carhartt uniforms and Sturgis motorcycle rally gear, the workers vowed this job would pay off their mortgages. They said the ecofriendly liberals needed to respect oilmen because they risked their lives so everyone could drive a car. Some lived in the Wild Bison parking lot, but their addresses, officially speaking, were in dying towns in West Virginia and Mississippi and Washington.

One afternoon, a matronly cashier advised me to be careful interviewing customers.

"There's way more murders than anybody knows," she said. "There's gangs out here, there's MS-13, there's drugs up the wazoo. It's scary . . . people don't understand how bad the oilfield really is. These people that come in . . . you don't know where they came from . . . don't trust them."

"Hey, can I get the receipt for fuel on Pump 1?" a man butted in.

She handed him the receipt and turned back to me. "Carry a gun."

Having lousy aim, I settled for pepper spray.

The wind blew so hard that it sometimes hurt to breathe while walking through the parking lot. It could take two tries to open the door. Elk heads that the owners had scored on a Northwest hunting trip were mounted on either side of the entrance. Dust was tracked in on the workers' boots and swept through with the gales. The displays of Twizzlers and Starbursts and chocolate candy bars, power chargers and bottles of coolant—they all needed regular wipe-downs. The camping fuel cans were so covered in dust that it looked like someone had taken them to the woods. The summer was overcast and even cold some afternoons, but at nine at night the sun seared through the window so brightly that some cashiers wore sunglasses as they rang up the lines.

The customers complained about the truck stop prices: a gallon of milk cost $6.59. "It costs a lot to deliver to Timbuk-nowhere," one supervisor told an angry customer. It was the same everywhere you went in western North Dakota. The customer compared it to the decline of the auto industry. "It's the labor force's fault. They think because you put on a bolt, that for some reason you rake in $80,000 a year, you know? I mean, think about it. What is the value of that labor action right there? So why not go overseas to get a Mexican guy or gal and put that bolt on for, I don't know, six bucks an hour?" But he would pay what the truck stop charged because there was nobody out here, Mexican or otherwise, who would work for so little.

While eating nachos in the truckers' lounge, I overheard a man complaining on the phone about the six cracks that formed in his windshield from flying rocks. He didn't know why the roads were so shoddy, with all the money coming in from oil companies. The man hauled drill cuttings after years of mediocre income as an over-the-road driver from central Michigan. The economy "is bad all over because the auto companies are going under . . . Michigan's the only place that Toyota is not moving in. . . . My house at home is $560, and then you drive by these places in Williston, it says why rent when you can own, $1,400 a month."

Another man in the lounge repeated this number incredulously. "Only reason is because of the oil boom," he said. "North Dakota used to be a place where you could buy a house for $25,000."

"Huh!" somebody snorted. "That was a long time ago."

At a time when liberals were pushing for a minimum wage of $15 an hour, an enclave of free enterprise was wrestling with the complications of a booming labor market.

"If you look at the economy now, you hear all these people complaining about the minimum wage. You give a state a $15 minimum wage . . . it's going to be the same problem you got out here.

You got all of us that are making over $100,000, all your prices and everything went up." By now the people in the truckers' lounge were rapt.

"Kids are making $17 an hour at Walmart," one man said.

"The more money you make, the more they take," the Michigan native said.

"They're robbers," somebody said, cursing. "North Dakota—these people are just stealing from you. Just because you can get it doesn't mean you should."

"*Capitalism!*"

Of course, a truck stop wasn't just a truck stop. It was a monument to transience in a region struggling to define itself. Come and go, get in and get out—a metaphor for what some residents feared their homeland would become. "If when we wake up twenty-five years from now and everybody's moved away because it's become a wasteland, it's become a huge truck stop . . . and we lost all these things we've come to value, then we've really dropped the ball," a tribal official told me on the nearby Indian reservation. Roaring and belching day and night, the eighteen-wheeler was the bearer of western North Dakota's wholesale industrialization.

Around the time Danny began driving a semi in 2012, the state's top officials were telling midstream companies that they couldn't build pipelines fast enough. "There is not a single thing I can think of that can do more to reduce the human impacts of rapid oil development," Governor Jack Dalrymple said at an industry conference. They wanted pipelines to displace most of these semis one day, given that the former was considered the safest, most reliable way to transport oil. The Bakken was so undeveloped then that the busiest areas still trucked 95 percent of their crude, clogging roads and necessitating major repairs.

Some residents were frustrated that the state's leaders promoted the great oil miracle without seeming to assume the burden for its ills. "You know what credit they don't take?" farmer Richard Johnson asked me over his kitchen table. He noted that more people died on the roads around here than anywhere in the state. "They should take credit for *that*. The infrastructure wasn't even here when they flooded this area with all the semis and all the people."

The turn from Highway 85 to reach the Wild Bison was considered an especially dangerous intersection in the oilfield. That year, a pair of twenty-year-olds would turn left onto the highway from the truck stop. The driver failed to yield, and a semi driven by an Arizona man struck the left side of the pickup, forcing it into a spin that landed it in the ditch by the Wild Bison. The force ejected the driver from the pickup, and he was pronounced dead at the scene.

But danger didn't always come from a reckless semi. One cloudy summer afternoon, a thunderstorm rolled in and lightning struck the saltwater disposal next to the Wild Bison. The tanks of oil waste caught fire and the flames shot up two hundred feet as black clouds roared. Firefighters saw the blaze from miles away as they struggled to reach the accident amid the unyielding traffic. "It scared the hell out of me," recalled one volunteer firefighter, who ran the county landfill a little ways down Highway 85. The tanks were so fiery that they seemed to be boiling on the inside, convulsing the ground.

A driver dozing at the Wild Bison heard several booms and felt as though his semi had lifted off the ground. The truck stop shook. The manager had a cashier call 911 and raced outside to ensure they weren't in danger. Remarkably, at one of the busiest junctures in the oilfield, nobody was hurt. "Do you know how close we were?" the manager asked his workers. Six fiberglass tanks of brine burned up entirely, unleashing 2,813 barrels of saltwater and 649 barrels of oil onto the ground. The fire was still smoldering the day after the explosion.

The Wild Bison

Weathered faces, blank from exhaustion, men shuffling more than they walked, nobody caring how they looked, shave or don't shave, didn't matter, burnt out at twenty-eight years old . . . The Wild Bison was their only respite from a twelve-hour shift, work and sleep, comrades here and gone—pepperoni pizza and Mountain Dew, a word with the cashier, perhaps TV in the lounge. Astonishing that the truck stop didn't even sell booze or movies, given how desperate people were to escape. You'd ask, *What are you in the oilfield for?* and it was usually a pointless inquiry because everybody just grunted *money*, and when one word was too much exertion they rubbed their fingers together in a telling gesture. Sometimes one word was too little and they'd spill something like *Just here long enough to pay off my child support and get the electric turned back on.* It was rude to ask too many questions. But everybody was smart enough to know that you got to be successful doing what most people thought they were too good to do—take the trucker who had supposedly had the third-largest company in Poland and went into hauling crude out here to make his fortune. Or maybe that was just another truck stop tale . . .

I met a Wild Bison customer who wore a low-hanging shirt that exposed an enormous tattoo across his chest that said MURDER. Another was a bounty hunter from south Texas. A regular was selling waste disposal services from rig to rig after his banking scandal drew the scrutiny of the Securities and Exchange Commission and the *New York Times*. An accountant from Baton Rouge was scouting for work after four arrests in three states. "May not be looking for a job," said a man who overheard this admission. "He may be running from the law!"

A twitchy hitchhiker with only $30 to his name washed in from Maine. The journey had taken a month and a half. He'd found his way to the truck stop after accidentally ending up in Miles City, Montana, five hours west. The hitchhiker asked how to get to Williston.

"It's twenty-five miles north," I said. "You can't miss it."

"Is it hard to get a ride from here?"

"I've never tried it. Looking for a job?"

"On the oilfield if I can," he said. "I'm trying to make the big bucks like everyone else."

He left for a while and came back.

"Truckers are that way?" he asked, pointing.

"Go straight back and there's a truckers' lounge," I said.

"Any casino thing back there?" He needed to make money fast, but had gotten North Dakota mixed up with Montana, where they had casinos in many gas stations.

He said later that he had found his way to Williston after all, not that it had done any good. The hitchhiker had been wandering day and night in search of opportunity. "No place to stay, no food . . . Salvation Army can't help me, churches around here don't help people . . . nobody seems to want to help anybody around here." He couldn't even find somebody to let him mow the lawn for a few dollars.

The brashest roughneck to come through was an Alabaman who wore a cap that said OILFIELD TRASH and labored on a work-over rig. He seemed invincible: he'd once rolled his Ford King Ranch after falling asleep at the wheel, and his only injury was a bump from a flying Mountain Dew bottle. Later he survived a heart attack on the rig. "All the food from the Wild Bison," said the roughneck, a bacon aficionado. He was still smoking his "cowboy killers" in violation of the doctor's orders.

In the truckers' lounge after a long day, two of the Wild Bison's regulars, Blackneck and Fish, regaled the other men with the story of how they'd talked their way past a patrolman just over the

border in Montana and managed to avoid being cited for an overweight semi. "I'm glad we didn't get weighed. We'd be in jail!" said
Blackneck, cursing. He considered himself a black redneck, thus
the nickname. He'd traveled here after work prospects at the coal
mine in West Virginia withered. Blackneck had the build of a mob
enforcer, and a paintball accident had rendered him nearly blind
in one eye. Fish had decided to drive a truck because he thought
it had to pay better than his old job handling bomb-sniffing dogs
in the Middle East for $50,000 a year. Like many oilfield work-
ers, he'd come to North Dakota after the government pulled the
troops out of Iraq. Blackneck and Fish had met at trucking school
in Salt Lake City and slip-seated, or drove as a pair.

The duo were paid by the quantity of water they delivered,
rather than the hours they worked, and loaded up the truck
heavier than a stampede of corn-fed hogs. That was the only way
they could make money on a three-hour turnaround between the
water depot and the frack. They didn't believe they could run legal
and profit. The men also fudged the numbers for how long they'd
been driving in their trucker logs, which usually exceeded federal
limits. They claimed to sleep five hours every few days. The truckers shared "bear reports" alerting their brethren over the CB radio
or text messages to avoid any road where bears, or cops, were on
the prowl. It was a reasonable gamble—the Highway Patrol lacked
the manpower to crack down on them, though the authorities
were stricter on the Montana side. "First come first serve, dog eat
dog," Blackneck described the oilfield.

Fish said people assumed he was making a killing, but he
wasn't when it cost $600 a month for food and he had so many
bills. He dipped from a tin of Grizzly wintergreen wide cut. It
was better than smoking, which was forbidden on the frack sites.
Of course, the supervisors—*pushers* and *company men*—got away
with cigarettes. "Put up with a bunch of crap around here," he
muttered.

That day, the Montana trooper had kicked their truck tires,
telling the pair they were underinflated but waving them along
without taking out his scale. "We were pulled over because he's

black," Fish, who was white, joked to the other drivers. Then he admitted that wasn't why at all: they just had a janky old truck.

Everybody was working, everybody except one man. He rolled up to the truck stop in a wheelchair nearly every day, holding a cardboard sign that read NEEDS WORK HELP IF U CAN? It doubled as a shield against the diesel exhaust that the trucks heaved as they drove in and out past him. A panhandler was a shocking sight in the oilfield, where jobs were so abundant that people had a saying: if you couldn't find work around here, you were unemployable.

Wayne Williams had scrapped metal and sold shrimp in Baton Rouge before he came across a *National Geographic* article about the oil boom and rode a Greyhound bus north. He hawked buttons at the McKenzie County Fairgrounds for a day and tried his hand at other work, but he wasn't a steady-job sort of fellow. Wayne slept for a while in the park by the Kum & Go, a gas station that had fed everybody in the oilfield at some point, but a manager threatened to call the cops.

Wayne sought shelter in a dumpster. As the temperature fell below zero and the January winds raged, he feared he would perish of hypothermia. *I don't want to die this way, covered up in a bunch of trash . . . nobody finding me,* Wayne prayed. He arranged some slabs of wood to try to hoist himself out, slipping again and again as he reached for the top. Finally he made his escape and staggered to a nearby bar, where he ran into some folks who had given him money before. They suspected that frostbite had ravaged his limbs and took him to the hospital. Wayne woke up with his legs amputated below the knee.

The accident horrified community leaders and the members of Wayne's church, but he was still struggling on the streets. A maintenance man at the Tumbleweed Hotel and RV Park down the highway had told Wayne he could try his luck begging outside the Wild Bison. The supervisors were nervous about Wayne coming so regularly to wait at the parking lot entrance, and somebody asked him to leave. But Wayne came back the next day.

So there he sat, next to a backpack and bottle of Gatorade. Hardly anybody stopped, though Danny had recently given him twenty bucks. ("Is he doing drugs with it?" Danny asked rhetorically. "I don't know, but his life is already hard enough.")

"But this place is hiring," I told Wayne, pointing at the tall sign along the highway: NOW HIRING.

"Oh, it is?" he replied.

Wayne remained there a couple more weeks before heading to California, where he imagined that residents were friendlier to the homeless. He drifted back at some point, though a church pastor suggested that Wayne began to take advantage of their charity.

Drive a few miles north, past a sign bearing the Ten Commandments, and there was a bar called the Hi Way Lounge where a lot of people from the truck stop hung out. It sold $3 Hi Way to Hell shots and let customers play shake-a-day, a dice game that doled out a free drink as the prize. I walked in one evening when the jukebox was blaring ZZ Top. *Clean shirt, new shoes . . . silk suit, black tie . . .* I began talking to a Wild Bison regular who claimed to have driven a newspaper truck back in the nineties for the *Philadelphia Inquirer*, where I had worked as a staff writer during the financial crisis. He said he had ties to the Philly mob—or his wife's father did. He had to wait until the man died to divorce her. Now he was on the run from tax troubles. "I can disappear up here . . . poof!" he said, pounding on the bar. "The IRS can't find me!"

He introduced me to his cousin, who drove a frack sand truck and went by the name "Cali"—he was from southern California. "I became debt free in ninety days up here," Cali said. It sounded like a line in an infomercial. I told him he should work for the state's new job marketing effort. "Find the Good Life in North Dakota," as it was called, was recruiting people to move their families here and build long-term careers. Cali agreed he could be on TV, intoning: "You, too, could be debt free if you're forty-three and homeless and needing a job! You could run away to North Dakota, where they're all running away to!" We started laughing.

Cali was likely not the type the state's marketers had in mind. He used to be a meth head who robbed big-box home improvement stores to support his habit. Cali had the misfortune of getting clean just as the financial crisis struck, and he'd worked only sporadically for years, sleeping in his truck. Then he heard about North Dakota and found a $90,000-a-year job with company-paid housing at the trailer park next door to the Hi Way called Dakotaland. Until that first night in the trailer, he hadn't slept in a bed in a year and a half. Before long, he was telling everybody back home that he had found utopia. It was the first time he'd ever met so many other outcasts. He was pleased to earn a high salary legitimately. Returning to robbery wouldn't have been an option nowadays, anyway. "Do you know how many technologies I'd have to circumvent?"

⁙   ⁙   ⁙

The Wild Bison began, as so many oilfield stories did, with the Great Recession. The Kysar family's longtime cabinetry business in Washington State was suffering when a relative told them about North Dakota. They left their idyllic life of fishing and hunting and made the twelve-hundred-mile trek east in search of new business prospects. They came upon a prairieland with far more jobs than places to live, where one could just about rent out a car for somebody to sleep in for $800 a month, as Derek Kysar joked. But it was the FOR SALE sign at an old two-pump gas station on Highway 85 that intrigued his teenage son Jackson. He saw the traffic jamming that route every day and knew the investment would be profitable. Jackson suggested to his father that they buy it. The family called the place Jack's Store. After six months it was so busy they knew they'd have to find a bigger area to accommodate semi truck parking.

They found nearly a dozen acres of farmland a few miles away, where the highway sharply curved east toward Watford City. "It was all timing," Derek recalled. "You couldn't touch it now." The Kysar boys and their dad worked to build the storm drains and roads in and out, painted the 13,500-square-foot building for the truck stop, and did the cabinetry work inside. They installed fifteen pumps and included a Hot Stuff Pizza and lounge, laundry machines and showers. They lined the shelves with all the necessities for truckers and other oilfield laborers: 2.5-gallon jugs of

DEF (diesel exhaust fluid), fuel injector cleaner, propane, premium octane boost, daily truck driver logs, trucker fans, pre-diluted coolant/antifreeze, cold-weather pigskin leather work gloves, Diesel 911 for cold-weather emergencies.

Business tripled quickly. The problem wasn't finding customers; it was finding enough people to serve them. Randy Roth, the manager, had spent thirteen years running a Pilot truck stop in central Montana, where he upheld high standards for hiring. But to maintain a similar ethic here would be impractical, even foolish. The abundance of high-paying oil jobs made it so hard for stores to find and keep retail workers that Randy had to hire nearly everyone who walked in. I was even one of them, taking a cashier's job in June 2014 so I could write an article about working in the oilfield.* Randy's main questions were whether I could learn to work a register and if I was a Vikings fan; then he gave me two yellow shirts with the truck stop logo to wear on my shifts. I left after four weeks, and this was not considered rude or unusual—workers seemed to treat the Wild Bison like an ATM. They would stay for just a couple of weeks or months until they found better jobs. The truck stop, like every other retailer, had to pay even the least skilled workers double the minimum wage just to stay open—at least $14 an hour, not that it did much good. In a recent five-month period, Randy estimated, at least twenty people had quit. He raised the starting wage to $14.50 an hour to keep new employees, though it was still not enough to match the $17 wage offered by many retailers in Williston and Watford City.

Many cashiers were women who had followed their men or families to North Dakota, or had grown up here—the friendly pregnant woman who tried to balance her hours with a boyfriend's truck-driving schedule, the pimply-faced jerk from Bemidji, Minnesota. There was hardly anywhere to live nearby, just south of the two-hundred-person town of Alexander, so some employees slept at the Tumbleweed RV Park and showered at the Wild Bison.

---

* Most of the material in this chapter comes from my time as a cashier, though some was reported later in the year.

One cashier always came a half hour early to shower and started the overnight shift with wet hair. He didn't hide his job search: after a week and a half, he landed a promising interview to run heavy machinery.

Then a couple of boys from Oregon rambled in. Chase had worked on a drilling crew around here a few years back until a coworker started reporting all of them for getting high on the job. He skipped town after the drug tests started: "If you don't take it, there's no proof." But Chase had blown all his oil money and needed to make it back. So he recruited his friend Drew and they pointed their car east and didn't stop driving until they hit the Walmart parking lot in Williston at 2:00 a.m.*

Their car had a lab of concoctions to pass the drug tests required for most oilfield jobs: vitamin B_{12}, milk thistle, cranberry juice, Certo. Chase had just celebrated his twenty-first birthday with a cocktail of LSD, cocaine, and molly, and Drew had done coke. Chase bought another friend's clean urine and heated it up on the dashboard of the car on the way to his drug test for a drill casing job, but he never got to use it. The company sent someone into the bathroom to watch him relieve himself. Fresh off that failure, the men slunk to the Wild Bison for a breakfast of biscuits and gravy and filled out job applications.

It was unlikely that Randy knew any of this when he asked, "Can you start at two?"

The Oregon boys went out to party one night at the Hi Way, and Drew kept drinking while he drove them back. The next day, Chase woke up monstrously hung over. I saw Drew step out of the car at the Wild Bison, ready for work, but Chase languished across the passenger's seat. He told Drew to inform the boss that he was too sick to come in that day.

Eight hours later, he was still there, sobering up. The car was packed to the ceiling with blankets, propane cooking gear, clothes, and multipacks of fire starters. An enormous Wild Bison jug rattled around the front, along with a red sleeping bag and a

---

* Because of their drug use, I've changed the Oregon men's names to protect their privacy.

crushed energy drink can. The back ledge of Drew and Chase's car revealed a Bible, a half-used roll of toilet paper, some CDs, and a mangled tube of toothpaste.

That night we went to the 4 Mile Bar with a reporter friend of mine visiting from Manhattan. The bar sat at the corner of Highway 85 and Route 2 heading north into Williston. The sign showed brown hills with the semicircle of a sun behind white clouds. The letters had worn off so much that they were hardly readable. The notice beneath them was clearer: FIREWORKS SOLD HERE. The 4 Mile was not, thankfully, doling out explosives over the bar; there was a tent set up next door.

Chase relayed a tangle of financial woes, like everybody within a fifty-mile radius. "Got to pay $3,500 to the state of Oregon, got to pay the boss of my last job between $5,000 and $10,000 . . . my credit isn't good . . . then my truck broke down . . . the transmission is $3,000 to fix, and I didn't pay that either . . . got a payday loan for $800 that's probably around three or four grand by now . . . got a cash advance for $500 . . . probably paid my weed dealer's rent all year"—he paused—"*twice* his rent . . . made a crapload of money here and spent every bit of it and then a lot more . . ."

They had camped at Fort Buford by the Montana border for a while, but the authorities booted them out for leaving a pellet gun and beer cans lying around. So they snuck over to the other side and ran into a man who claimed he was a big-shot real estate developer from Arizona. He invited them to his place and made a vulgar solicitation. "Drunk rich guy," said Chase. An elderly janitor at the Wild Bison took pity on the boys and invited them to sleep in the bunk beds in his trailer. They could only hope he would not be as libertine as their last benefactor.

"I'm trying to ditch it next week," Drew said of the truck stop.

"I don't give a damn about that place at all," Chase said.

I asked if they really wanted to be like the oil workers shuffling into the Wild Bison. But they couldn't imagine sitting behind a desk. They wanted to feel tired at the end of the day, as though they had accomplished something. A few weeks later, they hightailed it out of the truck stop for legitimate oil jobs, and the Wild Bison was scrounging for workers again.

The Wild Bison had a monopoly along this stretch of Highway 85, but other entrepreneurs had taken notice. One of them was looking to build a rival truck stop near Abraham Lincoln's head. For some mysterious reason, an enormous white bust of the former president stared out about thirty miles north from the Roosevelt head. Abe, with a long crack across his neck, sat near an RV park and billboard for a gravel site. He was just about the only government figure keeping eyes on this stretch.

Engineer George Miles told me his boss, a New York developer, wanted to move the campers farther back from the highway to make way for a $10 million truck stop that had already drawn interest from national chains. It would be bigger than the Wild Bison, with three times the parking spaces for trucks plus a strip mall, truck wash, and fast-food restaurant. He lobbied his boss to replace the presidential head with a replica of the Statue of Liberty—they could call the new truck stop the Liberty Travel Center—but that was a no-go.

"So are you going to steal business from them?" I asked.

"Probably—there's plenty to go around."

I sat with George a hundred feet from the bust in his pickup, watching laborers clearing a dirt lot for the campers. As he talked about the way to succeed in the Bakken, George brought up gold rush entrepreneur Samuel Brannan. The Mormon had arrived in California in 1846. Instead of digging for gold, he started businesses—newspapers, flour mills, a hotel, a store. He built C. C. Smith & Company at Sutter's Fort to offer tools and food at high prices for the gold miners, shrewd enough to see that supplying the miners would be more profitable than mining itself.

"He never mined one day," George said. "Most gold miners went broke. They didn't have any money. Most of these guys here, at the end of this, they're going to be a little better off but not much, realistically. The people that own the Bison, that are going to own the man camp here, the gas station up there, the hotels—those people are going to be the ones that have the money . . . it's the people supplying the stuff."

I soon got a tip from the Wild Bison's fry cook that suggested George was right.

The fry cook was affable and mild-mannered, with a military haircut, and had a sharper sense of what was going on than nearly anyone else at the truck stop. He had lost his leg in an accident on a rig in Wyoming years earlier, when a member of the crew made an error with heavy machinery while high on cocaine. The fry cook won a seven-figure settlement, got a prosthetic replacement, and moved to Denver to party with the windfall. "Lamborghini, twin turbo, supercharged engine . . . high-dollar hotels, condos, you name it! Parties . . . $10,000 Rolex, white gold crystals . . . It was like *Wolf of Wall Street*, out of control."

He became a professional pothead, spending his days in a haze on the couch. The drugs eased the ever-singing pain from his amputation. His brother was working on a rig and urged him to come to North Dakota. So the fry cook sold the luxury car and took a job as a hotshot driver, on call twenty-four hours a day to deliver tools to oil sites. During one run, a flying rock smashed a hole through the driver-side window of his vehicle so hard it sounded like a .22-caliber rifle going off. Fearing the glass would collapse on him, he pulled over and smashed the whole pane out. The fry cook was playing blackjack at the bar one day when a woman sat down and gave him her number. "In case you get bored," she said. He moved in with her at the Prairie View RV Park for a while, but was aghast to learn she was running heroin and crystal meth from Minneapolis and charging Bakken prices for the drugs—that is to say, double or triple the usual rate. The fry cook hustled out of there.

He dreamed of getting back into the oil industry, but companies balked when they discovered his lawsuit in Wyoming, even if he hid his disability well. Then there were the four drunk driving charges. When he failed to show up for his prison sentence, Colorado suspended his driver's license and issued a warrant for his arrest. He continued to drive in North Dakota, but oil companies wouldn't hire people without a valid license. We'd talk sometimes about when he should turn himself in, but the fry cook wasn't ready for lockup just yet. So he spent his days cooking gizzards and chicken fingers at the Wild Bison, lamenting the high turnover of the staff.

He was a long-timer, and it made his job more stressful. The fry cook also thought the place was a rip-off. People had to eat there if they didn't want to drive another twenty miles for a quick meal. "And you're forced to pay their prices," he said. The last he'd heard, the Wild Bison was about to be sold to a large truck stop chain. It was sad news, as the truck stop's appeal had been that it was a family business. The Kysars had even used sixty-seven-year-old pump jacks that Derek found in a Montana field to construct an indoor balcony that overlooked the floor. But one couldn't fault them for making a deal. They had played the Bakken game perfectly: get in early, invest wisely, sell at the peak.

Williston Brewing Company

*P*ast the Vegas Motel, McDonald's, Pizza Hut, Dakota Farms Family Restaurant, and Million Dollar Lanes, Williston Brewing Company stood in homage to the changing times. A brewery in the oilfield, that great preserve of Buds and dive bars! Intrigued, I turned into the parking lot and could hardly find a space. I pulled the restaurant's revolver-shaped door handle and found the interior so crowded that I had to hurry to claim the last seat at an expansive bar made from a redwood tree. I ordered a burger with blue cheese for $14, which was double what a small-town burger should cost.

The place had forty beers on tap and eighty in bottles: IPAs brewed in Utah and Michigan, amber ales from Colorado, porters from Oregon and Fargo, stouts from Montana and England—none of them crafted here. The misleading name could be forgiven, as the outfit also had a vast selection of cocktails with names like WBC's Oil Slick (Captain Morgan pineapple rum, fresh juices, and a dark rum floater) and Roughneck Lemonade (Don Q rum, lemonade, and blue curaçao liqueur). An enormous buffalo head shot a steely gaze from the wall. Ninety-inch TVs lit up with sports channels. A stalled mechanical bull sat near the blackjack table. The story was that they had installed the machine before realizing how much the insurance cost—the liability for drunken oil workers snapping their necks turned out to be too high.

The owner, Marcus Jundt, came from a wealthy Minnesota family. His father had managed a hedge fund and co-owned the Vikings football team in the nineties. Marcus had been a founder and chief executive of the Kona Grill seafood restaurant chain until a Connecticut hedge fund forced his ouster in a shareholder battle, alleging ethical lapses and mismanagement. Then he ran into trouble while building a Four Seasons Hotel in Vail, Colorado. The financial crisis hit. He was overleveraged and the bank called in the loans. Marcus filed for bankruptcy. He realized that he could revive his career in Williston after waiting two hours for dinner on a Monday night at Applebee's. Marcus would later tell me it was like catching a fever, finding himself in the renaissance of domestic oil production. He compared it to arriving in San Francisco in 1848. "This is it," he declared. "This is America."

The culinary scene was so sparse that a visit to Applebee's was listed among fifty things to do in a book about Williston's attractions. Transplants were startled by the bland offerings: a North Carolina woman told me she'd never met an egg that had no flavor until she came to the oilfield. The most fortunate received all of their meals from man camps, thus named because they housed mainly male workers. The camps served heaps of food to the laborers, as much as they wanted, anytime—beef stroganoff, shrimp and lobster cannelloni with a rosé and pesto sauce, corn dogs and onion rings, Asian-style grilled tilapia with ginger rice, southern fried chicken and corn on the cob, sloppy Joes and curly fries.

This tradition of all-meals-included camps gained widespread attention during the Alaskan pipeline boom of the 1970s. Pipeline camp diets ran up to 8,000 calories a day, as workers gorged on lavish spreads of lobster tails, steaks, pies, burgers, and cakes—prized indulgences amid their grim routine. When cost-cutting measures diminished their offerings, a group of welders overturned tables and rioted, injuring several kitchen employees. Eating was the laborers' only sensual pleasure, reported Associated Press writer Tad Bartimus in 1976. "It is the one major break in the monotony."

Yet in North Dakota nearly four decades later, many boomtowners still bought their meals from gas stations, truck stops, and the Walmart frozen food aisle. Some establishments tried to profit off oil workers' massive appetites. "Are you man enough for the FRAC-ATTACK!" asked Big Willy's Saloon & Grill, in a nod to the industry spelling that omits the "k" in "frack." "Everything you love combined in one massive burger feast!" Two grilled cheese sandwiches, two beef patties, caramelized onions, chili, red pepper cream, mushroom, bacon, fries, and crispy fried onions, all for $24.99. Eat it in half an hour for a free T-shirt.

Undaunted by his old failures, Marcus began raising money to build new eateries, much of it from his old investors. "Typical American dream," he recalled. "I picked up myself by my bootstraps and started anew." He and his cohorts opened a food truck, but those were quickly outlawed, and business was so lousy that they took in just nine dollars in revenues one day. Marcus took over Gramma Sharon's diner and J Dub's Bar & Grill. He transformed an old building east of the Walmart parking lot into a restaurant named Doc Holliday's Roadhouse after one of the nineteenth-century West's deadliest gunslingers, with a menu that included Frackin' Chicken ("a heaping portion of crispy chicken pieces seasoned to perfection").

Marcus set his sights on El Rancho Hotel's restaurant, which had been a beloved gathering spot before the oil rush. Families stopped for meals after church. They hosted their birthday and anniversary parties there, and the Rotary and Lions Clubs held meetings. But Marcus saw that it was ready for an overhaul during the modern boom, and transformed the home-style space into the trendy brewing company, his flagship property. The new establishment, with its sleek brick exterior and red lettering, was essentially a large sports bar with western décor, but it reminded patrons of their metropolitan hometowns. The Williston Brewing Company was a place where one could momentarily forget the trials of the outpost.

His adventures did not pass without trouble. An old shag-carpeted house he shared with employees burned down. They suspected electrical problems but could not be sure. Soon after opening Doc Holliday's, the restaurant staff had to call the police to rescue a drunken patron who wound up on the roof. On another occasion, Marcus was out on the town with some investor friends from New Jersey when a bartender who had been fired from one of his restaurants walked up and threatened to kill him. "Welcome to Williston," Marcus told his visitors sheepishly.

He was appalled that the gush of wealth seemed to reach too little of the community. Couldn't a town sitting atop the largest oil deposit in America be more than a mass industrial yard? Marcus considered local leaders too resistant to the recent transformations, overly concerned with protecting the past. He had invested at least $16 million in this town and wanted it to flourish. So when the mayor of twenty years said he was retiring, Marcus announced a bid to succeed him. He would run against his landlord, the owner of El Rancho Hotel: local commissioner Howard Klug. When I finished my burger that day and drove off, I saw a JUNDT MAYOR banner on the outside of the restaurant.

⋮ ⋮ ⋮

It was odd, in any case, to think that a mayor could have much sway over a crush of people and corporate interests so brazen in their drive for profit that this place sometimes resembled a third-world colony. Imagine honing a society from these multitudes: pioneers, outcasts, losers, tramps, dreamers, do-gooders, failures, drifters, deadbeats, felons, freaks, dodgers, bootleggers, scum, miscreants, missionaries, stumblebums, sneaks, bastards, loan sharks, hustlers, millionaires, hedge funders, laborers, prevaricators, vagabonds, criminals, believers, dropouts, vagrants, roustabouts, pipeliners, builders, daredevils, waitresses, escapees, bartenders, barracudas, shopkeepers, filmmakers, hotshots, tricksters, wretches, honchos, phonies, thieves, profiteers, adventurers, truants, bureaucrats, bawds, good-for-nothings, veterans, floozies, punks, hitchhikers, swashbucklers, drug traffickers, investors, marauders, quacks, fighters, profligates, streetwalkers, strivers, artists, junkies, killers, trollops, indigents, rooks, brutes, muggers, romantics, fabulists, ex-cons, fakes, globetrotters, barons, salesmen, delinquents, flimflammers, housewives, scapegraces, hellions, foreigners, usurers, bolters, pickpockets, scammers, liars, exiles, impresarios, peddlers, mountebanks, vermin, capitalists, fugitives, swindlers, trash, ballers, ruffians, opportunists, bilkers, pucks, screwballs, moguls, dynamos, cads, madmen, fleecers, libertines, wanderers, idealists, buccaneers, geniuses, hucksters, explorers, guttersnipes, merchants, maroons, creeps, psychos, scroungers, brigands, frackers, louts, prophets, grubstakers, drillers, industrialists, roughnecks, businessmen, harpies, kingpins, hawkers, pathfinders, skunks, workhorses, anarchists, crooks, mendicants, students, bankrollers, gangbangers, stargazers, drunks, rascals, rakes, gunslingers, writers, diddlers, humanitarians, financiers, optimists, tycoons, brawlers, robbers, safecrackers, predators, crackpots, gypsies, jerks, rebels, flakes, plunderers, malingerers, idiots, rustlers, finks, pilferers, heisters, nobodies, wayfarers, visionaries, cardsharps, debtors, fools, slopsuckers, malefactors, entrepreneurs, knaves, rabble-rousers, shysters, developers, schizoids, sinners, deuces, thugs, gold-diggers, connivers, poseurs, elites, bandits, goons, schemers, heels, louses, retirees, lowlifes, stiffs, lunatics, traitors, riffraff, saboteurs, prodigals, plebeians, hit men, strippers, double-crossers, bards, zealots, commoners, scullions, slackers, weirdos, paupers, racketeers, winos, defrauders, buncos, waifs, cheaters, colonists, floaters, counterfeiters, kooks, wastrels, scofflaws, prowlers, charlatans, utopians, looters, runaways, cab drivers, desperados, dissenters, molls, untouchables, turncoats, embezzlers, loafers, nutjobs, pedophiles, rapists, sickos, strays, strumpets, ne'er-do-wells, outlaws, hoodlums, transients, refugees, bums, rogues, imposters, derelicts, hobos, castaways, hellhounds, pariahs, rejects, degenerates, reprobates, grifters, renegades, con artists, crazies, deal-doers, hosers, meth heads . . .

How to build a lasting civilization out of such incongruence has always been the central dilemma of any boom. The "vast majority came to California not to make lives but merely livings, not to sink roots in the new land and build homes but to strip the land and return to their real homes," wrote nineteenth-century gold rush historian H. W. Brands. Booms also foster a mass indifference. A Scottish visitor's observation of the fortune-seekers in San Francisco during the 1850s could very well have applied to those of the North Dakota oil rush. "The community was composed of isolated individuals, each quite regardless of the good opinion of his neighbors; and, the outside pressure of society being removed, men assumed their natural shape," wrote J. D. Borthwick in his 1857 book *Three Years in California*.

I thought of this, of course, when a mangy man with a gray ponytail interrupted my interview with a pipeliner at a bar to say, "Shakespeare said this one time that the whole world is a stage and everybody's actors and that's the truth. You get in certain areas of the world like New York or Minneapolis and everybody plays a part. They're not really themselves. Out here you actually get to be who you are, ain't that cool?"

"Whether that be good or bad!" said the pipeliner, laughing.

"You can let it all hang out. . . ."

"Because we're all in the same damn boat," the bartender said.

The mangy man claimed he'd sent a robot into space for NASA, that his fifth wife had just left him, and that he'd done prison time for leading cops in central Minnesota on a cocaine-crazed, 160-mile-an-hour chase on his Harley. "But I'm just your average Norwegian Joe."

People went about their business in the emotional equivalent of wearing headphones. During my first visit to Williston in 2012, several workers mentioned offhand that they had seen men drag a passed-out woman from the bushes into the back of a van. "What did the police say?" I asked, and they shrugged. It hadn't occurred to them to call the cops. This disregard also had its benefits: it was one reason that there was little racial hostility in a region that, until recently, had been nearly all white. Nobody seemed to bother the crowd of African immigrants who gathered at the library every Friday for Muslim prayers. "I never cared for Mexicans, blacks, or Native Americans," a white oil worker from Montana told me. "But I had to learn to. They're not all that bad; I had to work with them."

At the time of the Williston mayoral election, in June 2014, an acquaintance from Idaho let me sleep on his couch for a month if I could be discreet, given his landlord's prohibitions on unapproved tenants. A lot of people were forced to sleep in informal arrangements like this. The couch was so small that my legs hung off the opposite armrest. My host worked as a floor hand on a workover rig by day and read Ayn Rand by night. He came home with terrifying tales: a prostitute had approached his work crew before noon; the neighbor lost his finger after some of his coworkers made drunken errors on their oil site.

All of this chaos was a striking turnaround from 2003, when the region was so desperate to stop decades of declining population that it developed a website called PrairieOpportunity.com to lure new blood. "Do you have what it takes to be a 21st-century pioneer?" the home page asked. "Odds are, you are not a candidate for NW North Dakota. You have succumbed to the cities. All of your pleasures must be provided, and you gladly stand in long lines to receive them. But if you are one of those who is wondering what they are doing in that line, continue on." The site touted businesses that know your name and milk cartons without pictures of children, though not all was rosy. "This is a very tough and unforgiving country . . . you need to make sure you can pay your bills without relying on NW North Dakota to provide you with an income."

The effort was led by Steve Slocum, who was a marketing officer at the First National Bank & Trust in Williston. The website wasn't particularly successful, Steve admitted, but neither was it responsible for bringing a bunch of Oklahomans and Texans who tore up the place and did whatever the hell they wanted. Many of the new migrants who began pouring into western North Dakota around 2010 were not the desired demographic of the old prairie website, or of First National, for that matter. A number of the men were subject to wage garnishments for child support and other debts—Williston was the new capital of deadbeat dads—so they preferred walking around with a few grand in their pockets to opening an account.

But no matter: a bank executive walked into Steve's office and told him to stop advertising for deposits. So much money was flowing in from longtime residents' oil royalties and lease payments that the bank's assets were rapidly multiplying. Steve made regular trips to the post office to pick up bags of cash sent from the Federal Reserve in Minneapolis. They used to go through a $20,000 ATM canister in about ten days. When the oil came, it was gone in a day and a half. They even had to buy bigger ATMs that dispensed $50 bills instead of $20s for larger withdrawals, so that the machines could hold more cash.

There were far more jobs than apartments when the oil boom began, so thousands of migrants stayed in tents, campers, and their cars during the early years. The first sight as one approached city limits was a complex of white trailers and cabins with gray half-moon roofs: the man camps. Then the neon lights of the Love's truck stop and billboard after billboard for Travel Host Inn, HomStay Suites, Carhartt, Subway . . .

The town functioned so erratically that one could see anything anywhere, for no reason at all: a white limo parked next to a billboard for the Super 8 next to two grain bins and dozens of hay bales across a dirt lot from a Mississippi barbecue joint ("Put a little South in your mouth") within view of four-hundred-barrel tanks. Much later, the developer of the land where the Pilot truck stop and other major projects were built took me on a drive and pointed out his majestic estate in a neighborhood where houses were about a half million dollars. It was just past a tractor store, trailers behind a chain-link fence, and abandoned greenhouses; the juxtaposition was shocking. So Williston was egalitarian, in a sense. The well-to-do were not entirely segregated from the upheaval.

The local boosters could no longer sell potential settlers on the slow pace of life. The rush was so frenzied that people waited in long lines everywhere they went. Now they didn't need to convince people to come; they had to convince them to stay.

Workers here had some of the highest salaries in the nation, but many big-box chains were hesitant to build because they relied on permanent rooftops and families, not singles in trailers. Lone men would build this civilization, but they could not sustain it. Man camp occupants trampled the roads with their pickups, showed up in emergency rooms, tussled with cops, and caused traffic accidents, all while contributing little to the wider economy. They were not bringing their wives and children, buying homes, or going many places aside from Walmart. They were just working twelve to sixteen hours a day, passing out, and flying back to Alabama, Florida, or somewhere else every few weeks.

In North Dakota, local leaders assured investors that the man camps were a temporary solution to a severe shortage of housing, that as soon as they built enough apartments they'd phase out the trailers. Developers poured in from around the globe. As the rest of the country emerged shaken from the aftermath of the housing boom, western North Dakota went on a building rampage. Rents were higher than those in Manhattan, San Francisco, and anywhere else in the nation: at the time of the mayoral election, a seven-hundred-square-foot one-bedroom apartment cost $2,394 a month. Officials believed the only way to bring rents down and keep more people in town was to keep adding apartments, so they erected housing at the fastest rate in the country and planned on adding more.

Marcus took out full-page ads in the *Williston Herald*. "Sick and tired of high rent?" asked one ad featuring an elderly woman clutching her face as she looked down in distress. "Williston has the highest rent cost in the nation! Vote for Marcus as mayor for positive change." Commissioner Klug took out promotions of his own touting his credentials as a lifelong resident and promising to preserve "hometown values." Marcus, by contrast, was a stranger. Suspicions of him had little to do with revelations of his bankruptcy. A lot of old-timers had gone broke during the 1980s oil bust and accepted financial hardship as one of life's inevitabilities. And the migrants who had come from out of state to work in the oilfield were scarcely in a position to judge. "Everybody had an aggravated assault or bankruptcy," as one oil worker put it.

No, the problem was that Marcus was not *from* Williston. The region had great affinity for his native Twin Cities, but that didn't count for much politically. Even his childhood ties to the eastern region of the state could not be leveraged for political gain. Official boundaries divided the Dakotas by north and south, but the real cultural rift was between the lands east and west of the Missouri River, which also marked the boundary of where it was acceptable to wear a cowboy hat every day. (You couldn't pull it off east of Bismarck.) Nearly half of the state's population lived on the Minnesota border, and decisions at the capitol were often made in the interests of this demographic. Western North Dakota was regarded by many of the state's own citizens as a backwater good for little more than weekend hunting trips in the badlands.

"Marcus Jundt has brought more to Williston in a few short years than most of us over a lifetime," one of his supporters wrote in a letter to the editor. "He didn't come here counting the days until he left, so isn't he one of us?"

Marcus knew they could never go back to the old days, but he imagined Williston could become like Calgary, which had flourished as the center of the Alberta oilfield, with skyscrapers and a riverfront with condos, jet boat tours, and a historic village. Many blamed the cold as a reason that nobody wanted to stay in North Dakota, but Calgary was even colder. It had a million people to Williston's estimated thirty thousand and went by the whimsical nickname of "Cowtown," even though that was a moniker better suited for our own humble city. (Williston planned to have as many as sixty thousand residents by the end of the decade, though this timeline was later revised to 2050.) Marcus felt that his new town's riches should be enough to overcome its inhospitable weather and isolation. This level of wealth could make anything possible. He believed the town needed a strong leader to convince developers to build a mall: Gap! The Limited! Cheesecake Factory! Nordstrom! More schools, parks, entertainment, shopping! He feared that without a bolder vision, northwest North Dakota would keep seeing oil money flow out. "Let's not become the industrial zone for Bismarck and Wall Street and Houston," Marcus preached.

Tall and blue-eyed, Marcus had a sharp sense of humor and a blunt way of speaking that sometimes crossed into the acerbic. Critics dismissed him as arrogant, though he struck me as no more so than any big-city pol. Marcus tried to reveal vulnerability.

He said in campaign ads that his first child had died of complications from epilepsy (his other two children were nearly grown at the time). His marriage later collapsed, which he attributed to being a workaholic. It became a bitter campaign given the genteel politics that normally presided in the city. Marcus accused city employees—largely supporters of his opponent—of taking his campaign signs from private property, and threatened to sue for violation of his First Amendment rights. He also fussed that the city was threatening to fine him $100 a day for displaying a mayoral sign outside the brewing company in violation of a sign ordinance. "It's a good old boy network thinking they can do what they want with no consequences," he complained to the *Williston Herald*.

Marcus was the leading candidate on an online newspaper poll days before the election, with the support of nearly half the respondents. But he won just 19 percent of the vote in the end, as the longtime residents pining for their old ways of life backed one of their own. "Marcus was a little over the top for Williston, North Dakota," the new mayor said. Marcus figured that at least he'd brought important questions to the fore, even if the election suggested that newcomers hadn't voted. Marcus was preaching change in a town reeling from too much of it. So he turned back to his restaurants, which were busier than ever. You never knew who would stop by, or what they were up to. One of his top customers, as it happened, was allegedly running the largest Ponzi scheme the oilfield had ever seen.

Great American Scam

T ales of the Bakken's riches quickly spread overseas, and two Englishmen arrived to claim their share. They seized on the idea of building man camps. Workers were so desperate for housing that the quickest way to get rich was to line up some trailers and charge people too much money to live in them. They began leasing land on Highway 85 some dozen miles east of the Wild Bison, on a stretch that was popular for man camps because it offered boundless space, along with escape from the regulations of proper oil towns. The duo solicited money from around the world with brochures that blared, "Property investment opportunity in the USA's largest oilfield." They called the man camp Great American Lodge.

Advertisements said the lodge would have "high quality executive hotel studios," though they were little more than what had become the oilfield standard: prefabricated beige trailers with a TV, microwave, fridge, and bed. The marketing pitches said the oilfield had an abundance of workers and not enough housing, guaranteeing that the man camp would fill up quickly. Bakken rents were the highest in the nation, after all, and the lodge's promised returns heralded the heedless optimism of the times:

UP TO 42% ANNUAL RENTAL YIELDS

AVERAGE ANNUAL RENTAL YIELD OVER 10 YEARS OF 56%

The flyers featured sweeping quotes from the US Secretary of the Interior, the *New York Times*, and the International

Energy Agency. They exclaimed that the region had more oil than Saudi Arabia and the United Arab Emirates combined, creating jobs for the next eighty years; that the forecast was for 150,000 oil wells in the Bakken; and that Great American Lodge would house employees of ExxonMobil, Halliburton, Hess, Schlumberger, Chevron, and BP. Never mind that regulators planned for just 65,000 wells over the coming decades, or that Chevron and BP didn't operate in the Bakken, or that man camps were never intended to last decades as more permanent homes were built. The company advised financiers that they could easily sell their stake to other investors or oil workers if they wanted to pull out. With their average $200,000 salaries, the company suggested, such employees would be interested in buying studios to save their rental allowances—a statistic that was wildly inflated.

The ads even said there was little competition, a questionable claim given the feverish pace of building. The local king of man camps was Target Logistics, a Boston company known for higher-end man camps. Target Logistics had housed military personnel in Iraq and displaced Hurricane Katrina victims. The company moved a trailer camp that it had used to house security officers at the Vancouver Olympics to Williston at the behest of Halliburton, which wanted to accommodate its oilfield employees there. That was the Bakken boom's first real man camp, and Halliburton and other major firms signed long-term contracts to house their workers in many of the other man camps Target Logistics went on to build. Oil companies preferred them because they were professionally operated, with a dining hall, laundry services, rigorous security, and bans on drugs, booze, and guests. Although lacking similar expertise, the British developers could nonetheless craft a convincing pitch.

Robert Gavin was chief executive of the firm North Dakota Developments, and lived in Malaysia, though he was a British citizen. The face of the operation in the oilfield was Daniel

Hogan.* He expounded on their progress in a corporate video that filmed the site of Great American Lodge when it was mostly a dirt lot with twelve rooms in a long modular unit. Hogan gestured at the trucks that had just delivered two more modular units and noted, "There's another lorry on the way." They would have more than two hundred beds open to oil workers in five weeks, along with a massive building for a restaurant, convenience store, and locker room for workers to store their dirty boots and coveralls. "A lot of sites are just literally RV parks for people to park on. . . . We are providing full-serving commercial lodgings."

Within months, the company claimed, it received an Overseas Professional Property Award at a ceremony in the Natural History Museum in London. The *South China Morning Post* reported Hong Kong investors had purchased studios at the lodge. The *Economist* wrote that the company was trucking in housing units from Minnesota and expecting to recoup the costs in a year. In a piece that discussed transient newcomers, *Forbes* quoted Hogan saying that he flew back to the United Kingdom every few weeks. A columnist for London's *Daily Telegraph* wrote a flattering account of his stay at Great American Lodge, saying it delivered healthy investment returns and gave oil workers shelter in the unforgiving cold. "It is not just a boom. . . . It is here to stay, it is an industry, and is lasting," Robert told the writer. The executive had attended the same grammar school as former UK foreign secretary William Hague, the column mentioned.

Hogan was a bald man with an aquiline nose and broad shoulders. He was, by all accounts, a flamboyant figure, his British accent clashing with the oilfield's Texan drawls and Scandinavian lilts. I never met him, but people tended to greet my inquiries about Hogan with the knowing chuckle. He was a high roller and a big drinker, the perfect embodiment of the Bakken's get-rich-quick ethos. The developer became a fixture at Williston Brewing Company, where he was known to order $400 shots of Louis XIII

---

* I refer to the developer Danny Hogan by his last name, to avoid confusion with the truck driver Danny Witt, mentioned throughout the book.

Cognac, blended from up to twelve hundred grapes eaux-de-vie matured in oak casks. He would also pay for large rounds of drinks for his associates, sometimes dropping hundred-dollar bills. A bartender who used to serve Hogan at the brewery laughed when I mentioned his name, saying, "He was a hoot!" Hogan even gave $500 to owner Marcus Jundt's upstart mayoral campaign. "He spent money like it was coming out of a fire hose," said Marcus. "You couldn't have a boom without people like that."

CNBC anchor Brian Sullivan interviewed Hogan at the Williston Brewing Company, where the man camp honcho was sitting next to the founder of Boomtown Babes Espresso at a table full of customers. "Did you literally come to Williston *just* for this boom?" the anchor asked. Hogan replied that when the financial markets crashed, they looked around Europe for opportunities— the United Kingdom, Portugal, Spain. Then they came to North Dakota, he said, where in two years they built fourteen hundred rooms.

Hogan often stayed at the Williston Boutique Hotel, a former Elks lodge in an old brown and white building downtown. It housed the town's most elegant dining spot, the Eleven Restaurant & Lounge, which served prime rib, pan-seared duck breast, ribeye steaks, and grilled lobster tail in a chandelier-lit dining room. The tables were draped with white tablecloths, a rare sight for an oilfield eatery. The executive chef recalled seeing him at the bar by midafternoon many days, ordering everyone drinks. At dinner, Hogan would ask for the most expensive dishes on the menu. "He was a pompous ass," recalled the chef, Jeff Burgos. "I'd see him and his whole entourage, everybody clinging to every word he said. He'd bring people in to impress them."

Acquaintances claimed he was a regular at the strip clubs, and often saw him with striking women. He was known to come calling with gifts of moonshine from a southern business associate. Some rolled their eyes at Hogan's spendthrift ways, but it was hardly suspicious behavior. The Bakken was making a lot of people millionaires, and everyone figured man camp owners were loaded. They had no idea he was blowing investors' cash. "Who knew," Jeff asked, "that he was spending these poor bastards' money?"

The company advertised corporate offices in Kuala Lumpur, Shanghai, and Central Milton Keynes, and began selling interests in Great American Lodge in 2012. A Greek expat told me he learned of North Dakota Developments at a property investment show in London and figured the boom was so big that it made sense to invest even if the returns were half of what they claimed. But Great American Lodge faced significant delays in becoming operational, and its occupancy was barely one-third even at the height of the boom. It didn't bring in enough to pay the original financiers—indeed, it never turned a profit at all.

The firm kept marketing the man camp to investors using misleading statements and omissions, and solicited investments for other projects. They began constructing another Great American Lodge in Culbertson, Montana, about forty-five miles west of Williston. They advertised another lodge near Watford City, though they never received government approvals or started construction. The developers even planned a 396-suite hotel in Parshall, an isolated Indian reservation town on the eastern limit of the Bakken's profitable drilling area. Associates all the way to Singapore hyped the Parshall hotel in an investment seminar, though the project was abandoned at the ground-leveling phase. The con men used funds from people buying into the later dubious projects to satisfy earlier rounds of stakeholders.

Years later, a group of Singaporean nationals who lost $800,000 in the scheme would sue a Singaporean sales agent, claiming that he played an important role in abetting the Brits' scheme. The plaintiffs alleged that he actively tricked them and other investors with misleading marketing materials while lining his pockets with undisclosed commissions of up to 20 percent of the plaintiffs' investments.

North Dakota Developments began investing in oil and gas in Montana, along with other transactions unrelated to any investor project. They bought real estate in Nebraska and spent $3 million of investor funds on several parcels of land in Williston.

I had lunch at Williston Brewing Company with real estate agent Ed Slater, who had befriended Hogan at a Chamber of Commerce social. A broker from Colorado, Ed helped the operation buy land in town that was supposedly for a lavish hotel. Ed thought it was an odd location, but some Texan investors were eager to dump the property.

"He would come in a place like this and blow ten, fifteen grand . . . and do it the next night over at the Williston [Boutique Hotel] and down at the girlie bar . . . just buy everybody all the whiskey they want to drink." Ed worked through a plate of grilled chicken salad with blue cheese. "He wasn't a bad guy. The money and the alcohol got to him, and he wasn't taking care of business."

Complaints from English investors reached the United Kingdom's Financial Conduct Authority, which determined that North Dakota Developments had been running an unlicensed investment scheme. The authority ordered the developers to issue refunds. Months after the flattering column from the *Telegraph*, British columnist Tony Hetherington investigated the matter upon getting a worried message from a reader who had not received his refund. "Why it takes a Buckinghamshire firm to spot a gap in the property market in North Dakota is an even bigger puzzle that investors might want to consider before signing on the dotted line," he wrote in the *Financial Mail on Sunday* newspaper.

But it appeared that nobody told investors from other countries—or authorities in America, for that matter. So people kept sending money. Gaston Procopio of Madrid pitched in $45,000 for Great American Lodge after receiving an email blast from a property investment website. The monthly payments never came. He spoke to someone on the phone about a refund but got nowhere. Gaston stayed up late into the night, sending messages and trying to track down other investors. In the United Kingdom, he tried the solicitor general's and constable's offices. I was surprised when he told me he tried the McKenzie County sheriff's department next. I had ridden along with a deputy sheriff around the time Gaston was faxing and calling in fall 2014, back when the department could scarcely keep up with overloaded trucks, knife fights, and domestics. The jails in western North Dakota were so full that officers spent much of their time driving convicts three hours east to the pen in Rugby, a little town known as the geographic center of North America. Stopping an international swindle would have been laughable. But Gaston was undeterred. He tried the county prosecutor. He tried the attorney general. He tried the FBI.

Jurisdictional complications stymied the case in the swindlers' favor. The company was not selling securities in the United States, and most of the victims were foreigners. But as complaints mounted, the Securities and Exchange Commission sued the company for running a Ponzi scheme. It was one of the largest securities fraud cases the SEC prosecuted in connection with America's modern fracking boom. Investigators found the bank accounts drained. Nine hundred and eighty investors from sixty-six countries lost $62 million. Hogan allegedly spent $250,000 of investors' funds on meals, alcohol, and entertainment. Contractors had also been stiffed on hundreds of thousands of dollars in construction work. The utility company shut down the power at Great American Lodge because it was $65,000 behind on the electric bill. The tenants were booted. The defendants never so much as answered the complaint. "This is a case where the system has failed us all," Gaston said.

·:·   ·:·   ·:·

Con artists have always loved a good boomtown. "Contracts are nothing in this land of liberty and gold," the *Home Journal* reported in 1849, in dismay over the California Gold Rush. "Men of irreproachable character at home and elsewhere, have often here . . . given themselves up to the guidance of personal interest."

During the Klondike Gold Rush of the 1890s, E. T. Barnette sailed north from Seattle and set up a trading post in Fairbanks to supply gold miners. After he became mayor, an old business partner turned up and sued Barnette for cheating him out of proceeds. Barnette's past prison term for larceny in Oregon emerged. He bought the Washington-Alaska Bank, which went bankrupt, and was charged with embezzling (and acquitted)—then he fled Alaska in disgrace.

Perhaps the best-known scammer from those days was Soapy Smith, who bribed cops and politicians and ran gambling scams in nineteenth-century Colorado. He went to Alaska as the gold rush got under way and opened a phony telegraph office and several saloons, as his associates steered newly flush gold miners to various enterprises where they could swindle them. A band of vigilantes tried to run Soapy and his gang out, issuing warnings around town: "All confidence, bunco and sure-thing men, and all other objectionable characters, are notified to leave . . . immediately." But they held fast, and the opponents retreated. It seemed that nobody was a match for Soapy until several of his gang members tried to rob a miner flush with gold and the victim turned a crowd against him. Soapy died in a shoot-out on Juneau Wharf in 1898. "The way of transgressors is hard," the minister said at his funeral.

Even McKenzie County's namesake was a frontier swindler.* After building a political machine in North Dakota, Alexander McKenzie traveled to the Alaskan town of Nome in 1900 to run a scheme defrauding gold miners. With the help of a corrupt judge, he arranged to be the receiver of disputed mining claims and hired workers to extract the gold hastily. Marshals arrived from San Francisco to arrest him. Authorities slammed open his vault to return the gold to its rightful owners. McKenzie served only three months in jail before receiving a presidential pardon, and returned to North Dakota politics.

An Irish real estate man recalled seeing Hogan at the Williston Brewing Company just before he disappeared in spring 2015. As his story went, the developer invited him out to party and boasted of his multimillion-dollar net worth. A few days later, the scandal hit the *Williston Herald*. By then, the word was that Hogan had flown out of the country.

---

* The Great American Lodge on Highway 85 west of Watford City was in McKenzie County, though Hogan spent much of his time in Williston, in Williams County.

"I don't know if I've ever been in a place where there are more
flimflam men," a businessman from Chicago said of the North Dakota oilfield. He told me at the brewing company that he even ran
into a crook who had screwed him over on a gas deal in Kentucky
a dozen years earlier, sitting right down the bar. "I never met so
many scammers."

One acquaintance of Hogan's would cringe when he heard
somebody say he was an *investor* in the Bakken; he considered it
a four-letter word around these parts. "They're all con artists, and
they showboat like they're high rollers. It's like a big poker game
up here."

Indeed, many people were not who they appeared to be.
It seemed that every woman had a story of discovering that her
boyfriend was married, wanted in another state, or using her for
a place to crash. ("He's not hot!" a woman told me upon discovering her suitor's ulterior motives. *"He's homeless!"*) Businesspeople
discovered that investment partners and contractors were ripping
them off. A real estate broker told me he didn't realize a massage
firm he represented was providing illicit services on Backpages
.com. Office administrators learned to double as parole officers to
track every employee with a rap sheet hurtling through. A friend
who found herself in one such position for a fly-by-night oil services
subcontractor would field phone calls about the ex-cons stumbling
around barely knowing how to turn on a power washer. Then the
boss's prison buddy from Texas took over and the embezzling got
under way. The whole operation went under and business owners
stormed the office to complain about unpaid bills. Soon my friend
was dodging calls from a federal prosecutor, and realized she had
unwittingly enabled the higher-ups' scam.

One's usual gut instinct didn't work; it couldn't. I occasionally met otherwise thoughtful, educated people who would rant
wildly about all that had gone wrong and everyone who was out
to get them, and took them for delusional types who brought on
their own troubles. Yet I would ultimately learn that they weren't
delusional at all; I began going off on paranoid rants myself. People who had never been to the Bakken gave me the same pitying

looks I had once given the ranters, and the people who had been here told me, "I can believe it."

This loss of trust hardened even good-natured people in ways they never imagined. Some North Dakotans would keep going when they saw somebody stranded along Highway 85, as lending a neighborly hand no longer seemed wise. "You can't put the police up at the gates of the state and say, 'You're in, you're out, you're in, you're out,'" oil lobbyist Ron Ness said. "Some of us, as North Dakotans, would like to do that."

·:·   ·:·   ·:·

The second Great American Lodge, in Culbertson, Montana, sat on land between a casino and a weedy lot overlooking a billboard for oil rig mats. The town was so small that it lacked the sewer capacity to accommodate the three-hundred-bed man camp, and a deal was made that Culbertson would expand its infrastructure and the company would contribute a half million dollars over the next five years. A former employee told me he quit after figuring the enterprise was corrupt, but he couldn't get anyone in Culbertson to listen. "They screwed the whole town over," he said. Investors called the town hall, asking if the scheme was legitimate. I found an email in a municipal file cabinet from a real estate agent in Alberta, asking, "Is it too good to be true?" Nobody had replied.

The lodge hadn't even acquired tenants when the SEC shut it down. Culbertson mayor Gordon Oelkers and I walked through the white trailers on the property. "They're pretty chintzy," he said. Dozens of the units had recently failed a required government inspection. Peering through the windows, we spied mattresses leaning against the wall. The mayor heard that workers were still bringing them in a couple of days after the scandal broke.

But the biggest mess was at the original lodge. Soon after the scandal became public, I arranged to trespass at the empty camp with Scotty Fain. He had put together the deal for the developers to acquire the property and had supervised the construction. Scotty disagreed with the SEC's move to halt activity on the site, saying that regulators should have allowed the man camp to stay open so that it could bring in revenues for the investors and provide dozens of jobs for cooks, housekeepers, and managers (the agency ultimately sold the development to Scotty in 2016).

An empty pickup blocked the entrance to Great American Lodge at the end of a rutted dirt road, abutted on either side by a chain-link fence edged with weeds and sunflowers. We stepped out of our vehicles and squeezed past the pickup. Rows of beige trailers with white skirting lined the lot in perfect formation, but the southeast corner was in disarray. GuardWrap curled off half-finished structures in what would have been the development's third phase. Seven roll-in showers sat on the tiled floor inside, along with rolls of vinyl flooring and boxes of construction materials. Wood planks for the walls stretched to the ceiling, insulation was torn out, and wires dangled askew. I tripped on a hole in the floor and saw more of them—shower drains, evidently. Gas tanks for the kitchen sat outside. Cement blocks lay in the grass like tombstones; tarp and cardboard packaging had been thrown about. We came up on the yellow grader that Scotty had used to smooth over the gravel pathways. He desperately wanted to take it back, but the SEC had forbidden them from moving anything.

We walked all the way around the development until we arrived at the red building that held the dining hall. I climbed the steps and looked at the notice on the door: GREAT AMERICAN LODGE WILL BE CLOSED UNTIL FURTHER NOTICE. Standing out front, I could see a workover rig, a crane, and several grain bins across Highway 85. The bustle depicted in the flyers was a sham. There was no battalion of workers in hard hats and FR coveralls. No pickups rumbling in and out. All we heard was the whistle of traffic passing us by.

Streetlights

The rig was a mobile skyscraper, erected here and there over a vast oilfield, and lately they had put it off Highway 85, towering over two lanes of madcap traffic. The crews had assembled it at the intersection of a route to Montana, to be precise, and the derrick soared as yet another waypost along roads that unfurled through a blank of winding plains. It was one of the closest rigs to the Wild Bison, so mesmerizing in its authority that it was easy to forget that nearly two hundred other rigs presided over western North Dakota.

A crew lowered drill pipe into the ground ninety feet at a time, as motors pumped mud and water down-hole to keep the drill bit turning through the hard earth. Muddy liquid coursed through long tanks, sending a putrid stench wafting through the steel grid walkway above. Shale shakers processed the used drilling fluid, separating out the solids, which would be later mixed with fly ash and dried before going to a disposal. Trucks hauled in cement and steel casing pipe, which laborers would run down the well as an extra barrier to prevent contamination below the ground.

Nevin Larsen monitored the operation from a trailer in front of the rig, watching the movements of the drill pipe on a screen mounted to the wall. It transmitted the data in real time: depth of the hole and drill bit, the rate and volume of mud pumping . . . Nevin worked at a long desk that had an array of computers and paperwork, including the daily drilling reports from Halliburton. He kept a sheet that listed the depths of geological layers—with names like Greenhorn, Dakota, and Pine Salt Top—down to their destination: the middle Bakken target, dolomite sandwiched between two layers of black shale in a formation that had begun 360 million years before.

A whiteboard had an L-shaped drawing of the drilling plan adorned with scribblings in red, black, and green. This was the trajectory of the drill pipe, which traveled two miles down and sideways in beginning, intermediate, and lateral stages. The notes marked the intersection of the two lines as the kickoff point, and the right end as TD, or total depth, around twenty thousand feet.

Men with dirty boots tramped in and out to talk to Nevin, a racket of voices:

"I was up half the night cleaning my shack. He left a pile of dishes in the sink, the bathroom was just disgusting, ate what food I had left in my fridge . . ."

"Keep the salesmen out of our hair so we can do our damn job."

"I tried not to kink this little bit of lateral too bad."

"He's going to go home and play with his hot rods."

In the eighties, Nevin returned from the army to roughneck in eastern Montana, working his way up to derrick man and driller. It was a wilder place, Nevin recalled, back when drugs were rampant and a rig worker could get fired and drive up to another rig for a new job without question. Then oil went bust. "We're done," his boss told him when he showed up to work one day in 1982. It was a line every oilman knew to prepare for, and Nevin reacted with the usual North Dakotan enterprise, taking odd jobs to survive. He poured cement, pipelined, and gauged oil tanks. Then Nevin bought the gas station on Highway 85 in Alexander—the same operation that the Kysar family from Washington would purchase as a precursor to building the Wild Bison decades later. Nevin had already paid off his home. He supported his wife and two children on $20,000 a year running that gas station, a feat that he admitted would be nearly impossible nowadays. "You would be on every kind of welfare known to man," he said. Many people in western North Dakota had tales like that from the eighties, when the oil downturn left business owners near bankruptcy and municipal governments mired in debt.

The industry slumped through the following decade, and by 1999 the state had no rigs running. That was the same year that geochemist Leigh Price wrote a paper stating that the Bakken had up to 413 billion barrels of oil, though many critics dismissed this as absurdly optimistic. The state had produced oil since 1951, but it had always been largely uneconomical to drill wells in the Bakken formation because the rock was so tight. Drilling vertically had a low success rate. Well after major oil corporations had given up on the region, geologist Richard Findley's research found that they had been drilling in the wrong direction. The industry found almost universal success in unlocking oil when it began horizontal drilling, in combination with fracking. In 2008, the US Geological Survey determined that the Bakken was the largest continuous oil accumulation it had ever assessed.

Nevin sold the gas station to his business partner in the early 2000s and found work as a roughneck again. He worked his way up to the position of company man for Whiting Petroleum, contracted to supervise a drilling rig for the company. (Hardly anyone on the rigs actually worked for the operator; the drilling crew and the rest were mainly contractors.) "I don't know of a better job out there," he told me of being a company man. "No college, spent three years in the army. I've got nothing special, hell no. Everybody's got to have a degree to do anything over a $50,000-a-year job now." People in his position usually made at least four times that.

A tall and lanky fellow, Nevin had acquired battle scars from decades in the business. While trying to latch pipe as a derrick man, he missed and smashed the same finger that he had nearly lopped off while laying down pipe another time. He didn't come down, just kept tripping pipe three days in a row with a swollen finger. He seemed a little wistful, sometimes, about how they'd toughed it out in the old days, before companies had gotten so particular about safety; Nevin would have been in the hospital filling out reams of paperwork if such mishaps happened now.

He had a kitchen in his trailer, though there was little time to cook. Nevin broke up Italian sausages, chopped tomatoes, and mixed them with spaghetti noodles. He ate a lot of pork chops, and liked to throw together ham, onions, rice, and eggs for breakfast. He drank a pot of coffee a day and tempered his stress with Copenhagen chew.

Nevin and the drilling crew worked from six in the morning to six at night for two weeks in a row, alternating with three other company men and crews to keep the rig running continuously. (Separate teams would come later to frack the wells and get the oil flowing.) He told me he was eager for his two-week hitch to end so he could take his Harley down to South Dakota. Nevin and his wife had looked at moving there a few years ago but decided to stay. "It ain't so bad," he said. Nevin noted that the long-awaited Menards home improvement store was coming to Williston; there was a new Buffalo Wild Wings, Famous Dave's, and Fuddruckers, even a few sushi restaurants—if only the road construction would cease. On his days off, he liked to make his own batches of wine and soap. He believed that people had grown too dependent on buying everything.

Sometimes people snubbed him, as if to convey that his high income carried little prestige because he was an oilman. Take the time he visited Des Moines and stopped at a high-end cooking store. He wanted to buy a $300 specialty pan, but the salesman seemed taken aback and told him he might want to check out a lesser store. His wife had to scoot him out before he made a scene. Another time, he sat down with his wife at a bar in Las Vegas and ordered a bottle of Bud Light. The waiter looked at him like he was a hick. Then he ordered a shot of Crown extra rare, just to show he had money.

"This could all go away at any time," Nevin told me during one of our first meetings in June 2014. I assumed he was speaking out of modesty, or perhaps like a lawyer noting a technicality. Of course anything was *possible*, but if you were standing on the edge of the rig site and watching the traffic jamming Highway 85, it seemed unlikely. The number of rigs running in the United States was approaching record levels. Oil traded for more than $100 a barrel. So I was startled, but he later elaborated that it was a dog-eat-dog oilfield. "There's no job security in the oilfield—none." Nevin relayed this with no resentment or criticism.

That it might all go away also seemed a far-off prospect given that Whiting was on the verge of making national news for acquiring Kodiak Oil & Gas. The deal would allow it to surpass fracking pioneer Harold Hamm's company, Continental Resources, to become the largest holder of oil acreage in North Dakota. Whiting planned to accelerate its drilling operations.

Nevin and I rarely spoke about corporate dealings; we were in a setting where people tended to simply focus on what was in front of them. I came to find that the oilfield was so remote, and our focus on work so singular, that we saw all the rest disappear into a blur—checking the phone to remember the day of the week, losing track of current events. Sometimes I would learn about a major news development through the TV tuned to Fox News in Nevin's trailer, near the screen where he monitored the drilling operations. I was half watching that TV when Fox reported that ISIS insurgents had declared a rebel state in Iraq. Nevin remarked that oil prices could spike with violence in the Middle East, but I didn't really understand the news because I had taken to ignoring the outside world. (Another journalist later told me that while I was in North Dakota for the month of June 2014, House GOP leader Eric Cantor had been voted out in a populist revolt. "He was?" I asked.)

∴   ∴   ∴

Over the next year, I sporadically stopped in to visit Nevin as he moved to rigs across Alexander, then to Stanley, and later just outside Williston. One night I drove east out of town down Highway 1804, a narrow road named for the year Lewis and Clark nearly froze on their journey through North Dakota. The darkness of Bakken nights was striking, effacing any edge and shadow of the pavement, the hills, the horizon. It was especially so on this route, where an obsidian shroud descended a few miles past the Halliburton complex. No one, it seemed, had put up lampposts in all these years of oil traffic. I looked for the flares to steady my mind, following the road as it lashed the hills like a tentacle. Companies burned off the excess gas that flowed up with the oil because they lacked the pipelines to transport it to market, and the gas was worth too little to conserve otherwise. It was easier to blast plumes of toxins into the sky. The flames appeared after I turned north onto a dirt road ten miles down, their fiery luster twisting high above the oil wells. A constellation of streetlights.

I relaxed in their glow as I drove over the ruts of the road labeled LIMITED MAINTENANCE. Perhaps a half mile before the turnoff west, I came around a bend and paused. The dark broke and there was the rig, bejeweled with white lights sparkling over the derrick and everywhere else. Behind it, hundreds of lights scattered across Williston a dozen miles beyond, as though it were a grand city and the rig were the gateway. There were surprises like this all over western North Dakota—rounding a curve and losing oneself in something spectacular.

It was a few minutes before one in the morning when I arrived on location, backing up into the row of pickups at the edge. They made everyone park that way so people could leave quickly in an emergency, without the hassle of reversing. I stepped out into the chilly air and walked toward the row of trailers. The rig had the clean, bright colors of Patterson-UTI, the drilling contractor out of Texas: a white derrick with an orange crown, a blue base, and tanks with orange railings. But its most remarkable feature was that it could walk.

Oil companies typically secured leases from landowners that required them to drill at least one well over a period of three to five years to hold their rights to the minerals. It made little sense under those conditions to drill wells efficiently—that is, to drill large numbers of wells close to one another. Oil companies had to rush to drill before the lease expired, or else they'd have to renew the rights to drill at a far higher rate. So after drilling one well, crews would disassemble the rig, hire a company to move it to a different site, and assemble it again. It was a haphazard dance that spurred mass chaos on the roads and in farmers' once quiet fields. Now that the leases were secured, companies turned to their old locations to drill more wells next to one another, deploying rigs that could walk a few dozen feet to the next well using a hydraulic system.

Nevin was presumably asleep, as he worked only the day shift. I stood outside watching with his night shift counterpart, a man from Nova Scotia. He told me they would move the rig with 270,000 pounds of pipe still stationed on the rig floor. The crew had been preparing for hours, removing the hydraulic catwalk, a device that resembled a wide slide used to transfer drilling and casing pipes up to the rig floor, and disassembling the equipment designed to control dangerous well pressure. The rig had what they called orange stompers attached to its corners, resembling boxy feet. These would walk the rig over. It seemed like an invention of science fiction, a rig that could stalk the oilfield of its own accord, but in reality the rig moved at a laggard's pace.

A worker pressed buttons (up/retract, down/extend) on a handheld device that remotely activated the system. Four others monitored the stompers intently as they shined flashlights on them, leaning over to ensure the hoses inside didn't tangle and using a crowbar to straighten them out when they veered off track. The stomper would rise up on the left side, slide over, and lower to the ground. Then the right side moved up and down. A man inspected the front left stomper with a flashlight from several angles as it moved, putting his foot on it and pushing. At times, when it tilted up, the stomper seemed to come clear off the ground. A forklift rolled up with a big slab of wood for the rig floor, which protected the ground from the machines. I stood there mesmerized in the cold. It took less than an hour for the rig to assume its new position. The workers prepared to spud the next well.

I saw the fire rolling sometime around three. It died and came to life again, erupting in a titanic burst of flame just beyond the perimeter of our site, dark clouds spiraling. The men were moving the catwalk with a telescopic crawler crane to the rig's new location; a forklift hauled a slab of wood nearby. I looked at the rig, then the men, then the rig, then the trailers, waiting for the shouting and running. But the crew continued working as they had, through the dull rumble of machinery. I hurried to the trailer where the company man from Nova Scotia was stationed.

"There's a fire outside!" I said, bursting through the door.

He came out. "That's just a flare—it's barfing up oil," he said, and returned to his desk.

I stepped out and watched the third explosion, just past the empty pipe racks over the rocks and puddles. The conflagration swelled with such fury that it seemed as if it might roll right toward us.

A safety official for Whiting once told me that at his last company, they had three worker fatalities in vehicular wrecks—men dodging helter-skelter oilfield traffic or making the long drive back to their home state half asleep. "Working on the rig is pretty safe compared to the roads," he said. But fire! Everyone learned to read those blazes over the prairie, the difference between flames contained and those that raged wildly. A flare had recently scorched forty-five hundred acres of forest near Watford City after spitting out some oil and igniting, prompting one county official to speculate to me that it was only a matter of time before a tumbleweed flew into a flare and set off another catastrophe. Lightning still caused periodic explosions at saltwater disposals, as it had next to the Wild Bison.

I flinched while thinking of dozens of burn victims in the North Dakota oilfield that had to be flown hundreds of miles away to specialized burn centers in Denver, Salt Lake City, or St. Paul, some arriving at the hospital so charred that doctors couldn't save them. In one of the earliest, most horrifying cases, a novice oil worker went on a rig in 2010 without flame-resistant clothing and was rushed to St. Paul for treatment after a fiery accident. He was permanently disfigured. I had recently interviewed a young man at the St. Paul facility whose legs were covered in third-degree burns after an oil treater exploded; he was searing with pain and nightmares.

So you understand my dread watching this inferno sear the night. I hurried to my car behind the trailers and drove over the scoria and up the hill, off the location, rounding curves shaped like a river's oxbows until I reached a battery of oil tanks. I idled for a while, until I could no longer see flames. I waited ten minutes to be sure and slowly edged back onto the rig, returning to the company man's trailer. We stood outside with the rig manager as the fire came back. Another flare peered over a faraway hill, reflecting purple beams.

"It's fucking burning!" the rig manager said. "I didn't realize there was a flare down there. I thought someone's house was on fire. I thought it was a workover rig burning down."

"There it goes again and again," said the company man. "Oh yeah, that's a good one." Huge flames billowed. It was ten minutes to four.

"It's a long way away," he told me as we settled back in the trailer. "It looks worse at night. You work in a dangerous industry and you get a feel for what's danger and what's not."

As the night waned, he completed his paperwork and ran through the usual oilfield lore—getting hazed in the early days on a rig in Wyoming, battling superstitions in Texas, meeting a lady roughneck in Montana that one time (some used to say that a woman on the rig was bad luck). Nevin shuffled in a little after five-thirty, having just woken up. The sky was lightening, and through the windows we saw pink and yellow streaking beyond the rig.

"You wouldn't believe what happened . . . huge fire and smoke everywhere," I said.

As usual, he seemed unfazed.

"We had giant fireballs," the other man said. "The last one was pretty good." He turned to me with amusement. "You were excited, weren't you?"

The clouds had turned purple with pink running through them. The lights still gleamed like emeralds on the rig, but their effect was fading with the rising sun. I drove off, past the two pump jacks and over a cattle guard, and turned right. As I neared the highway, I counted nine flares. I passed through Williston and drove south down Highway 85, where a thick fog oozed over the Missouri River. I could scarcely see ahead. The haze was white and day had broken.

A Fugitive at the Border

Just east of Montana and south of Saskatchewan, the stillness settled into the countryside like a fog, floating as hazily as the dust plumes from the oil trucks that rolled over dirt roads. It set in on the final northern stretch of Highway 85—past the frenzy of Williston and the turnoff by the Pilot truck stop, where it all went quiet. The languor reigned even during the fiercest gusts, as though this was where the horizon yielded to the end of the earth and time had fallen away. Dozens of miles below the international border, the radio stations gave the temperature in Celsius clear up to Saskatoon and phone carriers texted *Welcome to Canada Dial + 1 & 10-digit # to call U.S.* before reception faded.

Tips of grass jutted from snowy fields like a drunk's old stubble, yet in the spring they turned a singing green and the ice melted from the sloughs to reveal blue ponds fringed by cattails. The farmhouse sat just east of Port of Entry 7, down a rocky dirt road, south of the long, narrow sloughs that stretched to the Canadian border. Ducks congregated around the water, and black birds flew overhead. Pump jacks bobbed, drawing oil for Continental Resources. That was the Oklahoma oil company that famously wildcatted a well here in Divide County in 2004—executive Harold Hamm heralded it as the first commercially successful well to be horizontally drilled and fracked in North Dakota. He placed a monument there in 2011 inscribed with grand purpose: THIS WELL USHERED IN A NEW ERA IN THE AMERICAN OIL INDUSTRY . . .

Near it sat a boulder that honored the early prairie settlers who cleared the land of rocks and stones to make fertile farms, as if to remind us of what this place had always been and always would be, eons after the last drop of oil came from the earth. So it was to the old farmhouse that Jody Gunlock came to escape what oil had wrought. He boarded his John Deere tractor and looked out onto the land his father bought after returning from World War II. Jody fell into the rhythm of his boyhood as the tractor whirred along at five miles an hour, fertilizer and wheat seed falling into narrow lines in the haunted silence.

He had wanted to work a farm full-time, but that was an impossibility with a wife and children even in the early eighties. The farm was only two hundred acres, a paltry plot compared to the enormous agricultural enterprises taking over the industry. So he joined the army and moved from station to station, an adventure that sometimes gave him occasion to marvel at the long history of foreign civilizations. Pioneers had hardly even settled the northwest corner of North Dakota until the early 1900s. Many had starved, died, or fled—some, perhaps, driven to madness by the desolation—and only one-quarter of his native Divide County's population remained. Jody and his wife found a way to come home from his latest assignment, in St. Paul, Minnesota, when they reached the twilight of middle age and their children had grown. With his army pension, they could farm as a hobby while Jody worked as county emergency manager and his wife taught school.

The tractor was where he came to forget the stresses of the day—to feel, in some small way, that he was doing his part to feed the world when he went to the Noonan grain elevator to sell his crops. He could look straight north at the cluster of trees and see the fringe of Canada, measuring distances by the one gas flare that burned ahead—he knew it was south of the border by a half mile. In the mornings he turned south off the unpaved road past the Lutheran church, and again west by the New Ag station with its rows of white fertilizer tanks onto Highway 5. The corridor ran parallel to the border—Highway 85 dead-ended against this road much further east—like a lifeline connecting the Main Streets and grain elevators. Jody reported for work at the courthouse, a majestic century-old building distinguished by a domed ceiling painted with ranchers and Native Americans.

He would commiserate there with the sheriff and the other county officials about the unfortunate position of the border towns. They were too small and far away to receive the state dollars needed to offset the enormous stresses of energy development, and much of the frenzied oil activity was centered one and two hours south in the bigger towns of Williston and Watford City. The area along the border was the outpost of the outpost, where disreputable dealings remained hidden and unpunished. Out-of-state oil workers ran overloaded semis roughshod over dirt roads, binged on meth, poached wildlife, stole heavy equipment, and then ran, protected by the industry's use of so many subcontractors that rogue behavior was hard to trace. The jail was so full that they had to export prisoners to lockup in Montana, where a fellow with a long rap sheet tried to hang himself behind bars, leaving cash-strapped Divide County on the hook for up to $100,000 of his medical expenses.

Enforcing the law over such a sparse, sprawling area was impossible: they could double the police force and it would make no difference. The sheriff, who had grown up with Jody, had a tendency to joke about such things, as humor was all that could carry them through this. They used to brag around here that temperatures of 40 below zero kept the riffraff out, but then the oil drilling came, and the riffraff discovered Carhartt, North Face, and remote car-starters. Searing cold no longer guarded one of the most remote corners of the United States. The officers of Scandinavian descent could not decipher the accents of the men with names like Billy Bob from Louisiana crammed into the trailer parks. The sheriff derided them as "the swamp people" one saw on TV. He would arrest a man whose criminal record ran for pages, and when the sheriff called California or Idaho or wherever he had escaped from in order to inquire about extradition, his counterpart on the other end would too often bark, *"You can keep him!"*

Illegal dumping of oil waste was common. The water that flowed up with the oil in North Dakota was up to eight times saltier than the ocean, laced with metals and chemicals from the fracking process and containing low levels of naturally occurring radioactivity. Usually called saltwater or brine, the liquids had to be separated out from the oil and gas through a special treater and sent by truck or pipeline to a disposal that would inject it more than a mile down-hole. Saltwater disposals drew national attention for their connection to earthquakes in Oklahoma. This was not a problem in North Dakota; instead, the outcry was over unscrupulous contractors dumping waste pell-mell. While farmland could survive an oil spill, saltwater scorched any vegetation in its path and nothing would grow in its place for all of time. But truckers looking to boost their profits and save time had no qualms about dumping their salty freight on somebody else's pasture.

For instance, the sheriff's department learned of a man hauling gravel down a prairie trail who got his truck sunk in a slough. The man and his friend flagged down a semi loaded with saltwater off the road and hooked up a tow rope to it, only to get the second truck stuck, too. So they stole a county grader, and when that failed they stole a bulldozer to pull the trucks out. They dumped the saltwater out of the truck in the slough and surrounding field to lighten the load. Often the full stories never emerged, as many preferred committing Class C felonies by cover of night. Such cases were difficult to prosecute, but the county thought it finally had a case. The county received a call about a Utah man who drove a truck for Frick & Frack Transport LLC dumping saltwater in a slough off a narrow dirt road. Jody and a sheriff's deputy came out to investigate. The ground held a high concentration of saltwater. The defendant hired a lawyer who pushed hard in the courtroom: Did the county not apply some "gunk" on the dirt roads to control the dust when people blew by farms at breakneck speed? It was potassium chloride, which increased the saltwater level. "Nobody saw my client do anything," the lawyer said, and the accused got off.

The saltwater disposals strained the liquid through long, tubular filter socks that caught bits of sand, earth, and other sediment to prevent them from clogging the well and pumps. When a crew drilled a well, the soil and rock that came to the surface had naturally occurring radionuclides. Placing the mesh filter between the saltwater and suspended solids caused the radioactivity to rise and concentrate. North Dakota required the used filter socks to be transported to special waste disposals out of state—usually Montana and Idaho—because of their higher radioactivity levels.

As the pace of the boom became more frenzied, rogue truck drivers found it easier to dump the socks in the oilfield than drive long distances to lawfully dispose of them. An early report came in about a thousand pounds of filter socks stuffed in leaking trailers south of Watford City. The manager of the landfill off Highway 85, a little south of the Wild Bison, fumed that they were tinted orange and hot, with liquid sliming off the side—the biggest pile of filter socks he'd ever seen. Rick Schreiber, the director, grew angry when state legislators who lived far away told them the radiation levels were too low to hurt anybody. "How fast would things happen," he asked me, "if a bag of nasty gross filter socks ended up on the capitol steps?"

Then Jody fielded a tip in 2014 about a mysterious sighting of industrial-sized garbage bags hauled into a crumbling, long-abandoned gas station in Noonan. He drove east down Highway 5 and turned into the town, which was little more than a faded Main Street. The gas station sagged just before the train tracks and grain elevator. Jody peered inside and saw two hundred garbage bags of filter socks, strewn like corpses on the dirt floor. His best friend from high school managed the grain elevator next door and recalled that it was hardly a covert operation: the men had hauled in the waste by shining daylight. Jody typed out an email to state regulators with the subject line "Giant Mess."

Evidence was scant. But investigators trawling the six rooms of filth found a receipt in one of the garbage bags from a saltwater disposal called the Berg. It operated a half hour east in an even more obscure corner of the oilfield. The Berg had been constructed by a Texas company from an abandoned oil well in Black Slough Field during the last oil boom in the early eighties. It had passed through several more operators before its sale in 2010 to a company managed by Jack Johnston, a white-haired, genteel man who still spoke with the lilt of his Louisiana upbringing.

A fugitive named James Kenneth Ward turned up on the border from Wyoming, where he had been charged with stealing $100,000 of equipment from an oilfield trucking company—a Ford 350 pickup, belly-dump trailer, two winches, a utility trailer, a Yamaha generator, and tire chains—and faced a decade in prison for felony grand larceny. The fugitive agreed to transport filter socks produced at the Berg disposal to special waste facilities out of state. He even tried to sell Jack several properties, including the Noonan gas station, but Jack told me he didn't want to assume liability for the old tanks on the premises.

Jack didn't seem like the sort to be duped very easily—he pleaded guilty in 1993 to securities fraud. The authorities claimed he took in $15 million in a scheme involving undisclosed bank accounts in the Channel Islands and the defrauding of a pension fund for British postal workers. Couldn't a man convicted of running a con detect another man's con?

Yet the fugitive, it seemed, had been a skilled imposter. "He wore pressed pants and pressed shirts and had a haircut," Jack recalled. "You got guys up here who are a million times more successful and didn't dress as well." He said the fugitive and his wife had invited him over for dinner at the nicest house in town. "Neither one of 'em cussed, drank, or smoked."

The fugitive frequented a boondocks bar called Group Therapy, where a bartender described him as a quiet patron who favored Budweiser. "He was always one step ahead of the law," she said with a chuckle. One night, a group of men spilled into the parking lot to brawl around closing time when a Chevy pickup tried to run them over. A fighter told the cops they all dodged the attack, but the pickup backed up and hit the side of their vehicle, spun around, and screeched off. Authorities eventually charged the fugitive with leaving the scene of an accident, and he went on the run again. The fugitive turned up in Idaho and led cops on a chase down the South Yellowstone Highway before ripping out the wires of the Taser probes they shot at him. He did a short stint in jail.

The following year, the feds learned he was hiding out in Mexico and arranged for his deportation, dumping him in a prison transport van bound for the Cowboy State to serve out his grand larceny charge. The vehicle stopped at a rest area in Independence Rock, Wyoming, to allow the inmates to use the bathroom. It was one of the last breaks on the sixteen-hundred-mile journey. As they readied for departure a few minutes later, the security officers counted heads.

The fugitive was gone.

Surveillance footage showed him fleeing out the back door into the wilderness, wrists cuffed but legs free. The private prison company overseeing the van searched in vain for an hour and a half before calling the local authorities. The Wyoming police began a manhunt with the help of US marshals, trying to follow his footprints and searching fifty-two square miles by land and more than twice that by air. Their target: white man, 180 pounds, brown hair and brown eyes, last seen in khaki shorts, black shirt, and flip-flops, stab wound on his left side. They staked out the rest area. Surely, they figured, he would return for food or the pay phone. The fugitive outwitted them all. Authorities figured he must have hiked fifteen miles through the night. One man reported that the fugitive told him he'd been in an accident and hitched a ride, appearing disheveled and unshaven. Another told police about a possible sighting of the fugitive at a Love's truck stop, but the tip led nowhere. The sheriff of Sweetwater County, Wyoming, advised motorists not to pick up hitchhikers on Interstate 80. Six months after the last sighting, authorities in North Dakota discovered that the fugitive had apparently lied to Jack about properly disposing of waste from the Berg. They identified the fugitive as the culprit in the biggest illegal oil waste dumping that the Bakken had seen—it was likely among the largest in the nation's fracking boom. He was still on the lam.

∴ ∴ ∴

Waste disposal could be a savage business around these parts. Weeks after discovering the cache of filter socks in Noonan, authorities found more of them dumped on land owned by James

Siegrist, who had been serving a federal prison sentence on charges of possession of guns and ammo by a convicted felon. He'd accidentally shot somebody with a .45-caliber handgun, and his rap sheet included forgery, counterfeiting, drug possession, and theft. His company, Conservative Trucking, was sued by its primary customer, fracking pioneer Continental Resources, over allegations of stiffing contractors for more than $2 million. The suit against Conservative Trucking was filed after the contractors came after Continental for payment.

Jody was clearly disheartened by all of this as we drove out to see the gas station in Noonan, passing the new grain elevator and the crumbling childhood farmstead of the chief justice of the North Dakota Supreme Court, Jody's old fraternity brother from Grand Forks. The shambles at the gas station raised an alarming question for him: what other oil waste had someone dumped in one of these hundreds of dilapidated old buildings scattered across the oilfield, relics of the harsh frontier? They'd never find it all.

We turned into Noonan, pulling up next to the building, which had deteriorated considerably since the last time he was here. The cleanup crew in white hazmat suits had finished decontaminating the place, but the sight was no less disturbing: rusty tanks sat out back and the sides of the wood shack slumped as though they would fall into themselves. Jody warned me not to get too close when I walked around. He said the fugitive owner had gotten the place for practically nothing at an auction, and the culprit's mother in Montana paid the property taxes. Authorities sent her a letter directing her to fix the place, but Jody doubted that would happen, as cleanup would cost far more than it had to buy the building.

Since nobody could nab the fugitive, regulators stuck Jack's company with a penalty for failing to properly dispose of the filters at an authorized facility and allowing waste to leak into soil. The parties reached an agreement reducing the fine from $800,000 to $20,795—that would be enough to cover the cost of cleanup— and requiring that Jack's firm cooperate with criminal investigations and pay the full amount if there was a repeat offense. The

North Dakota Industrial Commission, which oversaw the state's oil development, believed more in cooperation with the industry than in punitive regulation. The panel, composed of the governor, the agricultural commissioner, and the attorney general, held the principle that the free market reigned supreme. It was standard at the time for the commission to knock fines against oil companies down at least 90 percent under the condition that they would have no repeat offenses over the next few years.

Jody drove less than a mile south to a building that used to be his school as a child—it closed after a coal mine shut down in the late 1970s. He and several local officials met to discuss their requests to the state for financial aid to offset the cost of oil development. One of them told me she was sad to come here because it reminded her of all the people who had left since grade school, how the mine's shuttering "put the knife" through the town. Afterward, Jody drove me around until we were very close to the border, within view of the steam rising from the power plants in Estevan. "It's not the edge of the world," he joked, "but by God, you can see it from here."

We went for lunch at Just Jude's by the county courthouse. The restaurant's bulletin board was known to post ads evoking the region's proud Scandinavian heritage: a celebration for Syttende Mai—Norway's Constitution Day—and the showing of a movie called Kon-Tiki, a historical drama based on the Thor Heyerdahl voyage of 1947. That afternoon, Jody ordered a bacon cheeseburger, and I had the hamburger potato casserole, a hearty meal for a day when the temperature was a few degrees below zero. It was so cold that a grimy layer of snow had frozen over the streets like another layer of asphalt, unyielding to the plows.

A Canadian at the counter began chattering to Jody about his daughter's engagement. Jody was not in a bright mood, fixated on how state regulators had betrayed them on the fine and just about everything else. In North Dakota, complaining about the oil industry used to be almost a breach of social mores. But as residents became increasingly upset and the stresses of the oil rush deepened, people became more emboldened in their criticism.

The two of us listened as a row of cops at the counter griped among themselves about the state reducing the fine for the filter sock dumping. Like Jody, they were furious over what they saw as yet another capitulation to the oil industry.

"We've been hosed," one of the sheriff's deputies said.

"What was that quote you had in the paper?" Jody called out.

"We got hosed," repeated the deputy, who had been a major player in the filter sock investigation. "The city of Noonan . . . got *hooooosed!*" Everybody laughed. "Got to drag it out. *Hooooooosed . . .*"

The deputy was angry that state regulators had reached the settlement without so much as notifying him. As the deputy rose to leave, he turned to Jody. "You know where there's a suspended sentence for a year and you have that big fine hanging out there . . . it's set up for failure. Terrible! Don't get me going. My blood pressure . . ." Everybody laughed again. "It's a nightmare for law enforcement. You do the charges and politics gets involved, and it reeks."

"Mm-hmmm," Jody told him. "Well . . . we have the best regulatory agency that the oil industry can buy."

In that month, December 2014, the Berg saltwater disposal that produced the dastardly filter socks injected eighty-eight thousand barrels of waste into the earth—its all-time monthly high. The disposal went up for sale the following year.

Edge of the World

*I*t was dark, the moon nearly full, when I began the hour-long ride from the border to my hotel, down roads lit only by here-and-gone oil tanker trucks and the red lights blinking from faraway farms. It was that time of year when 4:45 looked like midnight under a raven sky, the headlights revealing only the smudges of snowbanks.

Of course I still remember this. Long after I left North Dakota my memories returned time and again to driving. Endless travels on country roads, by turns foreboding and majestic and tiresome—the red roof of a Cenex gas station, elevators of grain, a lone barn or tree on an endless expanse, stopping for the roar of trains, the clang of a flagpole in the wind, signs numbering the miles to towns that were more a name than a place, the car's fuel gauge dropping, dropping . . .

On this evening—or was it still afternoon?—the rental car burned up gas much faster than my usual vehicle. I didn't notice until too late that the gauge was down to one blinking bar. It was twenty-five miles in any direction to get gas, and this wasn't the sort of place where one could count on AAA. The road had no shoulders. Roll to a stop and a semi truck would barrel up from behind a few minutes later going seventy miles per hour with nowhere to skid except into the car or over the snow. Stall out and die overnight in temperatures of 4 degrees below zero. It wasn't terribly cold for us in the Upper Midwest, but it would be deadly if one was stranded for hours. I thought of Jody's wisecrack—*it's not the edge of the world*—and it was of little comfort here on the brink.

I drove slowly through miles of this snowy gulf until the lights of a house shined beyond a gravel driveway. I stepped out and knocked. Nobody answered. I banged on the window and called out. An old man with shaggy hair opened the door in his underwear. I began rambling out my story and he closed the door and said he'd be right back. He returned fully dressed, urging me to come in.

I inched back, fearful. "I won't hurt you," the old man said. He smiled. "I'm the nicest guy you'll ever meet." Stacks of clutter hovered behind him. I didn't entirely trust him, but the glacial borderland beyond us was not in the least negotiable. So I waited in the kitchen as he fumbled around in a shed and found a two-gallon can of lawnmower fuel. The nozzle didn't fit the gas tank. The old man returned and called the house of a farmer down the road, but somebody told him he wasn't home. "Well, is Scotty there?" he asked. Pause. "Scotty? . . . You're drunk?" He returned to the kitchen and told me to follow him one mile south and down a gravel road to a farmhouse, where Scotty—well, he'd be too wasted to help much, but he could show us to the gas tanks.

I trailed his pickup, and he flew so fast on the gravel road that the taillights disappeared over a hill and then I didn't see him at all. I pulled up to the house, waiting five minutes before a pickup came swerving from around the back. Scotty ran out and told me to drive over the icy lot to the tanks. Back. Forward. Closer. Stop. There was a lot of whirring and clanging as they messed with the tanks—nobody could see in the dark—but the fuel didn't flow.

"Just keep firing the tank up," Scotty told the old man. "It's slow because it's cold." Then Scotty knelt by my window so his head was level with mine. He was drunk indeed. "I'm a Wisconsin boy, I know how to party," he said. "We lived together for a couple years. . . . I'm part of the mafia here."

"C'mon, don't scare the piss out of her," the old man said.

A middle-aged woman came out to see what was going on and insisted we come inside. She cut off my bumbling explanations as we hurried over the snow. We burrowed in the kitchen and she brought out chili and crackers with butter. Jimmy offered to drive the fifteen miles to town for gas. I fished in my bag for cash, but he refused, in the traditional North Dakotan generosity.

"He's such a good guy," said Scotty. He turned to the old man. "You are a very genuine person."

The old man laughed. "Oh, my goodness," he told me. "I bet you ain't never come across anything like this in your life." He began rambling about old presidents. "I am a conspiracy theorist. I am on to the Kennedy assassination."

"Who do you think did it?" I asked.

"Johnson or Bush."

"Open this guy's brain. You gotta crack his brain, crack him," said Scotty.

The old man left. The woman and I talked a little about the boom. She was a legal assistant for one of the county prosecutors battling an explosion of caseloads. My host lamented that there were so many people on the road these days who didn't know how to drive in the ice and snow. And that she used to leave her keys in the car and walk into the grocery store and know everybody, and now she couldn't, and she didn't. And they were building too much housing everywhere, and there wouldn't be enough workers to fill it . . .

My benefactor returned just as the woman's husband and two sons came home. He put the gas in my car and drove it right up to the house. I tried to give the old man money again, but he refused, one and two and three times, so we said goodbye and I rode back up the gravel road through the claws of the wind.

PART II
FREE MARKET RHAPSODY

The Sheer Emptiness of It

Highway 85 approaching Watford City from the south:
the faint slopes of the buttes, then a drapery of glittering
lights, civilization rising. Traffic cones, apartments, hotels. Theodore Roosevelt's head. Great American Lodge. The turnoff to the
landfill. The Wild Bison. A friend had told me to go a little ways
past the truck stop and turn right on an unmarked road. I was returning to the oilfield in fall 2014 and it was hard, as usual, to find
somewhere to stay; I had arranged through the friend's colleague
to stay in a spare room at a trailer park called Dakotaland. But I
couldn't find it on a map, nor by the vague directions I had been
given. What road? The sky was black, and there were no lights. I
couldn't see any of the landmarks. Where were the tobacco shop
and the post office? The Hi Way Lounge and the Hard Ride Saloon? The Shut Eye Hotel and the Ragged Butte Inn? I knew I had
gone too far when I hit Route 200, near where I used to visit Nevin
on that old drilling rig.

I turned around and drove a ways, but there again: the lights
of the Wild Bison. Still none of the old sights had appeared. Surely
I was hallucinating. I had that feeling often in the Bakken, that
sense of drifting into a mirage. The nights were so black, the landscape so stark, the aura so unforgiving. I was alone, driving back
and forth through nothing, and then I was not even on the road
anymore but just in my own mind. As I thought of giving up and
sleeping at the truck stop, I saw a vague turnoff and found myself
on a dirt and gravel road. A semi truck followed, blaring its lights,
and the road kicked up a plume of dust so thick that it blinded me.

The dust faded and the black resumed. I turned twice, drove up a hill, and veered left at the fork. Before me were rows of trailers and pickups. I pulled up to the one near the dumpster, with the cinder blocks out front. A roughneck from Tuscaloosa was supposed to let me in, but nobody answered when I rapped on the door.

I peered inside. The TV was playing *American Horror Story: Freak Show*. The sign on the door forbade smoking, but the trailer stank of cigarettes. The shower was running and a man yelled he'd be out soon. With three bedrooms, the trailer was expansive. I sat at the kitchen table, watching the freaks. There was a flash of tattoos and the roughneck from Tuscaloosa disappeared into his room, behind a door that someone had punched in a few times, to take a phone call.

Profanity punctured every sentence. "They ain't gonna fire me . . . it's hardcore . . . back in Alabama . . . a roughneck is not a position, it's a lifestyle. A driller used to be considered a roughneck, but now they're all computer automated. It's like playin' a Nintendo game, drilling holes." No, he insisted, it was people on the workover rig who were the *real* roughnecks. "Drillers are fluffnecks because they're all a bunch of fat lazy—" He cursed again, then remembered his guest and ushered me to a room on the opposite side of the trailer. There was an empty bed because a worker had had to be hauled off the rig in a stretcher. "I don't think he's coming back."

I sank into the mattress, wondering where, exactly, I was.

In the morning, I stepped out into the cool fall, the light. There it was: they'd built a massive bypass around the little town of Alexander and the streetscape I had searched for in vain. Residents had awaited it for years, desperate to stop the semis barreling through their community. The road had been widened from two lanes to four. In a few days they'd open another bypass around Watford City, prompting the governor to acknowledge he had heard the locals' concerns about taking truck traffic off small-town roads. I always remembered this when considering how fast the oilfield could change, that a visitor could be gone for less than four months and still lose her way on a road she had traveled dozens of times.

⋮ ⋮ ⋮

By this latest trip, the Kysar family had sold the Wild Bison to TravelCenters of America, the largest truck stop chain in the United States. "We're ready to go home," Derek Kysar said. The Wild Bison's appeal had always been that it wasn't corporate, like most other truck stops. But it was a shrewd move. They had described coming here as a move for survival during the recession, and they had done more than just survive—they had become an oil rush success story.

Some complained that the Wild Bison began requiring drug tests for employees, and several of the workers walked out. "When TA came into the Bison, it ruined everything," one muttered. The staff almost entirely turned over in just a few months, and some of them, along with the regulars, left the state shortly thereafter. But at least the new owner had added a beer cave and DVDs, to the delight of bored oil workers.

The truck stop planned for the area around Abe Lincoln's head never came to pass. Another project stalled west of Williston for a long time. TRAVEL CENTER FALL 2014, said the big sign on an empty lot:

A 64 ACRE MULTI-USE DEVELOPMENT

24,000 SF CONVENIENCE STORE

RESTAURANT, BEER-WINE SALES

GROCERIES & DRY GOODS

24 GAS PUMPS

10 HIGH FLOW DIESEL PUMPS

An outfit called Patriot Fuels eventually opened its own truck stop a few miles south of the Wild Bison, advertising LOTTO-CHEW-SMOKES-GAS-BEER-SHOWERS. The family that owned it came from Chicago, where there was too much government, they complained. Red-light cameras everywhere. Anywhere you went, the state of Illinois had its hand out. (It was a common topic of conversation to trash the liberal state or city from where one had absconded.) Of course, there were a lot of scam artists with their hands out in the Bakken, too, offering to go into business with Patriot. "No one comes with money," said an owner. "They're all here to use other people's money." Patriot Fuels had looked at the site of the Wild Bison years earlier, before anything was there, but figured that curve in the highway wasn't fit for a truck stop because it had been a two-lane death trap. Now the two truck stops were locked in a price war. Wild Bison employees would come by in their uniforms, taking pictures of Patriot's prices so they could knock theirs down a little.

All that fall, Danny trucked water to the fracks. He came to know an elderly truck driver named Stinky who was bald, save for two patches of hair on each side of his head. Some claimed he was a millionaire from Florida—a nonsensical assertion anywhere but the Bakken, given that Stinky lived in a semi with his dog. The man was not truly malodorous, just a rumpled mess. Danny met him to talk business over rum at Teddy's Residential Suites, which had the swankest bar in Watford City. Most memorably, it served the Fracker, a full bottle of Guinness poured over coffee ice cream. You could make it a Mother Fracker with a shot of Baileys. Stinky brought a stack of tattered books, including *Inspiration: Your Ultimate Calling* by Wayne Dyer. Danny gave him another spiritual self-help classic in exchange, *Battlefield of the Mind*. So many of them needed God, but oil didn't stop for church.

At one hotel in Watford City, they placed a Bible by the bedside that said *God's Word for the Oil Patch, Fuel for the Soul*. It had an offshore oil platform on the cover. *The search for oil and gas can be an adventure and also rewarding, but at the same time it can be disruptive and dangerous,* the Bible said. A corner of the hotel room mirror had a flier for an all-male Christian fellowship. Ministries started holding prayer groups at man camps on weekday evenings. But Danny's schedule didn't allow for any of that.

By necessity, he built a church on eighteen wheels. Congregation: one. Sitting at water depots and truck stops, Danny combed Stinky's gift for spiritual guidance: *Being in-Spirit isn't necessarily restricted to the work we do or the activities of our daily life . . . it's a return to that invisible, formless field from which all things emanate, a field of energy . . . called "intention."* God seemed to be rewarding him. November 2014 was the busiest month of Danny's career. He earned $12,000 delivering freshwater. The last frack was nearly 128 straight hours of work, running water to a site in eastern Montana.

It was a month that would make world history. I remember the frenzy of building in the oilfield then, watching in awe as they piled those bricks so fast it seemed to defy a human pace. I remember that tattooed roughneck at Dakotaland getting stoned every day after work, telling me they weren't going to keep paying for oil workers to fly back home every few weeks because it couldn't possibly go on like this. He didn't seem especially worried. "This place is for people who messed up their lives," he said of the Bakken as he split a bowl with the Texan rig worker from the trailer next door. When I asked why he would risk flying the drugs back and forth to Alabama, he said, "I'm a roughneck, darlin'. My life's already ruined."

What got him a few months later wasn't airport security but a layoff. The Organization of Petroleum Exporting Countries, or OPEC, refused to cut oil production at a meeting in Vienna on Thanksgiving, shunning its usual policy. Oil prices had been sliding gradually since June, the month I met Danny—that week at the water depot was their final gasp at more than $100 a barrel, and they might very well never be as high again in our lifetimes. The drilling frenzy created an overabundance of crude, while demand weakened in Asia and Europe. The oil cartel's move accelerated the decline, causing the worst crash since the eighties. OPEC leader Saudi Arabia had essentially declared war on the US shale industry, determined to put the frackers out of business. Workers in North Dakota were aggrieved when the bosses reduced their hours to forty and their pay to $85,000. There was no loyalty. I was reading Junot Díaz at the Hi Way Lounge one day, as the Wild Bison fry cook gambled at the blackjack table, when I overheard an oilman say he was looking at a job in Saudi Arabia.

"How do you feel about working for the enemy?" I asked him.

"Don't think that hasn't crossed my mind," he said. "But at the end of the day, you've got to think about your family."

Danny went to Panama for a few weeks in good spirits as he reflected on how much money he'd made. He had wandered around there with a surfboard years ago, and it was his favorite place in the world. He'd built decks and worked sundry carpentry jobs, read books on an island with no electricity, and drank with men rich and poor. He'd driven a small truck, hauling liquor, palm trees, guns, stereos, rock-and-roll equipment. For a little while, he claimed, he'd even driven one for a man who would become the Panamanian president. Danny and his comrades would load another truck up with tequila, groceries, and laundry for tourists at a surfing charter. He'd gone on a spearfishing trip and gotten lost at sea for thirty hours in a storm. Danny and his friends had opened a bar, raised a lot of hell, didn't make any money, and shut it down. On a later trip, he'd tell his expat friends about his job hauling freshwater to the fracks and they'd say, "But isn't fracking bad?" Danny tried to explain how exciting it was to be part of an oil boom, but they just asked who had the next turn at bocce ball.

He preferred the culture of Panama to America's cutthroat consumerism and hoped to retire there with his oil money someday. About the time I met him, Danny was corresponding with a woman in Panama. He fell in love and decided to marry her. It was an impulsive decision; Danny was an impulsive man. But this marriage seemed about the best decision he'd made in a long time. He had been too selfish, being out on his own. "Did you eat? Do you have on clean underwear?" she asked him every day as he hauled water. She was planning to join him in North Dakota the following year.

Danny returned in early 2015 to find oil prices had fallen by half from their summer peak. The speed with which it had happened was shocking, and the industry put most of the fracking activity on hold. Companies had also caught on to the inefficiencies of paying people to deliver freshwater. They increasingly ran overland polyurethane pipes resembling hoses along the roadside that could take the water straight from a depot or pond to the frack, cutting out the intermediary. "It will eliminate the need for thousands of water trucks traveling on already congested roads during the fracking process," one company wrote to landowners in McKenzie County. Trucking water was fast becoming an outdated occupation. Blue frack tanks with yellow railings were scattered all around like artifacts, dumped with plain disregard for thieves or the elements.

So Danny went back to trucking crude. No matter what the state of the markets, they would always need drivers to transport oil from thousands of existing wells. His employer transferred him to a town on the Canadian border called Lignite, near the Berg saltwater disposal that had produced the filter socks dumped in Noonan. It was the most remote place in the oilfield, a hundred miles northeast of Williston, two hundred miles from Bismarck, four hundred miles from Rapid City, two thousand miles from the Outer Banks. Near the turnoff into town were a half dozen grain bins and some fertilizer tanks, a tire warehouse, a convenience store advertising propane and room for trucks, and a welding shop. Yellow flowers sprouted like surprises. The big to-do in Lignite at the time was the state fining the fire department $659,000 for illegally selling water for oil development without state approval.

Danny lived in a green and beige apartment complex that had been hastily built for oil workers. The pickups outside had license plates from Arkansas, Utah, and Idaho. He admired the people who had the hardiness to make this their home, but he could not accept this as his: Lignite, population 155, named for its abundance of low-grade coal. The scenery was almost medieval. An abandoned church sat alone in a field across from the apartment, its phantasmal spire rising like the anger of dishonored gods.

Danny and I met at the 109 Club, a bar where the Norwegian flag hung on the wall and deer heads hovered above the jukebox. The family that ran the place was linked to the workers at the Berg saltwater disposal. An operator at the Berg, Josh Velo, later told me he'd invented a menu item called the Norwegian Mafia Burger, with two beef patties, bacon, grilled mushrooms, caramelized onions, and jalapeños. "I don't know if you're into heat," he said. "That's where that mafia part comes in—it's the heat in the burger."

But on this evening, I wasn't hungry. I asked a bartender with thick black glasses what kind of beers they had. He ticked them off: Budweiser, Bud Light, Coors . . .

"You have any Heineken?" I asked.

"This ain't the big city," the bartender snarled, but he looked more like a Fargo hipster than the workover rig hand he once had been.

I settled for a bottle of Miller Lite. Danny ordered a cheeseburger deluxe and his usual glass of Captain Morgan. "That's what sweet crude looks like," he said, holding up the rum. He paused. "Actually," he added, pulling my Miller Lite toward him, "that's what it looks like." Oil soaked his skin, seeped into his clothes, stank up the truck. But he found himself mesmerized by it, even the terrible fumes that made him dizzy when he walked the catwalk to open the top of the twenty-foot-high tanks. Amazing what a perfect liquid it was, how elusive it seemed. Hauling up to seven hundred barrels a day and never seeing anything more than a flash of gold through the narrow ribbon of glass on his hose. "I want to drink it. It's alluring—like diamonds, like fur, like Ferraris." He held up his rum. Sweet crude!

But that was the light crude an hour or two south in the heart of the Bakken. Sometimes his boss sent him to the wells around the borderland where the oil was black and the fumes were so dangerous to breathe that they kept respirator masks on-site for the truckers. "Dark, nasty, stinky—it will put you down—it will kill you."

As a man of the ocean, he couldn't take to Lignite—really anything along this wild convergence of Montana, North Dakota, and Saskatchewan. "This kind of desolation truly scares me . . . the isolation is what's getting me the most. The sheer emptiness of it." He threw his arm out helplessly. "It's raw. . . . I don't know . . . I'm kind of burned out on it."

This place was just—

Godforsaken.

Forlorn.

Ethereal.

Like the earth withered away.

It was the sort of place for somebody to trudge the embers of his regrets back and forth, around in circles, until the drudgery of trying to excise these old what-ifs seared his soul to the end. Here at the 109, Danny unloaded his burdens: he was estranged from his teenage son back in North Carolina after a bitter split from the boy's mother about a decade ago, and he despised himself for how everything had fallen apart. "When I think about it I can't function," he said as Bon Jovi blasted from the jukebox.

The oilfield was shaped and defined by fatherhood as surely as it was by the rigs and cranes, tanks and trunks. Workers would talk nonchalantly about the time they nearly died on an oil site, then collapse when reflecting on their failings as fathers. Many simply couldn't afford to live with their families, and considered it dangerous or impractical to move them to the Bakken. One man broke into tears during an interview as he realized how much he'd missed of his daughter's childhood because he worked such long hours. Another was overcome with shame as he recounted how the son he'd lost touch with after a drug addiction many years before had refused his Facebook friend request. One of the most common reasons people gave me for coming here was paying child support, often for offspring with whom they had little relationship. Many were divorced, often more than once.

This was all so embedded in oilfield culture that when I watched a particularly lavish fireworks display with several rig workers, one joked, "That's my child support check!" to a lot of laughs. What a father was, and what he wasn't—what made a good father and a bad one—these categorizations carved an underlying hierarchy. Jobs and relationships and life trajectories were so fractured that fatherhood was judged on a curve. It was better to send money than to be a straight deadbeat. It was preferable to be caught up on child support than owe back child support, and it was better to owe a little than to be on the hook for so much that it became a felony (this varied by state but could amount to being $10,000 or more in arrears). It was better to live far away from your family than stay at home and make minimum wage. Failing all else, as long as you mailed checks you were mostly absolved of other people's judgment, even if you didn't, or couldn't, do anything more.

Danny's first wife got into real estate during the housing boom on the beach and profited so well that he quit bartending to stay at home with his infant son for several years. Danny felt a great unease about not working in those days, and pride, still, at bestowing a father's influence as he put his boy on a tricycle and spun stories and threw a ball around. And now that was a bygone life and the years and memories had drifted by. He heard his son was a spirited surfer these days, and wondered if he had passed along some gift for riding the ocean even across this gulf of absence . . .

Danny knew he'd made mistakes, but he was too far away to make amends. One of his saddest memories was visiting his son in North Carolina and seeing his face fall when he realized Danny was leaving for the oilfield—letting him down again. Yet could he have found any other way? That time he returned to the Outer Banks after Phoenix didn't work out: Danny went back to work as a waiter and was wiping down a table when he saw his son's athletic coach watching him with disapproval, or at least it seemed that way. He was ashamed to be seen working such a mundane job. So Danny resigned himself to working in the oilfield, where he could at least make an impressive salary, sending child support payments for a child he never saw. Yoked to an oil truck in what he viewed as a barren wasteland—sitting at the bar here in Lignite, North Dakota—Danny supposed that was all he deserved and the only way to be anymore.

Nobody Lives Here

North Dakota had not been Aaron Chisholm's original destination. He applied for high school teaching positions all along the East Coast after completing degrees in social studies and geography in northwestern Pennsylvania, but there were too many applicants for too few jobs. Aaron figured he'd go to the Bakken and roustabout for a while. Though he was a bright, energetic man in his twenties, a recruiter was skeptical that he could do blue-collar work. "I'm not qualified for manual labor?" Aaron asked. "I've got two degrees!" Soon he began reporting to an office job analyzing spatial and mapping information for McKenzie County, where a geological jackpot had spawned a geographical quagmire.

The rush of oil necessitated new government buildings, hospital expansions, subdivisions, shops, and apartments erected so quickly that the county was perpetually under expansion, and needed Aaron to make sense of the disarray. Aaron and other government employees temporarily worked out of trailers near the fairgrounds to allow for the building of a larger courthouse to accommodate the surge in traffic tickets and assault cases, public works projects, construction permits, and other government functions. The county arranged for him to live in a trailer park off Highway 85, near Main Street in Watford City. Rent cost $900 a month plus utilities and required an additional county subsidy to offset the expense. It took ten months to secure an Internet connection. "Have you ever watched *The Big Bang Theory*?" Aaron asked. "I bought all six seasons and played them on repeat. After a while it was just background noise. I guess you've got to keep yourself entertained." He circled through the trailer park with me, pointing out the home three doors down that an unknown assailant had targeted in a drive-by shooting. The pickup truck out front had a bumper sticker that said GUN CONTROL MEANS USING BOTH HANDS.

After work, he liked to hike with his chocolate Lab, Addie, behind the trailer court or at Theodore Roosevelt National Park. He also labored several nights a week as a barback and bouncer at the American Legion on Main Street to help pay off $75,000 in student loan debt. It had the worst karaoke in the oilfield—the same old drunks butchering Johnny Cash and Kid Rock. A neon-yellow poster above the bar warned troublemakers: WE HAVE THE RIGHT TO REFUSE SERVICE! NO DRINKING OUTSIDE! ZERO TOLERANCE IF YOU FIGHT YOU ARE OUT FOR GOOD! WHEN YOU ARE CUT OFF YOU ARE DONE! DO NOT BEG, BORROW OR STEAL! IF SOMEONE BUYS OR GIVES YOU A DRINK THEY ARE DONE TOO! Oil workers jammed the bar from all over; the driver's licenses he checked at the door came from Oregon, Florida, Mississippi, Louisiana, Missouri, and Texas. Cops walked through the bar every Friday and Saturday night, eyeing the patrons menacingly. During a rib fest, Aaron had to pry a half dozen brawlers from under the pool table. One time a woman on the dance floor began taking her clothes off. Aaron's coworkers escorted her outside. "She was out there half naked and this van pulled up and she got in. Maybe she knew them?"

His first challenge on the county job—his official title was Geographic Information System coordinator—was that much of the new development did not appear on maps or GPS, or even have a proper address. Mail seemed to disappear into a hidden dimension. People used to call 911 and tell dispatch, "Go to Jim's house, take a right, and I'm down by the last tree," but nobody knew where they lived these days. Newcomers complained that Google couldn't find their house, and Aaron had to explain that it took a long time for mapping systems to catch up.

It was the first time in years that many people had to follow geographic directions uttered by a live person or scrawled on the back of an envelope; even the maps of oil wells at the Wild Bison truck stop were scorned for not being up-to-date. A civilization does not truly exist until it is recorded on maps, paper or electronic, and this was especially true in the Bakken, where there was so much grasping for place and legitimacy. Given that McKenzie County was the top oil producer in North Dakota, Aaron started requiring oil wells to have an address, as much for the safety of the workers as anything else. (Even that wasn't a perfect answer: cellphone service could be spotty, and a joke among oil workers was that they must have driven around until they found no service and decided that's where they would drill a well.) But how far should the endeavor go? Did the shacks, RVs, trailers, and shipping containers need an address? How to track them? He processed four thousand address requests in less than two years, and told me it could take another year and a half to catch up on the backlog.

But addresses mattered little if the system that underlay them was dysfunctional. The fastest-growing rural county in America didn't even know what lay in its jurisdiction. Authorities were aghast when they discovered an entrepreneur had begun building an unpermitted RV park in the path of last year's tornado, and scores of other shoddy encampments slouched around the countryside. Asphalt roads ceded to a morass of dirt, traffic cones, and dozers. I once absentmindedly followed a belly-dump truck into a construction lane where the driver was picking up a load of gravel, then had to find my way over ridges of earth back to the main route, which seemed indistinguishable from the path I had just left. I was startled to find the street in this condition not just for blocks but for miles.

It wasn't simply that too much was being built too fast; rather, it seemed to abide by no order at all. "We say McKenzie County has zoning, but they don't," a businessman complained to county commissioners in the new courthouse. He later told me that it was cumbersome for commercial enterprises to build and expand there because they didn't know what the government wanted, and floated the possibility that the free market didn't always work. But he insisted I put that off the record so he wouldn't be run out of town.

When he began the job, Aaron found the county depended on maps from the US Department of Agriculture's flights over the area every year or two. But the quality was too low to depict the massive changes taking hold in the region. So Aaron arranged for the county to hire a firm to conduct more detailed aerial photography. He hoped they could fly out regularly and deploy technology such as oblique imagery to track the area in greater detail so they could better plan road projects and assess taxes on buildings. "We can't rely on Google Earth," he said. "It's not good enough."

Perhaps the oddest phenomenon was how the culture of trailers and slapdash housing remained so entrenched amid this race to elevate permanent structures. Rents were still exorbitant, and people were making less as the oil bubble deflated. The free-market-questioning businessman had made his comment to the commissioners, in fact, during a meeting where the top oil lobbyist and members of the industry came to talk of doing away with all the ramshackle workforce lodgings.

Forcing out those homes posed a legal conundrum, but the county could at least account for them. So Aaron set about documenting the trailers, man camps, shacks, and other temporary housing dumped and scattered about, cataloging twenty-seven hundred square miles of shambolic, pell-mell, slipshod progress. He occasionally found himself horrified. At one RV park, he was taken aback by a little girl playing in a muddy puddle when she should have been in school. "We're not Uganda," he said. "This isn't a third-world country."

We set out one afternoon in the direction of the Wild Bison on Highway 85, passing the abandoned Great American Lodge before turning south onto a newly paved road. The county landfill peered from a hill—a grand gallimaufry of garbage, a truly epic dump. As the oil rush strained its capacity, the landfill leased a million-dollar Al-Jon Advantage 600 Compactor, which could crush, sardine, and cram in more refuse than ever before. The landfill claimed that was the heaviest trash compactor on the planet, so enormous that it took three trucks to deliver the sixty-two tons of machinery. The dump also claimed to be the first in the nation to install state-of-the-art radiation detection panels after haulers began smuggling in slightly radioactive filter socks. Several times the loads were so radioactive that they topped the scale. "Hot enough to give you chills on the back of your neck and run away," as one worker put it. They'd reject the toxic loads and fill out reports to send to the state, where regulators were so overworked that they sometimes called about the paperwork a year later. When oil prices swooned, workers on a rig shutting down would throw everything into a shipping container, which arrived at the landfill overflowing with coveralls, absorbent pads, chemicals, and liquids of indeterminate composition. "Just a be-all, catch-all hodgepodge of nastiness," said the director, Rick Schreiber. The landfill made creative use of the plastic thread protectors that covered the ends of millions of pipes transported to the oilfield. They were shaped like the tops of thermoses and colored as brightly as toys. Workers crushed the thread protectors and spread the small chunks over the rest of the trash as landfill covering.

If one took the road all the way up and turned west, the pavement extended just past the landfill and suddenly ended in the grass. It was common for asphalt to stop and start abruptly in the oilfield, where things only existed according to strict utility.

Aaron veered onto a dirt path, the vehicle bumping down at least an inch or two from the thick coat of fresh asphalt. Before us was an industrial park. The Kysars had developed the land here even before they built the Wild Bison truck stop, and had long since sold off the various tracts. I wasn't entirely sure why we had come. I had already visited the area a half dozen times on my own to interview employees of a workover rig, and I figured the sprawl of trailers held oil service equipment. But Aaron suspected that people lived in them.

We came upon an upside-down RV and, a ways ahead, a row of ten beige trailers with black window shutters and white skirting. Aaron and I stepped out to survey the mess. The wind had ripped off a deck and set of wood stairs and hurled them about fifty feet to the east of Trailer H, into weeds nearly a foot high. Orange traffic cones lay on the ground. A trail of scoria led to an office building. It was empty, the doors locked. The hatch to the mailbox hung open, dust filling the metal grooves. Aaron was pleased that the company sign included the address he had created, even if it appeared nobody had been here for a long time. He took out a handheld Trimble GPS unit. It gave him a list from which to select: road culverts, signs, bridges, cattle guards, shutoff valves, temporary housing. He clicked on the last one and worked through the system. Foundation: Piers. Name: Bloom Electric. Number of units: Ten. Comments: Abandoned.

Our adventure had the feel of urban exploration, that practice of trawling old factories and ruins in Detroit, Philadelphia, and other old, industrial cities. Yet how strange it was to be dissecting artifacts only a few years old in the countryside—hastily assembled, even more rapidly forsaken.

We drove a little further and stopped. Here—the trailer of a semi truck attached to a half-painted wood building, three stacks of tires resting against the side and several more on the roof. Four stairs leading to the back of the trailer, yet no entrance. There—a green shed with a sign advertising, FOR RENT. NEW 5 BEDROOM 2 BATH HOMES . . . COMMERCIAL LAND. LOW RATES. We turned left and came upon three more trailers, the window blinds in disarray. Two cabins sat nearby. Somebody might have lived in any of these, but who knew? "Number of units, we've got five," said Aaron, working the GPS. We came to an environmental cleanup company, where Aaron counted twenty-four skid shacks—trailers on skids that could be quickly moved. Across the way, he saw a company called Most Wanted Well Service. A white Pontiac sat, inexplicably, atop a tall shipping container by the entrance. "We have four for the Most Wanted trailer park," he muttered, entering the data into his GPS unit. We drove past the chain-link fence of a company called Black Gold and rounded the south side of the shop. Before us was a sight that defied the categorizations of his mapping device: a row of little white sheds.

Aaron began to count. "Two . . . four . . . six . . . seven . . ."

I cut him off. "Nobody lives here!"

He pointed to the evidence: satellite dishes poking out of each shed. I was starting to learn that there was always a "tell" during these sorts of expeditions. I once chased a tip that people lived in a junkyard and found myself wandering it uncertainly, imagining I had come to the wrong place. Then I came face-to-face with a grinning pumpkin outside a camper and shrieked. A freshly carved jack-o'-lantern was a sure sign of life in autumn. But that was another day, and here—

"There's no way," I insisted. They could not have been more than ten by twelve feet. I stepped out and knocked on a few of the doors. No one answered.

We left the matter unresolved and continued up the hill, spying a large pile of industrial waste. "You're right next to the landfill—why throw this stuff here?" Aaron said, sighing. "Just another day in Watford City." We reached the hilltop and turned right. There were four brown trailers lettered A through D in red, with an American flag covering the inside of one window. He added data via his GPS unit: temporary housing, no piers, mobile home, single-wide trailers. We turned onto another gravel road to 4T Construction. Two . . . four . . . six . . . eight trailers, all beige with white skirting.

"It blows my mind," Aaron said, shaking his head. "Living next to a landfill is not something people normally do. Living in a shipping container with doors is not something people normally do." Our mission appeared complete until a mobile home park called Almost Home Corporate Housing appeared beyond a chain-link fence. He chuckled at the name ("People here are so creative!") and snapped some pictures. We drove down a slight hill and onto the scoria lot, counting twenty trailers. Construction materials were scattered everywhere. We passed three tires on a wood stand and trucks with license plates from Arkansas and Oregon. White trailers with wood steps lined the perimeter. Mangled castoffs lay on the ground: a satellite dish, slabs of wood, a bale of hay, a four-hundred-barrel tank on its side. A car with Texas plates and a shattered windshield squatted in the weeds.

"It's an aesthetic thing, but it is quality of life, too," Aaron continued. "People shouldn't really be living in an industrial park, you know?" He began entering all of this in his GPS unit, deeming Almost Home a man camp. I disagreed with his assessment, as Bakken man camps usually struck me as hotel-like groupings of trailers that had meals and laundry service. It was a largely irrelevant distinction, given that dozens of people were living in an ill-kempt industrial park downhill from a landfill. By then, news of the settlement was already drawing scrutiny from Aaron's superiors. They were plotting how to get rid of the mess.

Evolution

W eeks later, I began visiting a frack job that was a fifteen-minute drive east. The crew labored down a scoria road past a sign that said DANGER EXPLOSIVES. Eight pumper trucks linked to a plexus of pipes. Two gigantic cranes leaned toward each other, forming a wide triangle in the sky. A line of trucks rolled in bearing millions of pounds of sand. Particles wafted everywhere; grit crunched between our teeth. The dust, the lonesome terrain, the artillery, the foreign enemy—it all had the feel of a military operation. A separate crew had already drilled the trio of wells, but to release the oil, they had to inject the sand, water, and chemicals to blast fractures in tight subterranean rock. The wellheads were colored as brightly as ornaments, and workers fracked the job in ninety-nine stages, going down the line—green-orange-blue-green-orange-blue-green-orange-blue—all day and night. A zipper frack, they called it. Over the first year, the wells would produce nearly 329,300 barrels of crude, a driblet in the world's growing surplus of oil.

The crew wanted dinner delivered by midnight, and I came for the first time with Jeff Burgos, executive chef at the Eleven Restaurant & Lounge. Value Place was the last blip of light before the highway turned dark as a vault south of Watford City. We passed a sign warning of livestock at large and rumbled over two cattle guards before turning onto a dirt path that rolled into a blast of light, the frack shining down a little hill. The chef steered around the mess of trucks and bumped over a large pipe as the tubs of fettuccine Alfredo lurched in the backseat. He parked, and we hauled the pasta heavy with chicken into one of the trailers. "They love their meat!" The chef already had ribs cooking for tomorrow's shift, figuring oil workers didn't like vegetables. At the restaurant, the chef liked to challenge patrons' proclivities for blandness by flying shark in from Hawaii. But the midnight meal on a North Dakota frack was not the place to be gastronomically risqué.

The men began filing in, scooping the meal into Styrofoam containers and plunking themselves down in front of the TV. "We're here for the good stuff," one of the guys said.

The chef's underling laughed and joked, "You came to the wrong place."

A wireline operator in green coveralls squeezed past me to get to the couch. "Sorry I'm greasy—sorry, sorry!" He ate with gusto, telling me this meal was the best part of his day. His last job had been running T.G.I. Friday's franchises in the Rockies. When I complained about the changes in mozzarella sticks, he sympathized. "That's just a decision they made to mess with things—I wish they wouldn't." He twirled the fettuccine around his fork. "I know way more about restaurants than this stuff." It was difficult being away from his family in Salt Lake City, but he couldn't fathom moving them out here. The region was so overly reliant on oil that he had no assurance of rebounding if the company laid him off.

"Ready to rock and roll, all right, fellows?" a man said over the radio. Outside they were preparing for the next stage. I was surprised the workers still had any energy; the rich, heavy cream sauce should have moved them to doze, not frack. But oilmen seemed to have a preternatural ability to work under any circumstance. "Thank you guys for dinner, supper, breakfast, whatever you wanna call it," somebody said, and they shuffled back into the dark.

⁘   ⁘   ⁘

On to the day shift. A fall chill descended and men moved across the scoria tract in methodical fashion. The din of pump trucks. High pressure. The next stage. The next stage, then the next, green, orange, blue . . . seventy-five . . . seventy-six . . . seventy-seven . . .

An impressive enterprise, still. But less dramatic by sunlight.

I walked with a supervisor into an artillery van and met a fellow preparing the wireline explosives. He was attaching a detonating device to a perforating gun. "This is pretty much an M-80," he said. They would pump the gun down to blast fractures in the Bakken shale. Then workers would drop a ball down until it seated in a plug, isolating the area below it to direct the blast of fracking fluids into the rock's cracks and fissures. The fluids were blended in a sophisticated mixology: heaps of sand and a sea of freshwater, with biocide to kill any bacteria in the latter; guar to give the liquid viscosity; breakers to eventually disrupt the gelling; a farrago of chemicals. A quality control operator would put some of the mixture in a blender to check the pH and temperature before bringing a sample to the supervisor for approval before starting each stage. The supervisor would examine the mixture as he tilted it over the edge of a cup, where it hung like a cow's tongue. During a week visiting the site, I only saw him reject the sample once, when it resembled a badly mixed banana bread batter—a little runny and full of clumps.

The supervisor was among a half dozen men who controlled the operations in a trailer called the data van overlooking the site, monitoring screens showing the movement of the slurry of sand, water, and chemicals second by second. This was considered one of the more desirable oil jobs because the workers were sheltered from the ice and gales, the cold and the wet. A blue line charted how many barrels of fluid per minute were pumping down the well (an average of eight); a red line displayed the pressure (an average of 5,300 psi); a chart showed the type of slurry and sand. In the beginning it took two and a half hours to complete a stage of fracking, though that eventually fell below two hours.

That week an investor from Dallas was visiting the frack with several cohorts. The oil company operating the site, Abraxas Petroleum, was based in San Antonio, and it was common for a lot of the oil sites to be run by a Texas outfit and have investors from that area. The group sat in the data van behind the technicians, in chairs that folded out like seats at a movie theater. Troy Eckard, the investor, watched the operations with great enthusiasm. He told me that this was like NASA compared to the old days. "Just looking at the equipment, the drilling rigs, the control centers, the technology, the advancements—it's unbelievable!" He compared North Dakota to Texas in the middle of the twentieth century, when the latter's oil industry was still developing. "Very friendly landowners . . . regulators are excited to see their state develop," he said of the former. In the Texas oilfield nowadays, "you get highly sophisticated landowners and lawyers, so it's not nearly as business-friendly."

Troy had looked at the other big shale plays but said he moved his oil interests to the Bakken because it offered the best opportunity in the country. He had financial stakes in hundreds of oil wells here that he came to check on several times a year. "My little saying is that North Dakota is the fattest chicken in the barn."

·:·   ·:·   ·:·

The crew moved to frack the green well a little after one-thirty in the afternoon—the eighty-fourth stage. I spent most of my time talking to the supervisor, Marc Bayne, an amiable man from San Antonio. About halfway through the job, the workers in the data van had each bet $20 on when they would finish the frack. Marc wagered on Wednesday morning, which was two days away. Additional crews would later come to oversee the rapid free flow of new oil into tanks, and erect pump jacks over the wells.

Marc asked if they wanted to bet on how many barrels of water they'd have to pump down to seat the ball. The last one had taken twenty-nine.

"This early I don't know where it's going to be," said one man, but he bet twenty-six.

Marc bet twenty-seven. "Anybody else?"

"Come on," said the man, looking at the screen. "Hit it! Hit it! Ahhhhh . . . *twenty-nine!*"

Marc stood up and announced he had to do his push-ups. He dropped to the floor and did seven. The deal was you had to do as many as the number of barrels you missed by, plus five.

Somebody called out that they had pumped nearly 25,000 pounds of sand, called proppant because it was used to hold the fractures open. The crew started the process with natural sand and increasingly pumped down ceramic sand to hold the fractures open longer, usually pumping down 225,000 pounds of proppant per stage.

"Do you have crosslink yet?" another worker asked.

The quality control man walked in to show a sample of fracking fluid, slinging the cow's tongue to and fro. I watched a train of frack sand trucks chugging up the hill, their trailers shaped like jagged fangs. One of the guys started talking about how his sister-in-law in Pennsylvania criticized him for fracking for a living. This set off a familiar oilfield debate. "My *aunt*, oh my God!" The man complained about her Facebook posts on fracking protests. "I told her to go live in a cave and go burn wood for her heat!"

An hour and a half passed. Someone yelled out: 224,572, referring to pounds of sand. It was a sign we were nearing the end of the stage.

"All right, guys, we're slowing down to fifteen barrels a minute . . . ninety barrels till we shut down."

"Drop three barrels. Drop a pump. Drop another pump."

"Drop another one. Is everything kicked out? Make sure everything's shut down."

The curve on Marc's screen leapt suddenly, showing the pressure spiking to 8,555 psi instead of dropping as it should have. They discovered that sand had plugged up the perforations, a condition called a screen-out. The hydraulic pumps shut down automatically, as a safety precaution. The crew prepared to open the well and force up several hundred barrels of the liquids we had just pumped down in order to clear out the detritus. We were going into flowback. Thankfully, the visitors had left by then; it was not the sort of mishap one wanted the money men to see.

A few of us walked outside. "That wind outside is a mess," somebody said. The flowback operator, a rumple-haired kid from Montana, came out of his truck. "If you could think of the gnarliest slug in the world and turn it into a liquid, that's what it is," he said of flowback. It stayed on your hands no matter how many times you washed them. He told me that if it were a cocktail, it would be made from bottom-shelf whiskey and grunge off the bar mat. We climbed the staircase to a walkway alongside the flow-back tanks, which resembled enormous rectangular vats. I peered over, clutching my hard hat to keep it from blowing off. A brown and white liquid lingered at the bottom. Within minutes, fluid from the oil wells discharged through a row of cane-shaped pipes at the tanks' edge. At first it fell through the spouts like an amusement at a children's wading pool—mostly water, free of fracking's additives and by-products. I was standing there with Gary Bayne, Marc's father. He had worked in the industry all his life, and had fracked back in Oklahoma and Wyoming decades ago, though it was a rather unsophisticated process then. As we peered over the tanks, Gary assured me the liquid would soon thicken.

It went from clear to brown as the sand came. Then the hue turned sallow, a sign of crosslink gel. The clumps of sand intensified. The discharge burst in buckets, rapid and deafening as it smashed against the rising liquid several feet below. I watched in astonishment as Gary put his hand under a spout to sample this toxic salmagundi. He held it up, revealing a milky gel speckled with silica. "There we go," he said. "There's my sand."

So the flowback churned. "Coming out of formation" is what they called it. We stood there watching in silence for a long time; talking was fruitless above the cascade. The ashen slopes hulked to the right of us, nearly the same dull color as the battery of oil tanks. Sepia ribbons swam in the vat; ivory bubbles bloated like abscesses, or a witch's warts, perhaps, a sign of natural gas. They shined and clustered and multiplied as flowback burst out. The gush paused, then renewed with fervor, disgorging like a drunk's morning-after purge. Indeed, workers commonly refer to flow-back as "vomit," and these were the excretions of the earth: its mucus, discharge, pus, puke, toxins, bile, ejaculate, piss, spew, sludge, egesta, venom, glop, scum, filth, rot, slime, dreck, sleaze, sewage, all fluxing and rising in a rhythm that seemed as natural as the cycles of the sun and the moon.

Gary looked for the green sheen that would indicate crude, and the sludge gradually turned a milky olive gray. Steam wafted. Gary reached his hand beneath a spout again to study the fluid.

"Good enough," he said, and we returned to the data van. The crew had since moved on to frack the next well.

"Swap that sand there, swap that sand!"

Someone called out another number: 174,557.

"Yessir."

"All right, guys, thirty-two barrels a minute; sixty-three hundred on the line."

As they neared the end, the supervisor said, "Let's hope this one doesn't do the same thing." He had the crew drop the pressure earlier than usual as a precaution. "Good stage."

Now they would flush out the well that had just flowed back, pumping water and gel to clean out any remaining sand so they could finish the stage. A production foreman came in, wiping droplets of a faint rain off his face. He handed me the ball that had barreled up from miles below. "Nice and shiny," he said. It was about the size of a ping-pong ball. The erosive power of rushing sand and fluids had made a dent. I studied it for a moment, then put it in my bag. The day shift was ending. Somebody said to drive slow because some rancher's cows were wandering on the road that led back to the highway.

I drove an hour north to meet the Texas investor, Troy, and several of his associates at Williston Brewing Company as I contemplated this steady influx of southerners. Longtime residents weren't always sure what to make of their interlopers. "Okies and Texans," Nevin once muttered to me, but he was reluctant to say more. He favored the strong work ethic of the North Dakota and Minnesota boys. Another North Dakotan who worked on the rig was blunter: "There's a lot of southerners up here that have absolutely no common sense." Others resented them for extracting North Dakota's resources and taking the profits back south, and distrusted them for their maniacal driving habits. A rancher told me that in the beginning of the boom, she saw the pickups with southern license plates flying down iced-out roads and exclaimed, "I'm going to die out here!"

Many southerners, for their part, found this place a backwater and were baffled by the residents' mild, trusting demeanor.

The sharpest assessment of the regions' cultural differences came from an ex-con I met in a Watford City RV who decided to migrate north after a judge in Texas told him he was getting twenty-five to life if he appeared in that courtroom again. "I'm North Dakota bound," he told the judge. "You ain't never going to see me again." As troublemakers do, he found himself busted again in the Bakken. He was shocked to find that the folks at the McKenzie County jail called him "sir," instead of grunting profanities as they had in Texas. "It was like the Holiday Inn of jails," he reminisced fondly. His astonishment grew upon his release, when the staff shook his hand and told him to have a good day.

On this evening, I found the Texans at a circular table near the bar. Troy was drinking a glass of Malbec. He brimmed with more enthusiasm for the Bakken's potential than even most North Dakotans I met. He gestured around the brewpub, which was crowded for a Monday evening. "This restaurant says what North Dakota is. How many guys are in steel-toed boots versus dress attire?" I was still in steel toes myself. "If you look around, it tells you that you're in an industrialized state right now." He saw a long future for the industry here, one that the rest of the nation would do well to take advantage of.

"If the federal government was smart," he continued, "what they would do is they would help build this up . . . and take all the people out of Detroit that don't have jobs and say, 'We've got plenty of jobs. We're going to build schools and we're going to build infrastructure and you get to come live in open space.' You take all these people that are congested in Los Angeles and everything else, move their buns out here. We've got fresh air and fishing. . . ."

He had invested with some twenty operators around here. The oil companies drilled and fracked wells and sent investors a bill when they began producing oil. Troy said it was very difficult for investors like him to even get on location, as I had seen him six hours earlier. His role was to cut the check and not ask questions. He spent lots of time fighting delays and excuses to get the operators to pay them their stake in the revenues. But he liked to say that were it not for the chaos in the Bakken, there would not be any opportunity.

Lately, Troy didn't like oil companies targeting new wells. The margins were too thin. But they did it because they needed cash flow to convince the banks that they wouldn't default on their loans. They were completing wells out of survival. He noted one benefit to the downturn, however: only the best workers were left. "You've got the A-team doing all the work right now." Around the world, 350,000 people in the oil and gas industry had lost their jobs since crude prices began their plunge.

We were sitting with a man from Halcon Resources, a Texas outfit that had some acreage up here. The Halcon man had just been joking that single mothers should be shot, but this remark spurred his compassion. "Let me tell you," he said, "you got a bunch of the A-team sitting at home, too—lost their jobs. A *lot* of them. It breaks my heart." He had to fire some of them, and not because they couldn't do the job or pass a drug test. "It's simply something that's way out of their control. *Way* out! It had nothing to do with them. They go home trying to pay for their house, their truck, their car, their wife, their kids. They suffered like that for *what?*"

"Honestly, I don't feel bad about it," said Troy. "Because the fact is, it's called a free market." Indeed, "it's a free market" was a common response in western North Dakota for any complaints about how the oil development had gone. "Think about the camera business. The iPhone has put cameras out of business. There's eight-track tapes sitting around, what happened? . . . It's an evolution."

Troy preferred the oilfield slower. He thought the frenzy had been ludicrous—companies overpaying for oil leases, gouging for pipe hauling. That was the amusing part of the oil industry's claims of how lean and innovative it had grown in response to OPEC's threats. Fracking firms used to wildly inflate their prices, knowing how quickly oil companies in North Dakota needed the job done. Prices had simply returned to a more manageable level. (The contractor fracking Abraxas's wells on this job gave the company a 38 percent "WTI discount," referring to the decline in the price of West Texas Intermediate, a grade of crude oil used as a pricing benchmark.) Troy still felt that most of the shale plays he looked at in America had the odds stacked against investors. Mineral owners in Texas, for instance, received a higher cut of oil profits. "Too skinny of a chicken," he said. But in North Dakota, he believed, he was looking at the largest real estate play in the last two hundred years.

I asked his associates what they thought of the place.

"Let me tell you what I think of Williston," said Troy's colleague, leaning forward. "I've already made sure my flight status is all good." Everyone laughed.

Troy believed the region had not built a civilization that would induce people to stay. "They're building a place where you want to hunker down like a freezer, make your money, and get the hell out in five years." He felt the Bakken towns sent the message *This is a drive-through restaurant.*

As they prepared to leave the brewpub, the man from Halcon told us he'd better start the forty-minute drive down Highway 85 to his trailer at the industrial park by the landfill, where he lived when he was not back home in Laredo. I was speechless. People in his position usually made several hundred thousand dollars a year.

Empire of Junk

To spend any time in the Bakken in those days required a boundless capacity to suspend judgment, as the way of things was not girded by the assumptions of most places in America. It would be easy to pity those who lived by the landfill, or berate the corporate occupants for exploiting workers, but neither reaction was true to the oilfield.

I learned this upon making regular visits to the landfill encampment on my own, without the encumbrance of Aaron Chisholm's county government vehicle. Intrigued by the sheds, I drove up one afternoon to the industrial shop of Black Gold, where I came upon the owner's wife. (It was not uncommon to see "black gold" in the name of commercial enterprises here, though most oil in the Bakken wasn't black.) Rena, as she was known, told me that their family business sent crews to build the containment walls around oil tanks and spray them with protective polyurea coating. The yard had stacks of circular foam pads used to underlay the tanks, along with a long dike for the crew to practice the trade.

Early in the oil rush, Black Gold rented a little building in Watford City—about a ten-minute drive south from the landfill—where the employees slept in cramped quarters. Crew members hauling garbage to the county dump saw FOR SALE signs outside the shell of a half-built metal shop, and Black Gold agreed to buy it. The firm lined up a row of sheds outside the south end of the building and equipped them with heat and air-conditioning, beds, TV, dressers, and nightstands. Black Gold initially housed two men in each, but now each worker had his own. The owner hauled water in from the depot across from the Wild Bison truck stop, and workers showered in a bathroom inside the shop.

Rena enjoyed mothering the crew, inquiring about their families and cooking meals—hamburgers and tater tots, mashed potatoes and tacos. She told me the "huts" were improvements, even if most people wouldn't live in them. "Why should they spend $1,700 to live in town, if somebody was giving them a livable place for free?" This was not much of an exaggeration: it was still routine to see a one-bedroom apartment in Watford City go for nearly that price. The hut inhabitants made $80,000 a year at their peak. Black Gold's employees included a man from Cincinnati who'd come after his restaurant did badly, another who left the fencing business in North Carolina, and a resident of central North Dakota who had four daughters and boasted that his mortgage was nearly paid off thanks to his free shed. "Shack life's all right," said a twenty-six-year-old worker, allowing me to peek inside his hut. It was a country studio: the interior was a light, rustic wood, FR coveralls hung on hooks, and a jumble of DVDs and electronic equipment sat on overhead shelves. He introduced himself as Nick Malakoff and said he used to work at a sawmill in Washington. "I learned that no matter what's going on, how bad things get, you just go somewhere else, you know?" said Nick. "I don't understand why people get all hung up on their horrible life when they can just abandon everything . . . all you have to do is get in the car and leave . . . just ride a bike. You could steal a bike if you had to!"

He believed blue-collar work wasn't valued the way it should be, but didn't fault the upper echelons. In fact, he admired them. "Most places you're not making enough money, but you're doing all the hard work," said Nick. "That's what's kind of cool about capitalism. . . . Someone decided, 'Why should I be doing all the hard work? Let me set it up so everyone else does the work for me.'" It was astonishing that everywhere I went, ordinary people remarked on capitalism and the free market, forces they had contemplated deeply and without my prompting. When I lived in Minneapolis, a liberal bastion, casual conversation did not include open reflection on the role of the state.

Nick's circumstances made him exceptionally resourceful. Outside the shed was a camper he'd built out of materials in their industrial yard. Nick had sprayed it with the polyurea normally used on oil equipment, then painted and stenciled the exterior in patterns evoking a haunted woods. After repeatedly spilling his beer, he found a small pipe holder in the shop's recycling bin and fashioned it into a cylinder that could fit a twenty-four-ounce can; he attached it to the side of the camper. Nick also built a canoe that he liked to take out on Lake Sakakawea and McKenzie Bay to catch pike and striped bass.

He didn't like to watch TV, preferring always to be tinkering with something. Nick had found his latest project just over the chain-link fence at the Almost Home trailer park, where he'd noticed the junked Honda from Texas. Nick arranged to buy it from the trailer park owner for $200. He couldn't get it running again so easily because the driver had taken off with the keys, which had a microchip. But at least the parts would be worth something. A worker from Most Wanted Well Service across the dirt road even offered to install a windshield. "You need any rap tapes?" Nick asked when I stopped by one afternoon while he was tinkering with the Honda, and he showed me an array of Bobby V albums left by the Texan occupant. Then he spied another by the country duo Montgomery Gentry. "I think I'm going to keep that one."

I found the people of Almost Home to be equally industrious. The owner of the mobile home park was a fellow from Wyoming named Darwin Williamson. I stopped by as he was puttering around the lot, hands black with grease from working the weed-whacker. He had me follow him into a trailer, which shook as the laundry machines ran. (ABSOLUTELY NO GREASY OR OILY CLOTHES! the sign said—an omnipresent warning around the Bakken that was often disregarded.) He washed his hands and we sat in his office, where his computer flashed a screen saver of him holding a pair of elk antlers. Darwin relayed a growing discontent with the county's accusations that the landfill industrial park was like a third-world country.

Darwin's father and uncle had run a water-hauling enterprise in western North Dakota during the 1980s oil boom. He followed decades later, after his family's garage door business was threatened by the financial crisis and the decline of the coal methane industry in Wyoming, both of which decreased the demand for new construction. They hustled for contracts here while working out of the backs of their pickups, building garage doors for the explosion of new apartments, government buildings, and industrial shops. He even erected the garage doors on the shop for Black Gold across the way.

Darwin's family roughed it those early winters, sleeping in a camper with no electricity when housing was scarce. They hauled water back and forth and relied on generators for heat. Other times they slept in his brother's home across the highway. The Kysar family, which had opened the Wild Bison truck stop, sold Darwin acreage by the landfill as the garage business grew and the freeze thawed. Darwin set about building a trailer park, moving mobile homes from Williston. He brought modular classrooms he got at an auction in Des Moines, Iowa, and refashioned them into a half dozen three-bedroom apartments. Darwin stayed in one of the refurbished classrooms, which he had once shared with two garage business employees. It was surprisingly cozy, with reclining chairs and a wooden table with benches; he hung pictures of his grandchildren on the wall. We stepped onto a wood deck out back, where a miscellany of tires sat on the edge of the scoria. The landfill was hardly visible but for a flag waving over the building.

"'This is a third-world country,'" he cracked, mimicking the comments made by county government officials. "Apparently these people have never been to a third-world country or watched National Geographic. We're not drinking out of mud puddles and pooping in our backyard!"

The company was advertising on the radio stations and in real estate magazines. I had been noticing Almost Home fliers at the taco truck across the landfill road on Highway 85, the Mexican food and check-cashing place near Main Street, and the Holiday gas station. Darwin and the other inhabitants of the industrial park had secured a permit allowing a zoning exception from light industrial uses. Indeed, McKenzie County's zoning had been running so heavily on conditional use permits, with so many grandfathering provisions, that it was hard to say what the original rules had been or were supposed to be. Darwin never thought any controversy would come of his operations here. So he was fighting for the million dollars he'd invested in this, and for all the money the other companies in the yard had put in, too. The business owners had meeting after meeting with the county, and in a few days would have a formal hearing.

He could explain the mess. The shingles were there for a building project—he kept some of his garage business materials here. The wiring was left over from a company that had departed. A welder who lived in a trailer at Almost Home kept the materials and equipment he used outside. More detritus had blown off a camper from a straight-line wind that summer.

One could be forgiven for wondering if Darwin was a slumlord at the first mention of the price: the cheapest was $1,000 for a one-room trailer with no kitchen (the bigger trailers, up to $2,000, were about as homey as a regular apartment). I once paid less to rent a one-bedroom condo on the Jersey Shore with a view of the ocean rather than trailers and a chain-link fence. But I considered him a decent and honest man. Almost Home—the whole industrial park, for that matter—was a bargain compared to rent for many apartments. County officials claimed that people deserved a higher quality of living than here, but residents believed it was preferable to what was in town. Peaceful, even, with the hum of frogs and birds. They'd put up fences, even though that interfered with pheasant hunting, and in recent weeks trimmed weeds and discarded trash.

Darwin's two daughters lived there with their husbands and children. One of them, Kyla, told me she'd like to move into an apartment and have a real yard, but they could forgo rent if they stayed at Almost Home. It was luxury living compared to that first winter in the camper with young children. Her husband worked on construction sites and she worked for her father, her bigger ambitions stymied by the scarcity of child care in the oilfield. But the sacrifices she and her husband made had nearly gotten them out of debt. She wanted to use the money they were saving in the oilfield for her daughter's and two sons' college funds, along with the purchase of a home when they returned to Wyoming. Not an almost home, but a real home, with a yard of their own. "You just have to put up with the opposite of the American dream when you're here. When you go home, that's when you can have it."

Kyla wanted to transform the shed behind her camper into a workout room, bringing in a weight set and putting some speakers in so that she did not have to go to the Watford City gym, where men leered. But the children were growing bored. They could only ride their bikes in circles so many times on this patch of scoria and spent much of their time indoors. Lately they had never watched so much TV in their lives. The kids attended school in Watford City, where the district claimed 40 percent of elementary students were homeless. The definition of "homeless" in the Bakken was a term of art. Did they qualify? Apparently not, as they had a real address with running water and electricity. A fine place to live, given the circumstances.

Yet there was something about the isolation of living downhill from a landfill, off the highway, and away from diversions that fostered discipline and achievement. I met a young man from South Carolina who lived in a trailer next door to Black Gold and hauled oil waste. He dreamed of being a playwright and wrote extensively in the trailer. When he wasn't writing, the South Carolinian lifted weights. "It's almost like you're in jail," he said. "You work out—that's about all you can do."

He was in perfect shape.

⊹   ⊹   ⊹

The residents crammed into rows of folding chairs in the red town hall of Arnegard. I arrived late, having forgotten that a portion of Highway 85 was under construction; traffic was rerouted in a big jam to the Montana state line and back. I slipped into one of the last empty seats. Nick was sitting nearby. Darwin was positioned closer to the commissioners, one leg propped against the other, hands clasped pensively. There was the new county planner, an earnest newcomer from Phoenix who was rightly aghast at the region's poor planning—and, alas, still naive enough to believe he could do much about it. He wanted the sheds and other trailers at least two hundred feet from industrial uses, though if he had his way, people would live much farther away, on a separate part of the land.

There was the chairman of the town council, Lynn Hovde. I'd visited his farm several months back, after he returned from a vacation to Norway. He knew as well as any of the locals about the trouble oil had brought. Lynn had given up several hundred acres of cropland because it was too dangerous and time-consuming to reach it by crossing Highway 85. A thief had taken one of their trucks for a joyride and dumped it in a lake, leaving the keys nowhere to be found. ("Uff da!" Lynn's wife said at the memory.) But that evening, he defended the settlement, saying housing was still too expensive, and the area by the dump had few emergency calls or other troubles. Housing employees in trailers on the property was a standard practice in the farming industry, after all, and keeping employees there prevented the usual troubles that arose when a bunch of men cavorted far away from home.

"I don't want this to be a sob story or anything, but if we were not to have housing . . . we'd probably hang our hat up and go south," said the accounting manager for a Colorado fracking company.

Officials conceded it was not normal to govern by conditional use permit. "Everybody was new to zoning," said Lynn. "It's like how wide do you crack the door if you make the wrong decision? And then you put a lot of something you didn't want—"

"Which happened anyway!" said the official next to him.

"I'm getting text messages from apartments and developers saying 'Get rid of workforce housing! We have empty apartments!'" said county commissioner Vawnita Best. "So you understand it's a very complex situation."

"Truth be told," said the planner, "those apartments are a *huge* part of the problem, no doubt." He was appalled at the exorbitant rents they charged.

"Sure they are," said Darwin. He was adamant that it was not the government's role to rectify other people's poor business decisions. Investors had thrown up all these apartments in a hurry, instead of building them gradually as there were enough tenants to fill them. "If you had a house with your husband and you had two kids, would you build a ten-bedroom home because you might have ten more kids? A lot of the people that came in here and built, they did just that . . . I feel for them, but"—he threw up his hands—"it was a gamble that they did take."

The meeting ended on an open note, as the commissioners saw that Darwin and the people by the landfill were a reasonable sort. The government's reach, after all, was limited. He and the other industrial park occupants took the county planner on a tour of their settlement the following morning and made all the right assurances.

Some weeks later, I stopped by Aaron's desk to see how the compilation of geographic data was going, and I gave him an update on the industrial park. Aaron noted the enthusiasm of the new county employees with a certain resignation. "I was at one point very energetic as well when I first started, but then life happens, and this town happens, and this place happens, and you just kind of have to take a step back before you get to do anything."

He was building more detailed addresses for each RV using new GIS imagery. Aaron clicked around on the map, sighing as he noted a beaten-up trailer. Their mapping systems were becoming increasingly accurate, making field visits like the one I'd taken with him by the landfill less important. After months and miles of sleuthing, Aaron presented his findings to the commissioners the following year. He calculated that if every RV park and man camp were filled, if every skid shack, FEMA trailer, and hybrid junkyard/shipping container/tool shed were occupied, their capacity was ten thousand people. The grandly named Island Empire had been invaded by a brigade of junk that was now in semi-permanent occupation. I loved that place all the same—a lot of us did—for its pastoral charm and warm community. I briefly entertained the idea of living in Almost Home, imagining all the writing I would accomplish in such seclusion. But I couldn't afford the rent there or anywhere else in McKenzie County.

Right-Minded People

I never wanted to live in Williston—it always struck me as a hostile place. But I was constrained by more than high rents. After several stints of crashing in spare rooms and on couches, in the odd trailer and farmhouse, I decided in spring 2015 that it was time to sign a lease. I began calling numbers on Craigslist ads, hoping to save money by sharing a house with several other transplants. To my surprise, people dismissed my inquiries upon learning I was a woman. "We've got to be careful now," said one man who answered the phone. "We don't want to discriminate, but we can't put anyone in a compromising situation." It had been difficult to find housing dating back to my first trip in 2012, when I was forced to sleep on the air mattress at the home of a friend of a friend of a friend, an arrangement that came to pass after I realized all the hotels were filled with oil crews. Now, I was relieved to see an ad for a house of all women. There was a vacancy for a basement room near the Williston Walmart for $600 a month, which was as favorable—and safe—a deal as one was going to find in the oilfield. "It's not like normal America," warned the landlord, a transplant from Ohio. "It's like the Twilight Zone." He had served in the military and managed an industrial plant, lost his job during the financial crisis, and couldn't even land work at McDonald's. Then the landlord came to North Dakota and made six figures delivering pizza his first year.

Soon he began running a cleaning company. Some clients hired him after other cleaning firms sent out women who leaned over their mops to reveal undergarments, signaling they would be available for extra services. But he assured me his operation was nothing of the sort. The cleaning company had acquired this squat tan house to lodge its employees and had plenty of extra space. I would have to go through a back door that led to a sparsely furnished basement, which had a kitchen and three bedrooms. My window was level with the rocky lot where tenants parked their cars. A billboard at the corner had a rotation of advertisements:

WEST PRAIRIE ESTATES—NEW HOME AUCTION

HOLIDAY SEASON SPECIAL GOLDEN CHINA SUPER BUFFET

(LUNCH $6; DINNER $8)

DEWATERING CONTAINERS FILTER SOCK SOLUTIONS SPILL-CLEAN-UP

LITTLE CAESARS $5 CLASSIC TURN LEFT NOW

Male guests were prohibited because somebody's boyfriend might trash the place; indeed, the landlord told me that oil workers had wrecked it before his firm took over. The Bakken was a patriarchal society, and gender segregation was de rigueur in oilfield housing. Male tenants in other buildings were often forbidden from having women over, in order to keep out prostitutes.

I only had one housemate at a time on the bottom floor, and those came and went. One afternoon I saw a young woman sitting at the picnic table in our backyard. She lived on the top floor, where I hadn't met anyone so far because they entered the house through a separate door. The young woman told me she had dropped out of college in Michigan and come out with her boyfriend. But unlike many of the women in their early twenties who migrated to the oilfield, she hadn't taken work as a cashier or waitress. She wanted to pay off her $20,000 in student loans and had taken a job as a pumper, checking oil tank levels for a company owned by ExxonMobil.

As the pumper and I chatted, a new stranger walked by with a load of boxes. I was startled when she told us she was moving into the room next to mine; I hadn't even realized the last roommate had left. Barbara, as she later introduced herself, had the most inspiring story of anyone I met in Williston. Back in New England, her boyfriend bought a conversion van for them to live in while he dealt crack. "He'd done ten years in federal," she said as we got acquainted at the picnic table. When Barbara tried to escape, he threatened to cut her neck with a butcher knife. He moved them into an apartment infested with bedbugs and gang members. Barbara's sunny demeanor briefly receded as she sighed, covering the top of her coffee cup with her hand, nails painted hot pink.

She escaped several times to a shelter for abused women, where she logged on to the computer to look for a job. She read about the explosion of high-paying jobs in North Dakota and spoke to some people over the phone about working as an Applebee's waitress or a housekeeper. Barbara negotiated with her boyfriend to find her an old vehicle, manipulating him with assurances that he could later meet her out there for work. She sold her jewelry at the pawn shop and her food stamps on the street for a discount in cash. Barbara departed at sunrise, singing to Katy Perry and running the string of tolls from Ohio to Illinois.

In Fargo, still six hours east of the oilfield, her car broke down. A man at a gas station there warned her against going to the Bakken, saying the men were dangerous. But she had just escaped a boyfriend who was a violent felon—could oilfield men be any worse? She went to a women's shelter in Fargo, where they arranged for her to work at a pasta plant for $12 an hour. Barbara saved up enough in a month to fix the car, fill up the tank, and get the proper insurance and registration. She drove across Interstate 94 to the southeast oil town of Dickinson and slept in the Walmart parking lot with a heated blanket. A man there offered to let her sleep in his hotel room but then began hassling her for sexual favors. When she refused, he told her he had money—a line common among newly flush oil workers. ("They can be the ugliest thing out here, but 'Me man, you woman, me have man money' and you're just supposed to bow down!" a female friend once complained. This had calmed down by the time I was doing most of my reporting there, but at one time men in the Bakken were famous for propositioning women in front of their own husbands.) Barbara reached in her pocket for the fifteen cents she had left. "I got money, too. And I have self-respect and pride and dignity."

She started making $1,500 a week working at a company that cleaned trailers on drilling rigs. Being a cleaning woman in the Bakken didn't have the low-class stigma it had in other places—the oilfield was a filthy place and everyone made enough money to pay other people a grand sum to clean up their messes. One rig worker broke a beer bottle and slipped on the shards, leaving splatters of blood from the refrigerator to the kitchen sink to the bathroom, and all over the bedsheets and carpets. "Just charge him double and clean it," her boss told her on the phone. Disinfecting, shampooing, using a Rug Doctor deep cleaning machine—it was arduous work.

Barbara wanted to be her own boss. With so many rigs running, anybody could start a business. She told her employer she was leaving and took some mops, buckets, and cleaning supplies on her way out. Barbara convinced a few company men to transfer their business to her and made the rounds to other rigs with new business cards and cake; she was beautiful and outgoing, so it wasn't a hard sell. Only a few men said they were too clean to hire a maid. "I like dirty men," she'd joke. "If you're clean, I don't have no work."

We realized that we'd stayed in the same farmhouse near the Wild Bison, though at different times, and traded gossip. The fry cook from the truck stop had let me use a spare bedroom when I struggled to find a permanent place. "José was deported," Barbara and I said at the same time, referring to one of the old residents, and burst into laughter. But as often happened in Williston, she disappeared without warning several weeks later. Her coffeepot was gone; her room was empty. A blond, portly South Carolina woman who worked at Walmart took her place. She cooked a lot and was generous with her food, inquiring about my well-being like a big sister. She had lived a different lifestyle years ago, she told me, but when I inquired further she told me she didn't want to say it out loud. A few months later, she suggested I take my printer off the kitchen table and put it back in my room because a shifty new housemate had arrived. "I think she's on meth," she whispered. But I never saw this junkie, and she, too, quickly vanished.

Among the upstairs tenants was a woman who delivered mail for FedEx and liked to come downstairs sometimes to hang out with the South Carolinian. "It's a hot mess out here, for real," she said of the oilfield postal system. I was glad for a new companion on the lower floor, but wondered for several weeks where Barbara had disappeared to. I found my answer during an interview with a fracking official at a Houston oil company's small office off Highway 85. I excused myself to go to the bathroom and saw Barbara in the hallway, working a vacuum cleaner. She got paid one grand a month to clean the place. Barbara said something about not liking our house and moving in with a boyfriend. Stepping out of his office, the fracking supervisor seemed surprised that we knew each other. But the Bakken was the only place a journalist would run into a cleaning woman during an interview and catch up on old times. Later my South Carolina housemate invited me to join her and the other Walmart workers at DK's Lounge & Casino, the rowdiest bar in town. Among her colleagues was a twenty-one-year-old who made the surprising admission to me that he was gay—this was almost dangerous to say in the macho oilfield—and he drank so much that the Walmart crowd carried him off the dance floor, feet pointed to the ceiling as they marched him up the stairs. The man staggered out and collapsed on the sidewalk outside as onlookers rushed to give him water. "No, he's going into a seizure, don't touch him! Don't touch him!"

"I'm afraid for this guy," said my housemate.

The ambulance rolled up just before one in the morning, as the temperature dropped to near zero. "Back it up, let's go," a cop said. "Okay, guys, give us some room!" The cop looked at me. "Ma'am, step out, give us some space, please. Ma'am, what part of 'some space' don't you understand?"

As I shivered in the dangerous temperatures, my crowd was so preoccupied with the ambulance that when two young men approached and offered me a ride, I agreed, given that I lived only a mile up the heavily policed main drag. When the driver pulled up outside of my house, he took out a bowl of marijuana and began taking hits. "You wanna come with us to a party?" he asked, and I scrambled out of the pickup. When I saw them around town a few days later, one said, "You're lucky we're nice guys," and it was a line I heard all the time.

Williston was, at last, drawing the contours of a proper community. The city had embraced a great expansion of retail recently, with new offerings as varied as Red Wing Shoes and Sportsman's Warehouse. They were not always well advertised: I was shocked when a real estate broker drove me around a new development up the hill, near Sportsman's, that was most visible for Sakura's Japanese Steakhouse—when we went around the other side we came upon a smoke shop and family clothing store that many people were unlikely to know existed.

Yet this place felt so small and remote that after a while I was stunned by how large Bismarck and Grand Forks seemed during a few reporting visits, flashing with big-box stores and chain restaurants. I attended a Chamber of Commerce dinner where the guest speaker was talking about how this region could be the next Silicon Valley—the successor to the California Gold Rush after all, a shining story of how a boom could create a lasting legacy of innovation. And it seemed so grand until I stepped out into downtown Williston after the event and looked down that quaint Main Street and slid back into 1960s America, in the very region that had some of the most sophisticated fracking technology in the world. Still, Williston hosted a great tradition of finding fortune beyond the usual pathways—a sense that it didn't matter if you had the right family, temperament, or education, that feeling a little on the outside might even propel someone to greater achievement. It was a state of mind people held even while working rather menial jobs. I knew a bartender at Doc Holliday's who had a business degree from the University of Wisconsin but realized he could make far more serving drinks and working in a clothing warehouse in North Dakota. He came here with $148 in his pocket and bill collectors hounding him. "It's crazy," he said. "I'm living out of my car and I make more than my parents."

I found the most old-school iteration of these values upon visiting a rib fest downtown—there was always a rib fest in the oilfield—where a good old boy from North Carolina introduced me to businessman Rich Vestal. "He's one of the richest men in town," the good old boy whispered. Rich was so plainspoken and casually dressed that I didn't believe this at first, but he was a classic oilfield success story. His mother discovered she was pregnant with Rich's older brother while his father was away in World War II. The father returned and married her, but the Catholic relatives blackballed them because the baby was conceived out of wedlock.

"We were outcasts," said Rich, who was one of four children. His father had multiple sclerosis and it was hard for him to keep a job. All they had to eat was the venison his dad hunted. Rich went to work in second grade chopping wood and packing coal for the lady up the street, making five cents an hour. He still remembered the time he went to a neighbor's house and she gave him a glass of lemonade with ice cubes and a lemon wedge in it—an unimaginable luxury. Luck didn't favor them in those days. His mother raised turkeys to sell for extra money on Thanksgiving, but a crank on a piece of farm machinery hit him on the forehead and his mother had to spend the proceeds on taking him to the hospital for stitches. Then Rich spent a summer doing farmwork for relatives who gave him a horse in exchange. "And then the horse was standing by a fence and got struck by lightning and it killed him."

In the late sixties, he took a job on a rig to put himself through college; then he went to work for a company that sold drilling mud to rigs. When the company went broke, Rich decided to start his own. Rich told the credit union he needed $15,000 to remodel his house and used the funds to buy equipment for his new company, Red River Supply. He built the business into a major wholesaler of mud for rigs and became known for flying his own airplane to oil sites.

Then came the eighties oil bust. Red River Supply would have declared bankruptcy, but the company couldn't afford to pay attorneys to file the court papers. So it diversified its holdings. When the next boom hit, they were prepared and picked up dozens of rig contracts. Rich amassed sixty-eight real estate properties. Red River Supply had a rail yard that took in ceramic frack sand from China and natural sand from Wisconsin. Cement arrived for road projects, such as the bypass north of the Wild Bison on Highway 85 and the Lewis and Clark Bridge over the Missouri River. Steel pipes arrived from Alberta and Kansas City. Guar gum, used for fracking, came from Houston, along with the calcium and magnesium chloride, barite, mineral oil, propane, and hydrochloric acid needed for oilfield operations.

The blacklisting of his family during his childhood had driven Rich to create and preserve success. "I guess that's why I put my head to the stone and said, 'I'm going to show them bastards,'" he said. Rich was proud that he was the only one of his first cousins to be a multimillionaire, though he was sometimes torn about this ambition, figuring it had cost him his first marriage and likely his second. He met a lovely woman at the Daily Addiction coffee shop on Main Street and they began dating. She had moved here from Alabama, eager to start a new life after working three jobs at a time to support herself. Rich conceded that this union caused some tension among his adult children, but he said he had no intention of remarrying.

Red River Supply had struck a deal to partner with a thirty-year-old entrepreneur named Bobby, who had used his earnings from working on a frack crew to start a business applying protective industrial coating on oil equipment. He was from a New York suburb in Connecticut, and had a sweatshirt made that said KEEP FRACKING; he'd wear it whenever he visited home, relishing the chance to rile up liberals. One afternoon I drove west past Walmart and the new Badlands Town Center featuring Little Caesars, a post office and nail salon, the Golden China restaurant, and the FBI office. Hundreds of apartments rose beyond— yellow-white brick, Tyvek wrapping, a sign that said NOW LEASING! ALL UTILITIES INCLUDED LARGE 2 TRUCK GARAGE INCLUDED!! GREAT RATES. I made a few more turns, past pipe thread protectors spilling out of bags behind a chain-link fence, and arrived at Bobby's shop. He was wearing a mask as he sprayed oil equipment with polyurea coating in a booth that resembled a torture chamber.

Curtains were draped to the side, and the whole place was a messy, blotchy, gory, bloody, savage, frightening red. I found the fumes so noxious I wanted to pass out, and moved a swivel chair to the driveway to wait. Bobby finally emerged, rolling his own chair out. He looked like a murderer because of the perpetual red splatter on his shoes and hands from the polyurea; scraps of red coating jumbled over the shop floor. A mutual acquaintance drove up in his Hummer. "I'd ask to use your bathroom but I know you don't have one," he said, laughing.

"I'm living in shambles here," Bobby muttered, lighting a Marlboro. He complained about how his landlord was ripping him off by charging six grand a month. Back home, "a guy like this would be buried in a fifty-gallon drum in concrete."

But he was about to stage an escape to Red River Supply. Bobby knew the landlord would become enraged when he moved out, so everything had to be carefully orchestrated after dark. For help, he relied on a Ghanaian immigrant who used to sell cars in Ohio and drive a cab in New York. A couple of evenings later, the assistant was clearing out the shop and filling the dumpster. Rich's thirty-something son, Tavish, pulled up a little after eight in a white Red River Supply pickup. The guys began loading the truck up with fifty-gallon drums, a generator, and other equipment.

"Ready?" Tavish asked.

"One more hose," Bobby said.

"You following me, buddy?" Tavish asked.

"Hold on, I got a few more things."

There were still scraps of industrial coating everywhere. Polyurea was renowned for its hardiness. A prospective customer who had come by earlier was skeptical when Bobby said it was bulletproof. Bobby told him he could test it, so the visitor went to his car, retrieved a .40-caliber handgun, and fired a shot. The coating was indeed impenetrable, or so the story went.

They arrived at Red River Supply a short time later and rolled the drums of chemicals off into the garage. The men began to talk about where to go for a late dinner. "Anywhere but the brewing company," Bobby said. So the three of us went to Famous Dave's. At the table, Bobby looked down at his hands. He wanted to wash them, but the spatter wouldn't come off. He ordered a cup of chicken wild rice soup. Then he recognized the waitress as the friend of an old fling.

"She's still drinking," the waitress reported.

We came back to the old garage a couple of days later to finishing cleaning. I listened to his usual rants about how he'd lost faith in humanity after coming to Williston. He admitted that this place had made him harsher, meaner. He thought he might be worse than Donald Trump. Bobby didn't know whom to trust anymore; he abided by the saying *Trust is good but no trust is better.* "It's an Italian thing," said Bobby, whose father was of Italian descent. He asked if I had ever seen *A Bronx Tale,* his favorite movie. "It's all about trust."

He and the Ghanaian man had grown oddly attached to a stray dog that had been squatting there. Wondering where the dog had gone, they found him asleep under the desk.

"Come here, buddy!" Bobby clapped. "See, when a dog rolls over like that, it's a sign of trust. I like dogs." He resumed cleaning. "If it comes down to happiness or money, I want to go back to happiness." He paused. "*After* I make my money." On his rare days of leisure, he would take his four-wheeler out to the Lewis and Clark Wildlife Management Area. The ATV wasn't working right these days. "Do you know why these are crap? Because they're made in America . . . *Junk.*" We shot a few rounds with his Hi-Point out there; I aimed at a vodka bottle that somebody had discarded on a pile of branches. It was unusual for an oil guy to keep such a lousy gun, but he wasn't terribly concerned with firearms—not like the people at the shooting range on the other side of the wildlife area, where machine guns blasted the pristine setting and shreds of paper targets were strewn about like confetti. Bobby mainly used the Hi-Point for security at the shop. The other night, a few men had wandered up in an old Mercury Capri, asking for work. Their eyes were blurred with drugs and they appeared to be hiding a gun. Bobby didn't take out the Hi-Point; he gave them $150 to go away. He wanted to see a therapist about what being around all this had done to his head. "I'll probably never recover mentally." Bobby paused. "It's like coming out of jail, that's how it is up here. You get rough around the edges." But he had moved back to the East Coast briefly, and "when I left I kind of missed the roughness—it's addicting."

·:· ·:· ·:·

Rich urged me to join everybody for the American Petroleum Institute's banquet, a premier event of the fall. Hundreds of people streamed into Williston State College, hobnobbing in a VIP room upstairs. The college leveraged gifts of oil royalties to give every local high school graduate free tuition, fees, and books, leading to a surge in enrollment. Bobby and Tavish were sitting in armchairs near the entrance. Tavish was reprimanding Bobby for his dirty hands and suggested, "Use apple cider vinegar." "Dude, I use harsh chemicals," Bobby replied. "Look, it's polyurea! It doesn't come off!" He would leave Williston amid business disagreements in six months, and eventually take up work as a construction supervisor in Queens, but on this night, Bobby was in high spirits. Everyone sat down for a dinner of potatoes, steak, and beans and watched leaders in the oil industry accept honors and give speeches. Red River Supply was up for an achievement award, but it went to the state's petroleum lobbying group.

Lieutenant Governor Drew Wrigley stepped to the podium. He was brimming with grand statistics about North Dakota: the fastest-growing wages, the best business climate. An island of prosperity in a troubled national economy. But he was dismayed by a national survey suggesting that just 49 percent of Americans believed free enterprise was the best avenue for lifting people out of poverty.

"In the greatest free market economy in the *globe*, half the people, not even that, say that free enterprise is the best way to lift people out of economic despair. The other 51 percent? They believe it's the *government!*" He was aghast that two-thirds of the respondents believed big businesses dodged taxes, bought favors, and polluted. "If not the North Dakota way, then what way? . . . America very much needs North Dakota, not simply because we're the number two oil-producing state in the nation . . . but because across the board we have industrious people, creative people, visionary people, tough people, who always pull through—in boom times, more challenging times, and all the times in between. Too many people in our nation are watching what's happening and thinking, 'It'll be fine . . . someone will take care of it. Someone will pave the way. Just move some more wealth around, that's all you have to do.' Attack the people who have more, give to the people who have less, vote yourself a raise. That is not America. That is not North Dakota. . . . Our way of life is at stake. Global peace is at stake. They need to know that it won't just happen. You *need* right-minded people who are pushing the ideas of free enterprise . . . and it's nowhere more present and obvious than in a room like this of doers, of creators, investors, people who have daring and challenge, who see opportunity."

Capitalism Is Legal

Gold prospectors arriving in California in the 1840s found a vast populace of Indians, and treated them as a hostile force. The miners attacked natives, pillaged their food and livestock, raided and burned their villages, usurped their fisheries, and drove game from their hunting grounds. They enslaved adults and children in gold-digging expeditions and brought diseases. "That a war of extermination will continue to be waged between the races, until the Indian race becomes extinct must be expected," proclaimed Governor Peter Burnett in 1851. California lawmakers financially backed militias and aided them in building a formidable arsenal. Recruits received better salaries than miners. Often hailed as a testament to the American pioneering spirit, the California Gold Rush wreaked devastation on those who lived there before. An estimated 150,000 indigenous people had lived in California preceding the gold boom. But white migration was so unrelenting that by 1852, the census counted 264,435 people in California—only 33,000 of them Indian, according to historian Benjamin Madley. Thousands of Indians died of starvation as the crush of newcomers chased them out of fertile lands into the mountains, where there was little food. Others took to raiding goods from white settlements, provoking violent retaliation.

As the gold rush drew a wave of white travelers across the Great Plains, the federal government moved to ensure that the Indian tribes along the routes of passage would not disturb their journey. The parties convened in Fort Laramie, Wyoming, a fur-trading post widely recognized by gold prospectors at the confluence of the Laramie and North Platte Rivers. Eight tribes signed the Fort Laramie Treaty of 1851, which set tribal boundaries and agreed to peace with other Indian nations and travelers alike. The natives would allow the US government access to their lands to build roads and trading posts, in exchange for receiving $50,000 a year for the next half century.

The détente was brief. Mining in California greatly increased the amount of gold in circulation, driving inflation, as a fury of railroad expansion and land speculation, decline in grain prices, and collapse of banks led to the Panic of 1857. Multitudes surged into Colorado upon the discovery of gold at Pikes Peak, desperate for fresh economic prospects after hearing that pickings had dwindled on the West Coast. Conflict abounded between whites and natives as opportunists encroached on tribal lands guaranteed by the agreement at Fort Laramie. The gold boom brought at least a hundred thousand prospectors, and they pressured the federal government to relent on the terms of the old pact. Tribal chiefs agreed to cede most of their treaty lands, but rank-and-file Indians were angry at this betrayal and skirmishes continued. One prospector named John Bozeman arrived in the Colorado goldfields to find much of the wealth picked over. He ventured to Montana as another gold rush was beginning, going into business as a tour guide for the miners and treading over old Indian trails supposedly protected under the Fort Laramie Treaty. Several years after he founded the city named for him, he was killed by Indians. Attacks continued on miners and travelers passing through on their way to the Montana goldfields or Oregon.

The government closed the Bozeman Trail. In return, the Lakota Sioux agreed to cease aggressions against whites by signing the second Laramie Treaty of 1868, an accord that also established the tribe's ownership of the Black Hills. Yet peace, again, was ephemeral. The discovery of gold in the Black Hills caused more disputes with Indians, as prospectors muscled into Sioux territory. Lieutenant Colonel George Custer arrived with an army to investigate reports of gold in 1874, a move that brought thousands of whites onto tribal land. After the Sioux War, the federal government seized the Black Hills. The US Supreme Court ruled a century later that the government took the lands illegally, but the Sioux rejected the $1.3 billion settlement. They claimed that the Black Hills were a sacred spiritual site that had never been for sale.

One party to the original Fort Laramie Treaty escaped such bloodshed, as they lived in isolated territory of little interest to nineteenth-century fortune-seekers: the Mandan, Hidatsa, and Arikara of North Dakota. But the Three Affiliated Tribes, as they were known, faced white encroachment nonetheless. The pact had drawn their tribal boundaries around twelve million acres from present-day Williston, where the Missouri and Yellowstone Rivers met, through Montana and Wyoming, into South Dakota, and up to Bismarck.

Over time, the federal government took back most of the territory to make way for the expansion of railroads and settlers. I often heard tribal members speak about the Fort Laramie Treaty of 1851 with some bitterness, as they recounted the vast diminishment of their holdings. The tribes were forced to sustain themselves on the remaining one million acres along the Little Missouri River, where the farmland was rich and coal and timber and wildlife abounded. By the late 1940s, the US Army Corps of Engineers approached the tribes about flooding their farmlands to allow for the construction of the Garrison Dam. Many of the elders were "no-budges," but resistance failed. The dam flooded 150,000 acres of fertile land, burying residents' longtime homes under what became Lake Saka-kawea. The water was named for the Hidatsa woman who guided explorers Lewis and Clark through the treacherous territory in the early 1800s.

A haunting photograph showed tribal leaders signing the papers approving the dam as chairman George Gillette wept and covered his face with his hand. The picture hung in the chambers of the tribal business council—an ever-present reminder that the government, and by extension whites, would intrude on that to which they had no claim. "With a few scratches of the pen, we will sell the best part of our reservation," Gillette lamented. Even decades later, tribal elders felt anguish as they looked across those royal waters burying such great betrayal. Thrust onto barren land, tribal members trudged on in poverty. By the early twenty-first century, 40 percent of people on the Fort Berthold Indian Reservation were jobless.

In 2006, the Houston oil giant EOG Resources discovered a major reserve of oil on the eastern edge of the reservation, about ninety miles east of Williston. The US Geological Survey later proclaimed that the reservation sat atop billions of barrels of oil, and other oil companies rushed in. Investors moved quickly, hiring land men to serve as intermediaries. Their job was to convince residents who held mineral rights to sign leases allowing the companies to drill and frack the oil on their land. In exchange, the companies would pay a onetime bonus and steady royalties based on profits from the oil wells' production. Some landowners didn't negotiate, assuming they had to sign whatever document an oil company gave them. For many, the lease bonus payments were the biggest fortune that had ever struck them.

Corporate representatives and mineral owners crammed the office of the US Bureau of Indian Affairs in New Town. The bureau was charged with approving all terms of oil leases, but it was understaffed and unprepared for an epic land rush. Frank Whitecalfe, a tribal councilman at the time, told me he often relied on revenues from the 4 Bears Casino & Lodge to plug budget shortfalls for a municipal government that was deep in debt. He considered the casino manager, Spencer Wilkinson Jr., a protégé and asked why he didn't put together a company of his own to compete with all the incoming oil interests. Spencer formed a company called Dakota-3 and teamed up with several companies off the reservation to develop the oil resources. He wrote that he wanted tribal members to be afforded the same financial security as those outside the reservation's borders. "Free enterprise is an opportunity that exists for all individuals on and off the reservation," Spencer wrote at the time.

But he drew controversy early on when the tribal council agreed to sell forty-two thousand acres of oil leases to Dakota-3 for a bonus of $50 per acre and 18 percent royalties. "Why is the tribe negotiating sweetheart deals?" demanded one tribal member at a 2008 meeting, when Spencer defended the sale. "There are a lot of kids here with nothing—while [Spencer] sits over there with a thousand-dollar suit," said another. Dakota-3 also signed many individually owned oil leases. Several Indian mineral owners sued, saying the Bakken could be the site of the biggest swindle of American Indians in US history. "History has repeatedly demonstrated that the bigger the prize, the more egregious the land grab and attendant exploitation of Native American rights and interests," the plaintiffs claimed.

They had sold their oil leases to Dakota-3 for a bonus of $400 per acre. Other residents got far less. They accused Spencer and his business affiliates of using political influence over the tribal council and Bureau of Indian Affairs to obtain leases at below-market prices and flip them for a massive profit. Dakota-3 drilled about two dozen wells and sold its oil interests to Williams Co., Inc. in Tulsa for $925 million, amounting to more than $10,000 per acre.

Calling it a "shocking windfall," plaintiffs accused the Bureau of Indian Affairs of failing its duty to approve leases only when they maximized mineral owners' economic interests. The bureau repeatedly stamped the paperwork "This lease is in the best interest of the Indian mineral owner" even as leases for white owners off the reservation sold for higher prices. They accused the government of breaching its fiduciary duty to Indian residents, forgoing a tremendous chance to win favorable payments for mineral owners and bring the tribes out of poverty. They said the bureau neglected to require the consent of mineral owners if oil companies flipped the rights to drill. Only later did the tribal council put restrictions on flipping, after most of the lucrative deals had already happened.

In 2013, rows of attorneys from Houston, Dallas, Oklahoma City, Washington, DC, and Seattle filed into a federal courtroom in Bismarck. Quite reasonably, the defendants' counsel argued that the plaintiffs opened the sealed bids, signed the leases, and submitted them for approval without protest. They never said they were denied bonuses or royalties, or that there had been personal injury or trespass, or that somebody had bribed or threatened them. Allowing mineral holders to push for higher bonuses and royalties years after a gusher hit would make it untenable to do business on the reservation, which was already a bureaucratic gauntlet. The attorneys argued that the tribes were happy to receive hundreds of millions of dollars in royalties, past and future, and that anyone had the right to ask the government to approve such deals. In fact, Spencer should be *applauded* for bringing in oil investors to the reservation. An attorney for one of Spencer's business partners told the judge that they had engaged in legitimate business conduct, spending significant capital to pioneer drilling on Fort Berthold. "'I didn't get a big enough bonus and I didn't get a big enough royalty,'" said the Oklahoma City lawyer, imitating his opponents' complaints. "Hindsight is great. It's called seller's remorse." His reasoning, in essence: capitalism is legal.

The plaintiffs claimed they didn't have reason to know the fair market value until years later, but that the Bureau of Indian Affairs was well aware of the oil wealth on tribal lands. Their legal challenge was unsuccessful (the tribal government, for its part, never sued). By then, massive oil companies from Texas and Colorado had tied up nearly all of the tribal lands' oil drilling rights. The reservation produced 17 percent of North Dakota's oil, but it had little control over the tumult that accompanied such development: hordes of shifty oil workers, drug traffickers, trucking accidents, pipeline spills.

One could walk the halls of the tribal administration building, where a "suspect at large" poster showed an outsider wanted for a shooting attack. Listen to the chairman of the tribal council give a distraught address about all the drugs and rapes. Come to an overlook of Lake Sakakawea, past the yellow pipeline warning poles and the fancy home a tribal member built from his oil royalties. Cross the soft yellow-beige grass and look at the magnificent sweep of turquoise water shining between the buttes that meandered like serpents, a scene as primordial as if Lewis and Clark had beheld it themselves. Generations of tribal members fished there for northern pike and walleye, hunted deer, and picked bitter chokecherries. A beautiful sheen over old exploitations, man washing history away.

Somewhere in the distance ran the scars of a million-gallon pipeline spill of brine—a by-product of oil production—that had flowed dangerously close to the lake. I was shocked to walk into a

Thanksgiving dinner of hundreds of natives in Mandaree and see that the owner of the pipeline was sponsoring the event: Crestwood Midstream Partners of Texas. Pipeline officials served dinner to lines of natives in a room draped with white Christmas lights. A tribal official read off numbers for the raffle. "9-0-0-2-0-7-4 . . . is that you? Yup . . . you get the iPad." The winner posed for a picture. "Enjoy," the man from Crestwood told her. "Bring that fifty-five-inch TV up here," the tribal official continued. "Don't drop it. . . . On behalf of Crestwood, I want to say thank you."

I was puzzled at the tribes' seemingly wholesale acquiescence to oil, unwitting as it may have begun, and met Frank at a café in the small reservation town of Parshall a few weeks later. I wondered what might have been if the tribes had controlled their energy interests from the start. Frank wore a cap that said TEXAS over his gray hair and a jacket with the insignia of the Indian Rodeo Finals, where he was a commissioner. Frank had left the tribal council several years before.

Over biscuits and coffee, he disputed the assertion that the council had sold leases for too little, saying that the values of the minerals had rightly increased with time. "Those lawsuits were created by ugly people that don't know nothing," said Frank. From his perspective, it was part of the "moccasin hotline"—the rumor mill among tribal members, some of whom didn't like to see their own kind advance. He was born the year the government flooded tribal lands for the dam, and figured it was better to have problems and oil money than straight problems. Frank didn't believe the council had acted in a corrupt manner, though the FBI had investigated the deals. He said the federal probe hurt the oil service business he started after leaving public office, and the controversies had ruined his friendship with Spencer. But Frank told me Spencer hadn't done anything that the corporate outsiders hadn't. "It was exactly the same," Frank said, "except that he's an Indian guy. There's never been a bad white guy in this deal, but there's awful Indians. Isn't that something?"

A Great Steaming Pile of Money

One man was particularly troubled by tribal interests giving away their riches so readily: Dave Williams, who was head of the tribal government's exploration and production division when the oil boom began. He grew up on the reservation and was one of the few tribal members with a long resume in the oil industry. Dave had worked on wells in Oklahoma, Utah, Wyoming, and Montana and liked to joke that he had earned the distinction of roughnecking in Texas in 120-degree weather and North Dakota when it was 90 below zero with the windchill. He was used to getting out on the rig no matter what; sitting back was simply not in his nature. So he was astonished to see the US Bureau of Indian Affairs and tribal leaders dole out oil leases so rapidly, and for such low prices.

He began asking why the tribes should settle for royalties between 18 and 22 percent when they could reap most of the profits and reinvest them in the community if they operated the oil wells themselves. Why were the tribes allowing huge corporations to take over the reservation's wealth?

Dave told me he was fired for insubordination several times. "They said, 'No, no, we don't need to do this, Dave, you're wrong,'" he recalled. "But this was about conviction and doing the right thing."

Tribal leaders relented several years into the boom and established the reservation's first tribal oil corporation, Missouri River Resources. Dave became the chief executive, and a roster of outside experts joined the board. An old colleague from Chevron became the chief operating officer. The firm's legal counsel had been nominated by President George W. Bush to be assistant secretary of Indian affairs. The senior geological advisor was an expert from the Crow tribe in Montana who had worked with the top oil companies before starting his own.

"The greatest value of oil is right at the wellhead," Dave often said, trying to steer people away from the lure of easy money from royalties. Tribal members need not worry about whether Missouri River Resources was invested in the community: Dave was one of their own.

In one tribal oil conference a few years after the enterprise started, Dave told the audience that as the Bakken took on global significance everybody was watching to see what they would do. "I believe it's Missouri River Resources' responsibility as a tribally owned company . . . to do today for our people what will make us prosperous in the future."

Tribes around the nation had been exploring how to generate revenue beyond casinos, and the Southern Utes in Colorado had become the model for economic sovereignty in Indian Country. Dave flew to Durango to get a copy of their business plan. The Southern Utes had formed the Red Willow Production Company with $8 million in seed money from the tribal government in 1992, and an executive named Bob Zahradnik called all sixty-three energy companies on the reservation to inquire about buying their leases. The other firms largely refused to take Bob seriously until the tribe made its first deal with ConocoPhillips.

The Southern Utes rode the boom in coal-bed methane gas, winning large profits from once-undervalued assets. As reserves declined, the Southern Utes began investing those winnings in other industries and regions. The tribe formed a pipeline company, with almost half of the interest held by Kinder Morgan, the largest pipeline company in North America. Most of the Southern Utes' income eventually came from dealings off the reservation.

Bob told me the Southern Utes acquired about a hundred thousand mineral acres in the Bakken, some of it on Fort Berthold

Indian Reservation, but drilled only a few wells on Indian lands before leaving. The Southern Utes determined that the richest oil reserves had already been leased to other players, and were concerned that the lack of pipelines required the transportation of crude by rail and flaring off natural gas. "The way to make money in the Bakken was to block up some acreage, drill a few wells that did well, sell, and get the hell out of Dodge," Bob recalled. "It wasn't to plan a thirty-year development." The Southern Utes concentrated their largest oil investments in the deepwater Gulf of Mexico, which they considered more economical. Bob seemed wary of chasing a boom-bust cycle; he reminded me, with some amusement, of the famous craze for tulips that gripped seventeenth-century Holland and collapsed in a speculative mania.

He came to speak to the Three Affiliated Tribes at the 4 Bears Casino & Lodge during an economic development summit in 2013. White oilmen mingled with tribal members in a large room where tribal insignia adorned the stage and a ceremonial tipi sat to the side. While many of the white oilmen privately griped about business on the reservation, they knew that oil on Indian lands was too profitable to pass up. Bob told the audience of flying on a Sikorsky helicopter to an offshore rig drilling where the Southern Utes had a stake in the Gulf, looking at millions of dollars' worth of equipment, and realizing they had made it to the big leagues. "You can *really* make a great steaming pile of money in the energy business," he told the crowd, "but you've got to do it right."

One of the proudest examples of Indian business success was Ho-Chunk Inc., the corporation started by the Winnebago Tribe of Nebraska in the early 1990s after casinos off tribal lands threatened the reservation's own gambling interests. Its chief executive was a Harvard-educated lawyer named Lance Morgan, who warned the Three Affiliated Tribes against settling for a pittance of oil royalties and told them they should be drilling and selling their own oil.

Lance joked about how the oil companies in the back were going to be nervous. He praised Missouri River Resources and its nascent plans to drill four tribal oil wells. "That is the tip of the iceberg," he told the audience. "Once you get the capital and the knowledge, think about what you can do next. Anything is possible. You might as well totally dominate and control." He spoke about his own company's success in construction, logistics and warehousing, and lending, expanding employees and interests into many states and countries. They were involved with NASA in New Mexico; they were contracting in Iraq and Afghanistan. Couldn't the Bakken tribes pursue the same ambitions?

But as Dave found, there was little mineral acreage left for Missouri River Resources. It seemed so absurd, scraping for oil leases when his own tribal government had sold so much to Spencer for a trifle. By the time the Three Affiliated Tribes approved a $30 million loan for Missouri River Resources and secured the rights to drill for oil, they had undoubtedly missed out on the biggest profits. They had dithered while oil traded at historic highs, and by the time the company erected a rig on a two-hundred-acre lot in 2015, prices had dropped by half.

The firm contracted Halliburton and Baker Hughes, two of the biggest oil services companies in the world, to help bring the wells to production. Dave's company also bought a stake in fifty-one wells operated by other interests on the reservation. "We want to be in the position eventually to get back what we can," Dave told an audience of several hundred people at an oil conference in Grand Forks soon after the wells began flowing.

We arranged to meet at his office on Main Street in New Town, along the reservation's main thoroughfare. Missouri River Resources sat on the same stretch as a grocery store, the newspaper office, a bank, Better B Café, and the tribal employment office, with the grain elevator towering a few turns away. The building was several miles west of the bridge across Lake Sakakawea; keep driving east and you'd come to the tribal administration offices and casino on the other side. Main Street was nearly impassable that summer, as laborers tore up the street for a massive road expansion.

A poster in Dave Williams's office showed the lake, sprawling in the shape of a lizard, a pump jack to the west and a drilling rig

to the east. Black and white feathers hung on each side. SOVER-
EIGNTY BY THE BARREL, it said. I asked how he had convinced the
tribal leaders to listen to his idea, and Dave pointed to the motiva-
tional poster on the wall that said PERSEVERANCE. He surrounded
himself with inspirational sayings and often listened to motiva-
tional speakers; his latest favorite was Kris Carr. Dave woke up
every morning thinking, *I want to have the best native-owned oil company in the history of the United States.*

He chose his words carefully whenever I asked him about
tribal leadership. The government had, after all, given Missouri
River Resources its start-up funds; he couldn't afford further episodes of insubordination. Even a driven executive like Dave was
dependent on the whims of tribal politics. It was a common dilemma: while oil development was a purely private enterprise in
the rest of the Bakken, 90 percent of the world's oil production
was controlled by government entities.

We drove a half hour south, winding through the badlands.
He spotted our destination from the gas flare piercing the horizon
of blue-gray buttes. It made him proud, even if flaring was one
of the oil boom's most controversial legacies. Dave was negotiating an arrangement to pipeline the gas soon. As he turned onto
a scoria tract he said, "There's our babies." We heard the rumble
of a swabbing rig that made it difficult to speak. Something had
gone wrong in one of the oil wells and the crew was running tools
thirty-five hundred feet down-hole to fix it.

I had begun to ask a question when I heard a plane, and I
paused, waiting for it to pass. It didn't. I looked at the sky and there
was nothing but the flare. Something in the oil treater had kicked
it into a high scream. "That's a beautiful picture," he said, looking upon the trembling flambeau. Dave began speaking to a contractor tinkering with the machines that separated the oil from
gas and water. Were they still heated to 110 degrees? Yes, the man
said; he'd lowered it a half hour earlier. Dave worried that the temperature monitor lacked protective covering. "The worst storms
come from this way," he warned. The man told him that sludge
was building up and assured him that Halliburton would stop by

and test a sample. Dave approached another worker, telling him to clean up the grass behind the containment area. "The last thing I want is someone coming out here and seeing trash."

The wells bore symbolic names: the Mandan, the Hidatsa, the Arikara, and the Nation. Four oil wells drilled and operated by the tribes. Just four out of thirteen hundred wells producing oil on the reservation. A third of a percentage point.

Those wells would produce 364,641 barrels of oil in their first year. Dave imagined this was only the beginning; he wanted fifty wells producing oil in three years. The tribal newspaper covered the success with a dramatic headline: "'Drilling Native Oil on Native Soil': Missouri River Resources Makes History with First Four Wells." It carried an enormous picture of the flare wafting in the spring winds. The rest of the paper was a reminder of the trouble that remained on the reservation. Beyond notice of the walleye tournament winners and the New Town rodeo was a front-page report of two men brawling after doing meth. One had dumped the other's body in the trunk of a car and was facing murder charges.

We walked over to the truck driver unloading oil by the rows of olive-green tanks. He told us he was from Kenya. The man had studied environmental science in Oklahoma but came here for the money. "Who you guys work for?" he asked us.

"I'm the owner," said Dave.

"So you going to keep giving me more work?"

Dave admitted that the plan was to put the oil in a pipeline.

"What am I going to do, man?"

"We'll drill more wells." Dave began telling him about the Native American ownership.

"Oh wow . . . I saw the names . . . I've been writing them in my log book."

"That's our name, the Mandan, Hidatsa, and Arikara." He pronounced it slowly, with great pride. "The Three Affiliated Tribes."

On the way back, Dave pointed out a native-owned oilfield services company on once-empty land. He liked to see oil development bring his people success. He was eager to start another round of drilling, this time with thirty-two wells. He had picked out land along the Little Missouri River that had been given back from the federal government in a land dispute. Scraps, but he'd take them.

I asked why it had taken them so long to do this. "It's just another example of failures on a reservation," said Dave. "Here we go again. We did it again, blew it again." He dreamed of the reservation becoming a model of nation-building, as tribal governments referred to it. He didn't want to have to borrow money from his government again; he wanted Missouri River Resources to find a way to convince banks to provide the next round of capital. Dave was still getting used to these meetings with lenders, and tried to keep a sense of humor about him. His first meeting had been with Houston oilmen in a conference room at the Denver airport. At the start of his presentation he'd quipped, "I don't know anything about finance, but I did stay at a Holiday Inn last night," cribbing from the hotel company's commercial, and the other businessmen laughed.

But it was hard for any oil business, much less a new tribal concern, to attract capital during the global oil price war. The banks were bracing for implosions of bad debt, as exploration and production companies' hedges expired and profit margins dwindled. The majors were slashing spending and delaying investments. Cash flow was tight; some firms were going bankrupt.

Having heard Dave's early pitch to start an oil company, former councilman Frank Whitecalfe told me he believed the government had acted in the right when it rejected Dave's proposals early in the boom. Frank hadn't wanted the tribes to wait years for a profit, liable for large debts—it could cost up to $10 million to bring one oil well into production. Frank believed, in fact, that Dave could have this enterprise only because of the other big companies that had built up the industry on the reservation. Dave had proven himself with these four wells, as Frank saw it, and more opportunities lay ahead.

But the delays caused Missouri River Resources to miss the fire hose of easy loans granted when oil was at historic highs. "We had all this New York private equity just dumping money into the oil business and anyone off the street could go out and get $500 million," said Bob, the Southern Utes' energy executive (he has since retired). "People were paying too much for leases, paying too much for rig contracts, and they all thought it was going to go to $200 a barrel. Well, it didn't. And everybody starts chasing that commodity, you get an oversupply like we did, and it busts, and it happens again and again."

·:· ·:· ·:·

By then, Danny was hauling crude in Mandaree, near where Dave took me to see the Three Affiliated Tribes' four wells. Just another white man kicking up dust on tribal roads, moving oil for outside interests—all profits the natives would hardly see.

Just another oilfield mercenary.

Ballad of La Bruta

*D*anny crossed the bridge over Lake Sakakawea as the currents glittered with white jewels cast from the sun's glare, and he went west and south a little way, toward a flare shining far on the horizon as the badlands sprawled into miles of primordial majesty. The torch disappeared and came back as the road curved and ascended, and finally we went beyond it.

Danny passed Missouri River Resources' four oil wells and looked in confusion at the GPS, which tried to steer us onto a route where the tribal government had recently outlawed semis. We took the long way, past hay bales stacked three rows high, and turned east. Two belly-dump trucks turned onto a gravel road ahead, breathing poofs of dust. He cranked the Jake brake as we swept downhill, and the compressed air released in a long snarl. The cows watched with empty eyes. Danny honked twice. He claimed that oilfield cows didn't care about truck noises—they failed to move in the slightest.

He turned onto BIA-12, which he considered the worst road in North Dakota. We bumped over craggy asphalt, teetering from side to side as we passed several headless pump jacks. The road was operated by the US Bureau of Indian Affairs and led to the heart of Fort Berthold Indian Reservation's oil riches. "The real rez" Danny called it. People usually only went there if they were tribal members or worked in the oil business, as it was secluded even by North Dakota standards. A half dozen people had driven me around Mandaree at some time or another, but I could never say where it began or ended; the borders seemed to run as freely as the strange confluence of wealth and loss at every turn.

We turned onto another tribal thoroughfare where the landscape sprawled into mantles of green and passed the home of one of the reservation's most outspoken environmentalists, Theodora Bird Bear. I knew she resented out-of-state truckers like Danny. I had sat with her and her sister Joletta on the deck one evening, surrounded by doves and killdeers, elm trees and cottonwoods. Theodora affirmed that the land must seem desolate to outsiders, but she still felt an ache from seeing her mother's anguish over losing the land to the Garrison Dam, the way her mother could not even speak of it. The stentorian snarls of the semis disrupted our pleasantries at first, then became unbearable. There were times they slept with a fan on to drown the noise of Jake brakes and still woke up at two in the morning. Joletta said it was an ever-present drone, as though they lived next to Boston's Logan International Airport or Chicago O'Hare. The Bird Bear sisters believed the truck drivers disturbed them deliberately, to intimidate the natives. They didn't know that Danny was only trying to control a hundred thousand pounds on precarious roadways. Such people had no occasion to mingle with one another; Danny couldn't fathom why anybody lived here, couldn't discern the meaning in this place that seemed more haunted than alive. He didn't know about the reservation's long history of fighting white encroachment and believed it was best to develop oil in thinly occupied terrain.

Danny turned onto a dirt road and honked at more cows. To our surprise, the animals jumped and retreated. I came to understand that he improvised these amusements—if one could call them that—as a way of enduring his solitary confinement. He saw more livestock than people. Danny still had the apartment on the Canadian border more than an hour north of us, so he had to trade one cage of isolation for another as he ran loads on the reservation, catching a night's sleep at whatever truck stop he could.

We began a steep descent, and Danny pulled his Jake brake hard. It sounded like an old man clearing his throat and spitting tobacco. *Hawwwwwwkkkkkk. Hawwwkkkk. Hawkkkkkk.* He steered around the bend, and the location appeared. Danny pulled the semi alongside the row of tanks—H20-OIL 1-OIL 2-OIL 3—and set a fire extinguisher and traffic cone in the front of the truck. To prevent static electricity, he unrolled a ground wire and clipped the end to the short wall that formed a square perimeter around the tanks. He then grabbed a toolbox and climbed the twenty-seven steps to the catwalk that ran alongside the top of the oil tanks. My heartbeat quickened as I followed. We were twenty feet off the ground, presiding over miles of rolling green marred by the olive-colored pump jacks on a slab of scoria. He turned his head away as he opened the top of an oil tank so that he would not be overcome by the blast of toxic gases.

Danny suspended a woodback thermometer inside the tank to measure the temperature. Then he took out a cylindrical glass device called a thief. Using a rope, he lowered the thief into the tank to take samples of crude. He spun a hydrometer inside to gauge the temperature and gravity. We waited the requisite five minutes, listening to the wind.

My chest tightened and I lingered by the edge of the stairway; my legs felt unsteady. I asked if it was safe to breathe this in, and he pointed to a monitor attached to his chest pocket. It would beep if dangerous levels of chemicals were detected. Everyone in the oilfield was on guard for hydrogen sulfide and the rotten egg smell signaling its presence, though it carried no odor at lethal levels. But this merely smelled like acrid gas. I tried to restrict my breathing, but it was still painful, and I didn't know if it was the chemicals or the panic.

We walked back down to his truck, where he put on his oily green gloves. Danny took a hundred milliliters each of mineral spirits and the oil sample and dropped them into a centrifuge that spun rapidly as it heated the liquid and separated the crude from water and paraffin. After a few minutes he held the vial of oil up to the sunlight, checking for impurities. "That's real good oil," he determined.

Danny was ready to load his tanker. He dragged a dull orange hose from the truck to a vessel they called a pumpkin. It resembled a barbecue grill sticking off the end of a pipe connected to the battery of tanks, and caught any fluids that might spill. The pool of oil at the bottom was tinted green. Danny unscrewed the end of the hose and attached it. He stepped over the lines of pipe on the bed of scoria, back into the shade of the catwalk, to open a seal on the tank that signified the purchase of oil. He went back and used a wrench to turn a valve behind the pumpkin. Danny pulled two valves below the truck to open the tankers. The machinery whirred loudly. "We're good; we're flowin'," he said. Oil rushed through a ribbon of glass on the hose. We watched the red digits flash second by second on the barrel counters attached to the side of the truck.

It was a firing offense for him to allow a passenger, let alone someone untrained in hazmat transport. He was angry, at first, that I had even suggested it. But he finally relented, believing I had put in the effort to show I was serious about reporting on the oilfield. He also disliked his boss's gauntlet of rules. "I'm a surfer" was how he liked to explain his personal rebellions. He even seemed mildly grateful for my company today.

We rumbled off the well pad, and Danny promised a trippy drive out. The semi wobbled severely as we made a sharp left turn. "This truck is a beast"—he switched to Spanish—"*la bruta, ani-MAL.*" Even the front of the truck looked vicious, with pieces of metal circling to form a feral maw. The truck was affixed with placards that said "1267," the federal hazmat code for oil. La Bruta grunted under the weight of 214 barrels of crude. Danny believed she liked to be heavy, liked to work. The truck picked up power and whistled. In the side mirror, I saw the dusty haze the truck made on the unpaved road. It trailed us like a shadow. Danny dropped to fifth gear and we sailed downhill.

"Woo hoo hoo!" he said as we rounded a steep curve. He let the Jake brake snarl. When I sneezed, he assured me it was just the dust. "I got a big old dent up here and I gotta run right through it, son of a . . ." He stopped. We swayed and cruised into a bowl in the asphalt, jolting at its far edge. "*Pobrecita*. Poor girl. She's a brute. She can haul, I tell you that."

Down and up through hills and more hills, each indistinguishable from the last. Even La Bruta seemed small in their shadow. Danny was becoming drowsy, numbed from the sameness of this, not just from hill to hill, but day to day. In this state of lassitude, drawn out by the afternoon sun, he slid over the ridges built to stop motorists from veering into the wrong lane. They snarled a loud warning. He jerked awake.

The landscape was a Pink Floyd album, one long and trippy riff of madness. The wild blur of badlands made us paranoid, wondering what spirit was coming alive over the next hill. One time I drove this route after dark and became certain I was being chased by a white pickup before it suddenly disappeared. When I mentioned it offhand to a few natives at the Mandaree tribal office the next day, they laughed and said this highway had a lot of phantom cars. There were bad spirits that wanted people to wreck.

"It reflects in the landscape," Danny told me. "Look how crude and rough it is. Now it's green but in a couple months it'll be frozen again, and it's just raw and rough and it's solitary, just like this job." He was moving through the world now in a savage cloak of aloneness, unmoored from family and community and church, the very ties cherished by generations of North Dakotans around him. His mouth was dry from days without uttering a word. Hauling on the reservation only widened the perimeters of his detachment. It was too far out, and the Indians didn't want him here, he knew that. He lamented that he couldn't even get to church to find any salve for his spirit. All he saw, in these small connections with humanity, was that his fellow laborers had come to make money and move on. They didn't seem to want to be here much more than he did, and it struck him that all of them were turned inward in their greed—or was it just survival? This way of life seemed so selfish to him, and yet he couldn't think of anywhere else to go or anything else to do.

That's all it is, Danny thought: *one man, one truck.* He justified the sentence he was serving in North Dakota the way most migrants did, shunning excuses. "What the hell am I doing out here, you know? And the answer is, a lot of poor, impulsive decisions in my life." I hardly ever heard anyone in the oilfield blame the government, income stagnation, corporate outsourcing, discrimination, dwindled pensions, crumbling schools, undocumented immigrants, or the devaluation of blue-collar work for their lot. Even the people who came because of student loan debt, foreclosure, and layoffs during the financial crisis rarely railed against Wall Street or the war against the middle class. They moved to North Dakota to do better. They didn't seek sympathy, and none was given. "I'm not blaming anybody but myself," Danny liked to say. If he complained, it was only because I pressed him about these matters. Otherwise, Danny turned his hopes and regrets over and over again in his mind until they blurred into miles of yellow lines and loneliness.

We emerged from the badlands, and Danny slowed dramatically. INJURED? WE'RE IN YOUR CORNER, said the billboard for a law firm. Danny turned past a saltwater disposal complex onto a gravel road to LACT 11. LACT stood for "lease automatic custody transfer," a system that would accept the oil and move it in a pipeline that delivered it to a railcar that sent it to a refinery across the country. Danny pulled into a bay and we stepped onto the dirt. He hooked up the dull orange hose from the truck to a receiving vessel and opened several valves. Danny and I were transporting oil from wells that had been drilled five years earlier by Peak Energy, a Colorado outfit that was a major player in the reservation's oil rush. It began advertising in community newspapers in 2007: "Attention . . . aggressively paying top dollar for . . . acreage . . . Call Toll Free . . ." The game was to gobble as much acreage as they could, then flip the leases to bigger companies for profit. But Peak was one of the few bright spots in the reservation's pattern of lowball land deals.

Peak hired several former tribal chairmen to open up access to the reservation—leaders who pushed for a bonus of $1,000 a mineral acre, which was several times what other companies on these lands were offering. John Mahoney, a white attorney who was close with tribal insiders, spoke with me about it over coffee at the casino one afternoon, after we escaped a particularly laborious council meeting at the tribal headquarters next door. We sat across from the gift shop by a window overlooking a thin layer of snow as Christmas songs played over the speakers, and for a moment it conjured the same generic comfort of a truck stop. John recalled the whirlwind of the old oil leasing days, when he would get big boxes of reports on mineral holdings from the Bureau of Indian Affairs office in Aberdeen, South Dakota, and scour them at all hours, looking for who owned what. Peak would order him to get more papers from the courthouse, and he'd tell them there was no way in hell they could do it in time. John would call the recorder's office late Friday afternoon to beg and call in favors and somehow they would fax them, "papers and papers, papers, papers, papers, and I'd fax them all to Peak and said, 'You guys often expect the impossible to get done?' and [an executive] said, '*All the time!*'"

He believed that Peak and companies like it had showed some sincerity in wanting to promote development for tribal members. But it was an adrenaline game to them, as he remembered it. *Here's a new play and we're going to go in and get it*—a spectacular gamble on getting rich. Spencer, the casino operator accused of bilking his own people, had drawn controversy for writing a letter to Peak's president accusing him of trying to lure away mineral owners who had already agreed to lease their oil to Spencer's company. Because Peak offered $1,000 an acre, the company posed a threat to his low offers. As a tribal member, Spencer wrote, he would take action to protect the agreements his company had negotiated.

Peak's gamble succeeded. The company sold its reservation acreage to the Calgary company Enerplus Resources for $456 million. Enerplus would go on to produce 27,800 barrels of crude a day on the reservation. Missouri River Resources, the tribal oil company, purchased a stake in some Enerplus wells.

⁙   ⁙   ⁙

Danny and I stopped at United Prairie Cooperative, a chain of local gas stations. At the edge of the parking lot was a new burger
stand, Bad Ass Burgers and Brats, offering an improvement over
the usual truck stop fare. It sold the Bad Burger Basic (one patty,
weighing a third of a pound), Super Bad (two patties), Ultimate
Bad (three patties), Big Bad Mama (four patties and all the fixings
on the menu), and Bad Ass Brats on a Bun. We ordered burgers
and walked inside the gas station while we waited for them to
cook. Danny ran into a trucker with dark hair and a mustache.
They began talking about their hauls in Spanish, then switched to
English when I came over. The men used to run freshwater for the
same company.

"I don't know, I like talking with people, man," his friend said.
"Over there, you're by yourself."

"It's nowheresville," Danny said.

The man said he was hauling freshwater to a frack. "They're
emptying out that pond right there, matter of fact . . . sucking water from wherever they *can*, you know?" He turned to me and said
the oil companies had to frack hundreds of locations by the end of
the year or they would have to abandon the wells.* "So if oil goes
down twenty bucks a barrel they still gotta do it, you know?"

"Or they could give up the money," I joked.

"They ain't giving up no money," said the trucker, laughing.
"Them fuckers, they money-hungry." He laughed longer and
louder. "It's all about that money, you know?"

We ate the burgers hastily in the truck. Danny checked Skype,
which he used to talk to his wife—she hadn't yet joined him in
North Dakota. He received many questionable solicitations from
foreign women, which he didn't care for because he was a faithful

---

* In 2015, there was widespread concern in North Dakota about a regulation
requiring operators to bring a drilled well to production in one year. Amid
the oil price collapse, companies didn't want to complete, or frack, wells they
had already drilled because it didn't make economic sense. Some expected a
renewed frenzy of oil activity as companies raced to frack their wells by the
deadline, but later that fall, regulators gave them an extra year.

husband. The latest had been writing every day from Ghana. *How are you, dear? I am a queen. My family is royalty. My father is dead. I have to get control of the land. I need money for a lawyer.*

We turned back onto the reservation, and he nearly stopped the semi as the ravaged asphalt opened before us. Danny steered to the edge, negotiating the rim with care, but came upon another within a hundred feet. He danced around a pothole shaped like a three-leaf clover and another like a diamond and another—just a sprawling mess, one and two and three inches deep. "It's the rez, man," he muttered. "They're not going to fix anything."

Here in Mandaree, just about the only place to stop was the convenience store and the community center, which sat next to each other. Lodgings on wooden platforms hulked nearby, and the streets were lined with squat, aging houses. The people here used to revel in walking a mile or more to their hunting grounds; these days there was no adventure in shooting elk or deer when they could just drive a car over the scoria roads that ran over the fields like arteries. There was scarcely a spot in Mandaree where you couldn't go over a hill and see a pump jack or flames. Some claimed that when the rigs began drilling on tribal lands, ghosts of weeping old women appeared.

Danny passed the land where tribal member Kristie Jo Hunts Along grew up riding horses. She had been poor, and then oil was discovered and Kristie began receiving $100,000 a year in royalties. She told me she got into meth and heroin while cashiering at the Mandaree gas station, serving oil workers, and aided Mexican drug traffickers in addicting her own people. Kristie was off drugs now. The royalties were drying up. "We see white people having all these nice things, and these big houses," she told me. "Everybody wants that." Four pump jacks operated by Exxon-Mobil bobbed on her family's land, and we had stood there one afternoon listening to the machinery as it squawked like cars skidding in the rain. A flare blasted on Heart Butte, that idyll from her childhood. Just another oilfield story . . .

Danny crested a hill and the wells of our destination came into view. Danny made a sharp turn and pulled alongside two rows of tanks. We climbed the stairs, and he popped the thief hatch on the oil tank and lowered his tape. Danny had offered to let me do it but said I would owe him $500 if I dropped the reel in the oil—as he had done once—so I declined because I was too nervous to hold it with a sure grip. I walked up and down the catwalk, looking over the hills of Mandaree. Danny held the tape to the sun, studying the palette of brown-yellow-green. We returned to the ground, and I followed Danny's instructions to test the oil. I walked back to the tanks, maneuvered some valves, then came back to the truck to push the valves under the tankers so they were ready to receive the oil. Danny barked orders. "Squeeze it down . . . open this one, squeeze it! Errrr, all the way over. Now! Push this handle down." We watched the oil rush through the sight glass of the hose. "Now we're pulling Bakken crude!"

It would take at least forty-five minutes to load the tanker. I walked toward the gas flare. I heard its roar even from a distance of a few hundred feet. It harmonized with the motion of the pump jacks and the rush of oil flowing through the hose. I felt the heat of the flame; I was already sweltering in my FR coveralls from the sun. I walked to the edge of the pad, closer, where the black pipe that connected the tank to the flare rose to my chin. I turned around and saw Danny sitting on the short wall that enclosed the oil tank area, looking glum. I ducked below the line and walked down a bank of overgrown grass, where a dozen cattle lingered, then went yonder until the pump jacks and tanks looked small. I stood in the field for a while, looking around, then walked back until I was in front of the pump jacks. I listened to the rhythm—fast, slow for dramatic effect, then fast, like that amusement park ride in which the ship sails back and forth until turning upside down. *Pup pup pup pup pup pup . . . pup pup . . . pup . . . pupupupupupupupupupup pup-pup-pup . . . pup . . . pup . . . pupupupupupupup . . .*

Back at the tanks, I told Danny how loud the flare sounded. Violent.

"I know," said Danny. "It's an angry flame—an angry well."

The barrel counter for the back tanker was moving very slowly. Danny rubbed the dust off the sight glass and looked closely. It appeared there was too much air—something wrong with the hose. He wanted to stop so he could cram in another load before it grew too dark.

"Man up, girl!" he said as I struggled to turn a valve. I removed the hose and laid it alongside the oil tanker.

He concluded that I might have promise as a crude hauler, if I could stomach the fumes. "You might as well do it," he said. "You're already in the truck. You know the area. . . . You're basically training for this job."

The industry wanted to do away with oil trucks like Danny's. A few years before, the top oil lobbyist gave a presentation to the Three Affiliated Tribes, flipping to a slide showing a line of trucks on a snowy road. He brought up another slide showing a brown swath over a hilly tract, marking the construction of pipelines to transport crude. The lobbyist said the only way to reduce the trucks was to encourage and develop more pipelines; it was the number one issue in the Bakken. It would stop the dust and make the roads safer. They wanted to remove twenty-five million truck miles a year from the roads. He encouraged landowners to allow the easements to let the pipelines cross their property.

Yet pipelines carved their own wounds. Go down to the tribal-owned ranch near here, where the buffalo were forced to adjust to the groans of industrial traffic and flares. Look at the land beset with scars—fifty-foot-wide stripes colored lighter than the surrounding grass, all the way to the horizon. The animals rubbed up against pipeline warning poles and knocked them down. Surveyors ran roughshod over grasslands with their four-wheelers and left open the gates, so the whole herd would flee across town. The ranch manager once had to call a helicopter to chopper over the buffalo and drive them back home, as they had wandered so far they were in the eastern badlands. He received small royalties from Enerplus, the company whose oil Danny was transporting that day, but sometimes he would rather all this oil stayed in the ground.

Danny drove off at almost half past seven. He shook a Starbucks double energy drink and slurped it up. The moon was a magenta wedge as we turned into LACT 11. This time I would have to take over the unloading. I unrolled the static wire, pulled the orange hose off the truck, and dragged it over the dirt, hooking it up to the vessel that would transport the oil to the pipeline. Danny eagerly assumed the role of my trainer. "Pull it with all you got!" he said as I struggled to open the valves. "Look and see that the oil's going through it. Oil's moving!"

I stepped back in the truck because the dust had caught in my eye. I tried to rub it out and my contact lens fell into my hand. I wrapped it in a crumpled napkin—there was no contact lens solution, or even water, to clean it—and stepped back out, half blind. The sky was a faint purple, lit up with eight flares. We loaded up and resumed driving. I was nodding off at a stoplight, my head against the window, when it turned green and we found ourselves barreling down a rutted dirt road, bouncing out of control. I straightened up and began yelling. We had been on a paved road and suddenly it was not paved, for no good reason. Danny found an Oasis Petroleum well pad and pulled in to turn around.

"That could have been bad," he mused as we found our way back onto the main road.

He pulled into a gas station, took a squeegee to the windshield, and wiped off the sheen of dust and dead bugs. My coveralls smelled of oil; mud ringed the bottom cuffs. I fished in my bag for the Lunchables I'd bought at United Prairie Cooperative. My fingers were covered in grime from working the valves, but I was too famished to care, rapidly eating the crackers and ham and cheese and dirt. I was hungry as soon as I finished.

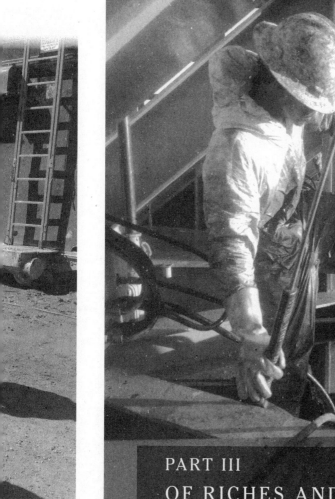
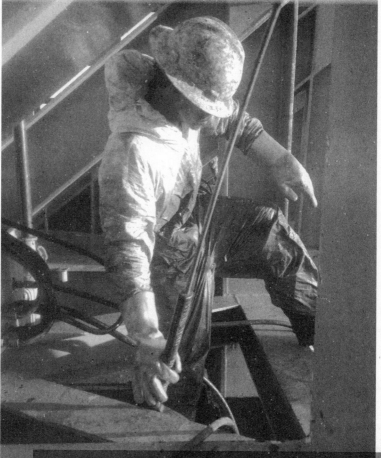

PART III
OF RICHES AND REALITY

The Dinner Party

The businessman peered into his pot of Bolognese sauce. "I don't know if it needs anything," he mused. The golden maroon delicacy had simmered on the stove since morning, the base churned from celery, carrots, and onions, sautéed with garlic, added to a dozen pounds of veal, pork, and beef, blended with tomato paste, flour, and wine, and seasoned with thyme and basil.

The dinner party was starting soon. The four-layer lasagna stuffed with zucchini, squash, and spinach was ready for the oven. Another tray held servings of chicken parmesan dipped in egg batter and—it was all he had in the pantry—fish fry crumbs. The businessman, Dave Noack, poured marinara sauce over the chicken breasts.* He chopped the Gouda cheese he had brought back from Wisconsin and set out the crackers. I was skeptical of his plans to grill the Caesar salad, his favorite item on the menu. "You'll see," he said.

Noack was fond of hosting social gatherings, his gourmet fare drawing friends and associates in a town beset with hunger and ennui. Everybody in the oilfield was desperate for a savory meal, their palates parched from truck stop specials, frozen pepperoni pizza and sixteen-ounce Mountain Dews, beef jerky, the McDonald's drive-through, sushi from the Twin Cities, potatoes and a rock of country-fried steak, plastic-wrapped sandwiches at the Kum & Go gas station, gizzards and chicken fingers, ham and

---

* I refer to Dave Noack by his last name here to avoid confusion with tribal oil executive Dave Williams.

Swiss cheese Lunchables, Walmart produce, microwave dinners, and Applebee's entrees. I hadn't enjoyed a fine meal myself since some RV dwellers invited me to share a Thanksgiving dinner of turkey, homemade pies, and green chili enchiladas in the junkyard they called home.

But I had, thankfully, moved up from scrap heap cuisine. I was visiting Noack's pied-à-terre at the Ridge, one of the finest housing communities in all of Williston. New York private equity firm KKR had launched the 164-acre development several years earlier, and the owner of the local Jiffy Lube transformed a parcel into premier two-bedroom condos. Noack's front door opened into a living room with a fireplace. It was separated from the kitchen by a long granite countertop, where he kept *Bobby Flay's Mesa Grill Cookbook: Explosive Flavors from the Southwestern Kitchen.* Noack was very pale, with penetrating blue eyes, and wore a baseball cap over his bald head. I watched as he arranged another pan of chicken parmesan and talked about how he hadn't eaten a cheeseburger in his three years in North Dakota—surely a record. He favored restaurants such as Sakura Japanese Steakhouse, where he was known to bring a platter of his flatbread pizza or lasagna to the immigrant staff who had tired of their own offerings. He also brought food when seeking business with drilling rigs: Moroccan chicken with tomato mint salad and Greek yogurt sauce; Asian soup filled with pork, mushrooms, scallions, and bamboo shoots; and dried cranberry-stuffed pork tenderloin with peach jam, ancho sauce, and a touch of rosemary. "North Dakota people are looking at me like, 'What are you thinking?' They don't eat any spices or sauces."

Noack especially enjoyed cook-offs. Some time ago, he had found a worthy competitor in a saleswoman who used to crash at his place. She chopped vegetables obnoxiously through the night—*whack! whack!*—and blared in Chinese over the phone to investors in Asia about selling ceramic sand while he was trying to sleep. The Chinese sand, which resembled poppy seeds, was commonly used in fracking operations. The saleswoman made excellent marinated pork and left behind some dehydrated Chinese mushrooms that were a hit when he passed them around to the company men who supervised the rigs. But she had decamped for Houston.

Seeing me scribble quotes in my reporter's notebook, Noack said, "You've got to put that paper away when people come. You've got to have fun."

His neighbor walked in. She was an ex-stripper from Las Vegas who went by the name of Mama. Tall, black, and slender, Mama had long hair and an angular face; she wore a tight purple shirt and dark pants. Mama asked if I'd like to come next door to meet her family, assuring Noack that she'd join the dinner party later. I followed her out, hoping the meal would be served by the time we had gotten acquainted. She opened a bedroom in her condo where her sons and their friends were hanging out, and the air was so thick with smoke that I had to suppress a coughing fit. We returned to the living room, where her daughter-in-law was on the couch. She was a young blonde who danced at Heartbreakers strip club.

Mama was out of the game but recalled it fondly. People thought dancers' success was proportional to their beauty, when it was really about charm—"the gift of gab," as Mama called it. She knew that a dancer must not take offense if a man preferred another woman. "They all have their own fantasy," she said. She had been so skilled at her trade back in Las Vegas that one of the strip club's patrons married her. He was a doctor from Coeur d'Alene, Idaho, a decade her senior, and she proudly described herself as his trophy wife.

Mama and her children kept homes in Las Vegas, but the doctor maintained his practice on the Idaho panhandle, where he had a 4,700-square-foot house on the lake. Mama said she traveled back and forth to North Dakota to sell hair extensions; there was nowhere for a woman to get her hair done around here, and the boom in strippers to entertain oilmen offered a market for hair products. I didn't wear hair extensions, but I understood what Mama was talking about. The first time I went to get my hair colored in Williston, I trembled in fear of a butchery (the stylist did a fine job).

It was common to meet ex-strippers from Las Vegas in the Bakken, and people here peddled every ware imaginable. Still, I wondered how she could sell enough hair extensions to afford a luxury condo in Williston. Did the doctor pay for it? Was selling hair extensions a lucrative enterprise? I hadn't much time to dwell on the matter, as the dinner party was about to start. Noack was on the front patio, grilling the lettuce in the late autumn chill. His guests were arriving.

There was the Chicago businessman, who came with a Texan colleague bearing bottles of wine. The businessman claimed to have been cheated out of his multimillion-dollar fortune in the natural gas industry and had left the comforts of his Michigan Avenue home for an oil job in Williston. He liked to remind me that those who came to North Dakota to reinvent themselves were not just the bums featured on the news—some had been quite wealthy—and he was determined to succeed here because he was sending his children to Georgetown University and did not want them to have to take out college loans.

There was Marcus Jundt, the owner of the Williston Brewing Company. He came from Minnesota money but went bankrupt when the economy crashed. "If that hadn't happened," he lamented of the financial crisis, "I'd be worth over $100 million today . . . in Vail, skiing at my hotel." He had started coming to Noack's get-togethers during his mayoral run the year before in order to meet more people, though Noack was rather critical of his offerings at the brewing company. ("His Brussels sprouts, they're horrible," said Noack, who fancied his own version flavored with balsamic and red wine vinegars, caramelized onions, and garlic.)

There was Jack Johnston, whose company had been fined in the oilfield's largest illegal dumping case—the one involving the Berg saltwater disposal on the Canadian border. He had recently driven up from his home in Colorado, a trip he was making more often now that he and Noack were going into business together.

These were mostly people of means with college degrees, some who had been in the top financial echelons at one time or another, and they had found themselves in Williston on a fine Sunday evening. But the oilfield was not all bad. The fireplace was going, the grilled lettuce was as delicious as promised, and the Bolognese sauce was divine.

More people showed up. The property manager from Greece. The surly man who went into the cement business here after his real estate investments soured in Minnesota. Bobby the entrepreneur, who used to live with Noack—they'd met through the Chinese saleswoman. (Their old place near downtown Williston had been the site of many festivities, drawing such a large and varied group that even the alleged Ponzi schemer from the UK, Daniel Hogan, passed through a time or two before his federal case went down.) I went to tell Mama and her entourage that dinner was ready, and they came to join the get-together. The dining room table wasn't large enough for everyone, so some guests perched on the couch, others on stools at the long countertop. Noack performed his hosting duties with aplomb, moving about to fill glasses of wine as they dwindled.

Hundreds of miles to the east, the Securities and Exchange Commission was most displeased. The agency's attorneys had filed papers in Milwaukee federal court several weeks before, complaining about Noack's "stingy proposal" to limit the amount of time they could depose him to two hours instead of four. Noack's attempt to narrow the time "has nothing to do with the search for the truth," the lawyers fumed. "It has everything to do with limiting the SEC's ability to pose hard questions about documents that cast a dark cloud over the defendants. . . . This court should . . . give the SEC the latitude it needs for a fair examination about this $200 million fraud."

I wondered if most of the party-goers knew about Noack's troubles. But I didn't say anything. While the oilfield was a famously rude place, bringing up the host's securities fraud investigation would have been a terrible gaucherie.

An attendee explained to me later that people were not judged too harshly for their pasts out in western North Dakota. This was more a matter of practicality than anything else. "If you insist on having only pristine friends, who have never had any mishaps in their life," this acquaintance said, "you're going to be awfully lonely up here."

Peyton Place on the Plains

New Year's Eve 2015, an hour before midnight. I was walking across the parking lot of Racers gas station to pick up a snack before meeting acquaintances at Cattails in downtown Williston. The store lights blasted across the cold darkness. Someone called out as I neared the door. "Maya!" I stopped and looked around—nothing. Night was too deep to discern anything beyond the store, and I resumed walking. "Maya! *Maya!*" I squinted and began walking back toward the parking lot. There I found Mama sitting alone in an idling SUV.

We had talked about going out on the town sometime when I went to her house before the dinner party, but these plans had never come to pass. She said to text her daughter-in-law, a dancer at Heartbreakers, but the woman never texted me back, and I forgot about it. I stuck my head through the open passenger's window and asked Mama what she was doing for New Year's. Clutching her stomach, Mama said she was staying in because she felt sick. She was flying back to Las Vegas in a few days because she was arranging some house-flipping deals now that she had finished taking a real estate class.

I felt a tinge of envy—I had always wanted to flip properties. People here were so entrepreneurial. They traveled to Williston and out of state, indulging in this business concern and that, meeting with investors, always on the cusp of some grand venture. Mama and I said something vague about getting together over the weekend, but I had too much to do and she left for Las Vegas. That January, Mama went to visit her husband in Coeur d'Alene, Idaho.

He was a craft beer aficionado. She didn't like beer, but he found her a Belgian peach variety she loved: Lindemans Pêche Lambic. "Enjoying my hubby," Mama posted on Facebook.

Six weeks into the New Year, federal authorities arrested Mama for running a $1.3 million drug trafficking ring that stretched from Las Vegas through Idaho, Montana, and North Dakota. Her real name was Loren Toelle, and she sold heroin, oxycodone pills, and meth as part of a criminal organization that would see eleven people arrested in all, including four of her five adult children. Another defendant was her daughter-in-law, the Heartbreakers dancer whom I had met at Mama's house (she'd also tagged along to the dinner party). Their mug shots were blasted across the news. The authorities seized Mama's homes, jewelry, and cars, including her Cadillac Escalade with the license plate STAN4ME, a reference to her doctor husband, Stanley Toelle. Authorities busted the doctor for laundering Mama's drug proceeds through his bank account, though the doctor insisted that he'd been duped by his wife.

His attorney, Nick Vieth, told me that the doctor had traveled years earlier to Sapphire Las Vegas Gentlemen's Club after going through a divorce. There he met Mama, who was a dancer, and the pair began a courtship. He soon became her fourth husband. Mama told authorities that the doctor gave her and her children the money and emotional care they needed after her father's passing. The doctor maintained his gastroenterology practice in Idaho and gave her a monthly allowance. He bought her cars, paid her credit card bills, and helped her purchase homes as they regularly visited each other.

Five years after their wedding, in 2010, Mama was sentenced to three months in jail for distribution of narcotics in Idaho. She promised the doctor she would stay away from crime, and they resumed their whirl of travel and fine excursions. The couple vacationed in Hawaii, boated on Lake Coeur d'Alene, and went for romantic dinners and shopping trips in Spokane Valley, Washington, just over the state line. In Las Vegas, Mama took him to the Bellagio on the Strip for his birthday. She grew irritated that friends began soliciting her for money. "He's a doctor, not a banker," she posted on Facebook. She refused to keep going to her husband to pay everyone else's bills. "I'm trying to build an empire and it takes money to build an empire."

The doctor's largesse allowed Mama to open the Vegas Stylz House of Beauty, a salon that offered eyelash extensions, braids, weaves, twists and locks, manicures, pedicures, and waxing. She continued enjoying the scene in Las Vegas, even socializing with the likes of famed boxing analyst Al Bernstein. During a visit with the doctor, Mama posted a picture of them holding what appeared to be margaritas as she leaned in to kiss his cheek. "This man right here is making me a millionaire," she wrote on Facebook. She frequently posted about their relationship: "Me and my husband [are] bringing love and marriage to another level . . . Proud to be in love . . . also proud to be a gold digger . . . don't hate 'cause he gives me everything I want."

Soon after Mama's jail stint, the feds got word that she was back in the drug game. They caught a break when a bust for oxycodone and heroin in Spokane pointed to Mama as the supplier. Afterward, Mama and her crew packed up their apartment there and shifted business to North Dakota, according to Traci Whelan, assistant US attorney in Coeur d'Alene. Mama expanded to the oilfield "because she was a savvy businessperson and realized she could make a lot more money," Whelan said.

They ran drugs to Williston, Fargo, and Fort Berthold Indian Reservation. Drug lords from around the nation had targeted the Bakken because they could inflate the price and target a large market of vulnerable people flush with oil money. Tribal leaders pleaded for law enforcement to stem the influx of drug traffickers as their members grew mired in addiction and violence. I was taken aback by the angst in chairman Mark Fox's voice as he addressed his people about the reservation's struggles to enforce the law, in a meeting a few months before Mama's arrest. "It's the violence, it's the people shooting people . . . it's the drugs being sold—I'm sure this evening you can step out and buy it right outside this

place. There are so many damn things we're working hard on. . . .
I'm frustrated. I don't sleep."

Investigators observed suspicious activity in the doctor's bank
accounts. Someone would deposit sums in Williston and Missoula,
Montana, banks; a short time later, there would be a withdrawal
for similar amounts from a location in Las Vegas or Coeur d'Alene.
Cops began recruiting witnesses to testify in closed hearings and
make drug buys.

Prosecutors alleged that the family used Vegas Stylz House
of Beauty to launder drug proceeds, and that the salon barely did
enough legitimate business to pay the rent. Mama gave her associates train and airplane tickets between Las Vegas and North
Dakota. Authorities discovered that Mama's enterprise would con-
ceal the drugs in hair gel bottles as they traveled on Amtrak. She
"recruited her children, roommates and other family members to
be her mules, dealers, and money launderers," investigators said.
"She controls the family by controlling the money earned in the
conspiracy."

A maze of law enforcement agencies coordinated the take-
down of Mama's drug empire: the Drug Enforcement Agency,
Internal Revenue Service, US Border Patrol, Department of
Homeland Security, US Marshals Service, FBI, and various task
forces and US attorneys' offices in multiple states. In North Dakota
alone, the case enlisted the Williston Police Department, the Divide County Sheriff, the Williams County Sheriff, and the North
Dakota Bureau of Criminal Investigation. Jack Johnston, the waste
disposal entrepreneur, recalled driving past the swarm of feds outside Mama's Williston condo. "It was a sight to see," he marveled.

It should be fitting that this book features a case that began in
Las Vegas, which sent a stream of fortune-seekers to the Bakken in
the wake of Nevada's housing bust—from one nakedly capitalistic
outpost of the American dream to another. A businessman who
came from Las Vegas to work with Marcus Jundt at the brewing
company told me that Williston needed a new slogan that played
off the one from Sin City: "What happens here doesn't happen
anywhere else—and that's a fact." Here's what doesn't happen

anywhere else: a reporter attends the soiree of a man facing a civil trial for securities fraud and is so absorbed with thoughts of financial derivatives that she never considers that the neighbor is a drug lord. I had a misguided tendency in the Bakken of using mainstream logic instead of anticipating total absurdity. (Though neither the dinner party host nor his other guests, beyond Mama's associates, had anything to do with her criminal scheme.)

The doctor claimed that he was too busy practicing medicine to pay close attention to his bank accounts, and Mama passed a lie detector test saying that her husband didn't know about her criminal activity. He divorced her soon after the drug bust. Why had Mama given up a seemingly luxurious life for all the trouble of drug trafficking? It appeared that she could have made money well enough otherwise, just as the British Ponzi schemers could have profited legitimately. Authorities said she didn't even do drugs. She merely sold them. I sent a message to Mama through her lawyer seeking an interview, but she never responded.

Just before the doctor's trial, the feds dropped his money laundering charges but nabbed him for several misdemeanor counts of tax evasion for not declaring Mama's strip club income. Nick, his attorney, had to hire forensic accountants to investigate the cost of G-strings and other stripping wear—he just wanted to know when HBO would come calling to make a series about the case. "You can't make this up," Nick told me, chuckling.

Mama pleaded guilty and agreed to forfeit $2 million in cash and property.

"You seem very intelligent," US district court judge Lynn Winmill told Mama as she sentenced her to seventeen years in prison. "You could have done so many other things in your life."

"I did what I did and I deserve to be punished," Mama said.

Secrets, scandal, intrigue—the Bakken had it all. How could these characters have all turned up in this windswept outpost in the middle of America? When I mentioned this to a local real estate investor, he laughed and shook his head.

"This area," he said with a sigh, "is Peyton Place on steroids."

Deal Junkies

Weeks after the dinner party, businessman Dave Noack traveled home to Milwaukee for the Christmas holidays—and his deposition with the Securities and Exchange Commission. Both sides agreed to spend three hours hashing over Noack's role in the investment deal from hell. The deal from a lifetime ago—before the oil boom, before the financial crisis—back when he was a senior vice president at the bank Stifel, Nicolaus & Co. and wore dress shoes instead of steel-toe boots.

Wild snow across southeast Wisconsin canceled flights, knocked out power, and caused hundreds of motorists to crash. Noack walked through the freezing, blustery winter into the twenty-two-story Chase Tower downtown and entered Suite 1400. The court reporter swore him in.

"Good morning, Mr. Noack," said a lawyer from the SEC.

⁙   ⁙   ⁙

It had been a very bad day, in retrospect, when Noack addressed the school board of Whitefish Bay, Wisconsin, about how to pay for retired teachers' health benefits. "What's the best investment? . . . It's a collateralized debt obligation," he said. Noack suggested they buy complex instruments usually sold to investment banks and hedge funds. He assured the officials that other school districts had already made similar investments with his bank's help. The investment scheme was "very, very conservative" and there would have to be fifteen Enrons to see a default, he said.

177

Noack had been a longtime financial advisor for the district, and the Whitefish Bay board members trusted him. But that day in 2006, they didn't know that Noack had never sold CDOs and had little understanding of how they worked. They didn't know that several banks had declined to participate in Stifel's program over concerns that the deal had too much leverage and school districts weren't sophisticated investors. They didn't know that another Stifel official had internally questioned the CDOs' high credit ratings. They didn't know that the first such investment that Stifel made for another school district had suffered an unusually large number of downgrades within weeks of closing, or that Noack had inquired about repurchasing the notes, to no avail. They didn't know that Stifel had done nothing to address the problems in the portfolio after the investments' poor performance. The St. Louis–based brokerage and investment banking firm considered school districts' retiree health care liabilities a substantial business opportunity, according to authorities, and wanted to sign them up for such investments quickly to gain an advantage over competitors and expand the program nationwide.

Following legal approval, Whitefish Bay joined four other eastern Wisconsin school districts in putting up $37 million of their own money and borrowing $163 million from the Irish bank Depfa. Then the school board used the funds to invest in notes tied to the performance of synthetic CDOs with a portfolio of at least a hundred credit default swaps linked to corporate bond obligations. The instruments were sold by the Royal Bank of Canada (RBC), with Stifel brokering the deals. The returns were projected to be higher than the interest on the borrowed money and yield greater returns than traditional fixed-income investments.

Noack's prospects seemed to be rising. He received a $1 million signing bonus for his expansive client base upon moving in 2007 to another financial institution, Robert W. Baird & Co., according to a court deposition. But CDOs weren't the winning investment that Noack claimed. The schools' investments were among the billions of dollars in risky financial derivatives that fueled the worst financial crisis since the Great Depression. After years of easy credit and predatory lending, a massive wave of homeowners began defaulting on subprime mortgages that had been bundled into securities sold on Wall Street. The school districts had unknowingly insured a layer of the worst debt in the CDOs. Standard & Poor's AA-minus rating of the instruments was a sham. The school districts' investments didn't need fifteen Enrons, or anything close, to default. The value of the investments plummeted and the schools lost all of their money, even as the banks involved reaped lucrative fees. Depfa was purchased by German titan Hypo Real Estate shortly after the schools' investments, and German taxpayers had to bail them out for $75 million as the financial crisis spread around the globe.

Initially, the school districts claimed Noack and Stifel weren't at fault; they blamed RBC because it had put together and sold the investments. But the school districts eventually sued Stifel. Whitefish Bay alleged in court documents that Stifel used deceptive sales practices to further a conspiracy and had falsely claimed that hundreds of other school districts were interested in participating in the program. The lawsuits continued: Stifel sued RBC, and RBC sued Stifel. The SEC sued Noack and both banks, claiming they had defrauded the schools by pushing unsuitably risky investments and making material omissions and misstatements.

Noack told the commission that he was "terminated" from his banking job in 2011, the day after the SEC filed suit. Weeks later, North Dakota governor Jack Dalrymple appeared on CNBC's *Mad Money* with Jim Cramer to implore Americans to fill thousands of job openings in the state. Booms thrive in times of financial crisis. The Klondike Gold Rush happened in the wake of the Panic of 1893, as the overexpansion of railroads led to the failure of hundreds of banks and businesses, the contraction of credit, mass layoffs, foreclosures, and a plummeting stock market. People stole; they protested; they fled; they starved; they killed themselves. They were so desperate that the bitterly cold trek to the Alaskan mines was worth the risk. More than a century later, so went the Great Recession. Lehman Brothers went bankrupt. The jobless rate hit double digits. Banks foreclosed on houses, and families moved into their cars. Trillions of dollars in consumer wealth vanished. The same variety of toxic financial instruments that Noack sold in Wisconsin wiped out so many jobs that when North Dakota faced a shortage of labor to develop the oilfield, thousands of people rushed in for a chance to start anew.

People like Jeff Burgos, the executive chef at the Williston Boutique Hotel. His eatery in Arizona collapsed; he saw hedge funds snapping up hundreds of distressed properties in Phoenix without even looking at them. "I lost my business, I lost my house, I lost my family—I lost everything," said Jeff. He was so desperate that after he escaped to North Dakota, his first job was washing dishes at a Halliburton man camp.

People like Cali, the trucker I knew from the Wild Bison truck stop. One of his jobs during the financial crisis had been cleaning foreclosed homes in southern California. He witnessed the wreckage of people's lives: refrigerators full of food, dishwashers full of dishes, dressers full of clothes. Sewage clogged the toilets; candle wax speckled the floors. People lived there for months after the electricity and water got shut off, fleeing only when the sheriff's department came to evict them. "It was the bottom of the barrel of life, but I was just glad to make $125 a day," Cali said.

Noack was one of more than ninety senior corporate officers sued by the SEC for misconduct that led to or arose from the financial crisis. The scandal made the *Wall Street Journal*, *Financial Times*, NPR, CNN, Bloomberg, Reuters, and the *Milwaukee Journal Sentinel*. Noack "got a little greedy and big for his britches," huffed a blogger for the *Economist*. The *New York Times* featured the case in "The Reckoning," its series exploring causes of the financial crisis. A book called *The Looting of America: How Wall Street's Game of Fantasy Finance Destroyed Our Jobs, Pensions and Prosperity—and What We Can Do About It* posited, "In fact, if we can understand exactly what Dave Noack sold to Whitefish Bay and why, we will also understand how the economy collapsed."

Noack told me that he came to North Dakota after a friend of a friend contacted him about recycling oilfield wastewater. That didn't work out, but he wound up selling waste disposal services from rig to rig. It wasn't as though he hadn't been to North

Dakota before—I was surprised when he said he'd consulted for the Three Affiliated Tribes before the oil boom, when they were deep in municipal debt. He noted, as I later confirmed, that the tribal government had to borrow $30 million from the Shakopee tribe in Minnesota to stay afloat. "I said, 'Guys, just stop spending money.'"

In 2014, Noack traveled from the Bakken to Milwaukee to be deposed by the SEC in the ongoing investigation of the schools' CDO deals. He said he didn't plan to return to the financial industry and that he was a partner in a waste disposal business. The facility was near the Wild Bison, where he'd been a regular ("The food was so bad and they charged so much money," he complained to me about the truck stop). Of his business activities, Noack told the commission: "We have a solid waste reinjection site in North Dakota . . . that processes oil fuel waste and reinjects it back into the earth." Financial bubble, fracking frenzy—both involved toxic waste, riding a huge boom that would eventually collapse under its own excesses and enable catastrophic job losses, overbuilding, and overleverage.

Noack said that he had urged the districts to take their time considering the investments, and that law firms on both sides had reviewed the transactions. "I wasn't working in my basement doing something that nobody knew, okay," he told the SEC. He explained that a group of fifteen to twenty people were back in the office analyzing the program, while he spent much of his time on the road visiting clients.

Regulators found that the bank's chief executive had been directly involved in the transactions. In a 2008 talk with the FBI Noack recounted how CEO Ron Kruszewski, of St. Louis, flew in for a brief meeting with him at the Waukesha, Wisconsin, airport around the time the financial crisis exploded. Noack said the executive told him they were on the same team, despite past disputes. He said that he told Kruszewski that they had never disclosed the subprime risk (and told the FBI that Royal Bank of Canada never shared it with them), and said the CEO responded that Stifel didn't have to make the disclosure, according to a summary of the meeting. An attorney for the SEC questioned Noack on his statement later, asking whether he and the CEO had discussed how to spin the transactions. But Noack brushed off those assertions in his deposition, saying all he remembered was that the executive was in and out of the airport.

His latest deposition took place in December 2015, days after *The Big Short* began playing in movie theaters nationwide. The movie used celebrities from Brad Pitt to Margot Robbie to depict the nightmarishly complex CDOs to laypeople, but the whole drama carried the aura of the distant past—moviegoers might have been surprised to learn that the SEC was still chasing down bankers over transactions nearly a decade old. Securities regulators lobbed a long and varied line of questions at Noack that wintry morning in the Chase Tower. Was it true that he had thought Stifel's CEO was conceited and prone to lying? *No.* Had he ever asked RBC in 2006 whether the school districts' investments had exposure to subprime mortgages? *Yes.* What did the RBC official say? *She said no.* Was the program Noack's creation? *It was a group effort.* Had he wanted to cooperate with the districts? *Yes . . . they were my clients for twenty years, okay, and we were trying to solve a long-term problem with a long-term solution . . . [there were] obviously things that RBC did not disclose.*

"Happy holidays," concluded the SEC lawyer. "And we'll see you again."

Noack returned to Williston, appearing frustrated that the case had dragged on for so long. "I lost five years of my life," he told me. "I lost time with my kids." (He got divorced for the fourth time the year of the SEC suit.)

A trial was set for April 2016; that was delayed to September. Just before their day in court, Noack and Stifel reached a deal with the SEC in which they agreed to pay financial penalties and admitted that they had violated federal securities laws. A final judgment barred the defendants from making public statements that contradicted their admission of misleading the school districts. The schools were made financially whole through several court settlements. "Seriously, Maya, I'm just a nice guy," Noack said nearly a year before the judgment. "I'm just nice."

An oil tester I met during a tour of a frack came to Noack's condo with a heap of fish from North Carolina after the Christmas holidays, giving Williston's resident gastronome a new challenge. "What the fuck am I going to do with all this fish?" Noack asked. Noack laid out recipes for Super Grouper and Flavorful Flounder. As dinner party guests mingled, I began chatting with Ross Graves, who came to Williston at the behest of wealthy Turks he met in Vail. "They wanted to diversify their portfolio," he said, taking a sip of wine. "And they ended up in this godforsaken part of the country . . . Everyone was coming up, chasing a lot of deals. It was a place for deal junkies. I'm a deal junkie, and a deal junkie is someone who knows where the action is."

The Turks had Ross help them develop the upscale Brooks Hotel—and a Fuddruckers—and it was at the hotel that he started a breakfast for all the other deal junkies. "You had Manhattan, Wall Streeters . . . [Noack] and everyone would stop by and we'd talk about deals all day long. . . . If you were dressed well, people would sit down. . . . 'What are you working on, you need a warehouse, a piece of property?' And you'd say, 'I know something,' then you'd have lunch and end up at the Williston [restaurant] at night and just cut deals."

Ross was trying to start an agricultural research center. He said he was hoping that some of Noack's friends in the import-export business in the Twin Cities would finance the project. "I'm just doing a capital stack—that's how you layer financing. You raise money by mitigating risk on debt and equity, stack this stuff on insurance wraps."

"I should hook you up with my buddy out of Fargo," Noack said, having overheard us while chopping fish.

"Who's in Fargo?" Ross asked.

Noack mentioned a man in the ag tech business.

"I've never seen so much fish," said Ross as Noack put the mahi-mahi in a deep fryer to make fish tacos. "What the hell?"

A fellow from Statoil walked in the door, and Noack called out, "Hey, I hope you didn't bring fish because I have enough for an army!"

The Greek landlord arrived. She and Noack began recounting their cook-off involving the pheasant a friend had hunted. The landlord cooked green chili pheasant taquitos with avocado and cream sauce, while Noack prepared a dish with ancho mushroom sauce. But his offering had, apparently, turned out a bit dry. Ross and I continued our conversation. "It is void of culture, ostensibly," he said of Williston. "But . . . it's a really exciting place to be." For his latest deal with the ag center, "I'm going to the National Potato Show in Las Vegas on Monday."

Oh, the deals in Williston! At the time, Noack was involved in a new business to repair oil pipes with Jack Johnston, whose company had owned the Berg saltwater disposal on the Canadian border. They had met through friends. Jack, too, had been in trouble with the SEC once—back in the early nineties. The pair was doing business out of the old Pacific Steel building on West Dakota Parkway. (Jack later confirmed that they ended their business partnership the following year, but declined to say more.)

A representative from the Williston Chamber of Commerce walked into the pipe shop to drop off registration papers one afternoon, and Noack showed her around. The woman put a leaflet for an upcoming event on the table. *Take your business and career to the next level,* it said. "The other good thing is we have Eggs and Issues and we have some *pret-ty big* people coming this time." She noted that past guests had included a city councilman, along with the chairwoman of the state agency that would approve the massive Dakota Access Pipeline to Illinois. The representative told Noack about a small party at the home of Cindy Sanford, who ran the job service. That was often the first stop for people who came to Williston looking for the high-paying gigs they had seen on TV, even years after the Great Recession had supposedly ended. Cindy was quick to remind people that there were still reams of job openings in the Bakken—employees just had to have more specialized skills. The upcoming get-together was to look at jewelry and oils from Swarovski. The chamber wanted Noack to cook appetizers for the event. "You can make it simple."

"Well, people love my empanadas," he told her. "And I can do my shrimp wontons."

Going to War

Metal buildings, man camps, dust, explosions, male camaraderie, generators, cranes, military precision, dirt country roads that gave them flashbacks to hidden roadside bombs . . . a lot of oil workers looked around North Dakota and saw the Middle East again. Just another deployment. Former CIA director General David Petraeus himself said the Bakken resembled a "war zone" during one boom-time visit, years after leading the surge in Iraq.

"Iraq was where I learned to love money," a frack crew worker recalled during dinner at Doc Holliday's. He used to be a grunt for KBR, the former subsidiary of oil services giant Halliburton contracted to rebuild Iraq after the American invasion. When the troops withdrew in 2011, Halliburton announced it was hiring eleven thousand people in North America, many of them in the North Dakota oilfield. Veterans and military contractors streamed in for high-paying jobs. A marine told me that he and a lot of other vets were battling post-traumatic stress—knowing you had to get out of Iraq but wishing you could go back. The oilfield was purgatory on American soil, that halfway version of the old battlefront pulsing with loud noises and dust and patriotic mission.

So when I met an actual Iraqi out here, I was eager to hear his impressions. His name was Mohammed Neamah, though everyone called him Doc because he used to be a doctor in Iraq. "It is like Iraq, a little bit," Doc agreed. He was shocked by a shoddy encampment off Highway 85 where people were crammed into shipping containers and RVs; he couldn't believe that Americans lived that way. "There are places in Baghdad that look like that."

He grew up in Baghdad as a Shia Muslim, though now he considered himself an atheist. At the time of the American invasion in 2003, Doc lived in a mostly Sunni neighborhood. His rides on the bus to college in a Shia area became increasingly dangerous, and necessitated carrying a fake Sunni ID. One day a militiaman demanded to see his identification as gunmen waited outside the bus, and when Doc couldn't find it he was saved only because the other passengers shouted his aggressors away. Back home, his neighbor was found decapitated on the street. Doc slept with an AK-47 under his bed.

He began working as a doctor at a government hospital for $800 a month. He doubled his pay by moving to an American military base to train workers. Doc went on to manage one of the American crew camps and received a series of raises as he got into army contracting. Meanwhile, the war liberated Iraq's oilfield from government control, opening it to development by Western oil giants such as BP and ExxonMobil; companies like Halliburton found an expanded market for their oil services. Doc began working for a military contractor that did business with the oil industry in Iraq. The company branched into North Dakota and sent Doc here to help supervise electrical work for oil sites.

When Americans apologized to him for invading Iraq, Doc told them he was thankful. Dictator Saddam Hussein had executed two of his uncles. What mattered was winning freedom; how his countrymen used their independence was another matter. *Free will, free market.* Doc had seen socialism kill innovation and opportunity, and his time under an oppressive regime had convinced him that one could never rely on the government. Working on American military bases and oilfields had given him a growing appreciation of capitalist ideals.

Leaders in the North Dakota oilfield often framed the success of the Bakken as a matter of national security that would move the country away from dependence on foreign oil. America had, in recent years, become the world's top oil producer. "Here's what it comes down to," the guy from KBR told me. "It's either go to fucking war with another country and have some . . . innocent people

killed, or it's a little [fracking] pollution. You want your kids coming home in a body bag fighting for oil?"

I met Doc at a friend's party at Madison Heights, an upscale
apartment building in Watford City that had investment backing
from a fund run by Wall Street billionaire Henry Swieca. I had
been astonished at the breakneck pace of its construction the previous fall as I drove by with a trucker who was delivering dirt for
the expansion of a nearby water treatment facility. Now, as our
group played card games and enjoyed wine and cheese, it felt like
socializing in a big city again. Yet it was startling to look out into
pure dark when I stepped out onto the balcony with Doc and our
hostess. Some lights glittered from downtown to our west, but
straight ahead was nothing but fields and a few pump jacks afar.
"For me it is really the American dream," he said of being in the
Bakken.

Doc's employer helped him and his girlfriend, Sumayah, buy a
$300,000 house, and they invited me over several times. It sat in a
line of a half dozen new houses on a quiet field and was elegantly
decorated, with hardwood floors. He hadn't understood why there
were chips in the wooden door frames, and the real estate agent
had to explain that it was a rustic style. Doc hung the Declaration
of Independence on the wall and marveled at the sights of wild
horses and rainbows from his yard. He felt blessed to be here—in
Iraq, he could never have owned a house—though he didn't believe in luck, unlike Sumayah.

"You didn't get shot in Iraq," she told him during one of my
visits.

"I don't like luck."

"Well, what else do you want to call it?"

"I don't know, things just happen in the world. People get shot,
people don't get shot. If I got shot I wouldn't call it my bad luck."

There seemed nothing further away from this bucolic harbor,
where he could finally live as he wished. Once a man in line at the
post office overheard Doc speaking in Arabic and told him to speak
English, saying he had served his country. Doc calmly thanked
him for his service and said, "I served as well." Still, his time in

North Dakota had been mostly pleasant. In McKenzie County, the fastest-growing rural county in America, Doc was exactly the sort of new resident the locals wanted to attract (indeed, I found that the growing number of immigrants were the most committed newcomers to the Bakken). But his future was uncertain, because Doc's girlfriend preferred the city over rural living, and she hadn't taken to it the way he had.

He had just returned from a trip to Iraq, where his boss periodically sent him to manage projects building oilfield machinery. Of course, he noted, the increasing production in Iraq was worsening the global oil glut. Iraq was the second-largest oil producer in OPEC. "So I'm working both sides," he joked. Lately everybody was talking about the Middle East again. It was far cheaper to produce oil there, and Saudi Arabia, the leader of OPEC, wanted to put US shale producers out of business by flooding the market to depress prices. The newest geopolitical battle involved economic and technical ingenuity, not military prowess, and thousands were losing their jobs, not their lives.

The Derrick Goes Sideways

S o the rig Nevin Larsen supervised kept drilling as crude over-
flowed the markets; as oil prices kept falling; as rigs shuttered here and in Texas and Oklahoma; as night blackened from
the wane of derrick lights; as weeds grew around discarded frack
tanks and water barrels and shale shakers; as red pumper trucks no
longer needed for fracking filled the Halliburton yard a short drive
west; as a Bloomberg News headline said that the crash could be
the worst in more than forty-five years; as oil service companies
that used to gouge clients touted discounts; as bartenders who
once groused about drunken oilmen bemoaned their declining
tips; as hordes of workers broke apartment leases, abandoned man
camps and trailer parks, and hightailed it out of town in pickups
about to be repossessed.

Of course it was still the old routine. They drilled the beginning, intermediate, and lateral stages in twelve-hour shifts, in-
termittently bringing in cementing and casing crews. Rig down,
move to the next well, rig up, drill the three stages again. A pipe
in a hole doesn't know the price of oil. The change was on the
drive to the site—unsettling in its ease, on account of thousands
of semi trucks vanishing from the highways. A trucking official
came by with papers for Nevin to sign and asked if there was anything more he could do.

"Bring oil up ten bucks," cracked Nevin.

"Ten bucks? I'll work on that this afternoon after lunch."

The rig's directional drilling contractor stopped by Nevin's
trailer. He'd been a history major—this was an unexpected career

trajectory—and was back into reading again. "I got into these god-damn *Game of Thrones* books recently. There's only so much TV you can watch." But his employer, Baker Hughes, had cut his pay 20 percent. Another round of layoffs was coming. Halliburton had made a bid to acquire the firm on the cusp of the oil crash, though the deal was later killed over antitrust concerns. "It's ugly," he said. "I heard they're hiring in Saudi Arabia."

Even the rig-to-rig salespeople brought increasingly paltry offerings.

"Figured I'd just swing in and bring you some walleye," said one salesman, who had been supplying tools for the lateral. He dropped two packets of frozen fish on the ledge. "You guys working your intermediate?"

"Yeah, just waiting for the cement truck," said Nevin. After the salesman left, he eyed the fish with disapproval. "Not even fresh-caught."

And another . . .

"I heard you're out of cashews, so I thought I'd come by . . . if you ever need a hydraulic choke, I'm right here."

"He's got good cashews," Nevin said later, "but we don't get anything compared to what we used to. They'd bring ribeyes for the whole crew. Brisket, ham, turkey!"

In flush times, some salespeople even offered company men trips to Alaska and Las Vegas, along with fishing and hunting trips and golf outings. Not that Nevin would have accepted them, as he didn't want to compromise his judgment, but their disappearance was one more augury of gloom. Nevin and his counterparts considered many of the salespeople a nuisance even during boom times, and the least they could do was stop bothering everybody—

We heard a fumble at the door again.

"There's another one," Nevin said, cursing.

"Just checking up on you guys," the salesman said, launching into a futile pitch.

Workers were vowing to do their job better, faster, as if their own individual efforts could protect them from the vicissitudes of OPEC. The problem was that the rigs worked best when they had a longtime crew whose members understood the others' customs and foibles, from the floor hands to the derrick man to the driller. They would rather *know* the men they trusted with their lives. Now they were meeting and losing people all the time.

I was surprised when the workers told me that this was because drilling contractor Patterson-UTI (oil workers referred to it as simply Patterson) laid people off based on seniority. I had wrongly assumed that the industry's cutthroat nature and lack of labor unions would have arranged layoffs the other way around. But the Houston company would fire junior workers, then shuffle those with greater tenure into their places, sometimes giving people large demotions to save jobs. You knew the market had swung dramatically when you walked onto a rig and there was hardly anyone under thirty. It was that way at the bars and Walmart and everywhere else. A roughneck I had talked to on Nevin's rig during the boom was a twenty-two-year-old novice who paid for his house in Wisconsin in cash, but that was an old story nowadays.

I was sitting in the rig manager's trailer as the day shift ended and met a Texan with a funny name. He told me Patterson had just bounced him over here from what they called a warm-stacked rig—still standing on the same site but not running. This was a rare practice in the Bakken. When companies wanted to take a rig out of service, they usually had it disassembled and transported to a separate yard: a cold stack.

An official with Liberty Resources, of Denver, told me it would have to pay $20 million to buy out its contracts with the warm-stacked rig and another Patterson rig idling down the road. Liberty opted instead to pay the $12,000 a day to keep them in limbo. Patterson paid a few men to stay there for maintenance and guarding purposes. The Texan had spent a few weeks on rig watch duty and found it chilling. "It was too quiet," he said. "Eerily quiet."

So I drove out to the site that weekend. It was past an intersection with a broken pump jack, down a dirt road near an abandoned white farmhouse. Cows with yellow tags pinned to their ears lounged at the fringe of the tract. I found the lookouts resting inside a trailer. There was a man named Kenny Dirk and two other drillers who said they spent their days painting and repainting the rig. "Oh, we got Michelangelo here," Kenny said, pointing to one driller, "and Picasso"—pointing to another—"and I'll be Leonardo." They were still making a driller's salary of $120,000 but without the bonuses for safety, fast time, and other metrics that applied when the rig was operational. One of the drillers said he wanted to pull his face off—he hadn't done real work in six months. But at least Patterson was trying to keep them on the payroll. Months earlier, a war veteran had driven from Tennessee to North Dakota for his next hitch and got fired. He and a counterpart in Texas sued the company for violating the federal law requiring a sixty-day warning for mass layoffs.

Kenny's roommate back in South Dakota must have made more than $300,000 the year before as a directional driller, but one morning Kenny was awoken by the repo man coming for the roommate's pickup truck. There were a lot of people who had made money for the first time in their life and were going to lose everything because they'd spent it all. The roommate was trying to sell off his assault rifle for extra cash.

"How much?" one of the other drillers asked when Kenny mentioned it.

"It's a Mossberg AR-15," Kenny said. "Tactical hard case, two magazines, and a Burris AR-536 scope, all new. He wants $1,700."

We walked outside. I couldn't imagine it until I saw it, this tower of enterprise just an inert machine. The painters used to sit in the doghouse—the enclosed area next to the rig floor where the driller ran the operations—raising and lowering pipe down-hole, knowing the fate of the crew on the floor was on them. The clanging metal, the buzz of trucks, boots in the thick of mud, pushing pipes in violent gales and mean cold. It had been as frenzied as a Wall Street trading floor, and now . . .

The accouterments of a functioning drilling rig were still strewn around: rows of white bags sagging with fly ash, 691 joints of drill pipes laid out over the racks, casing pipes that still had plastic thread protectors on the end.

Oil was $55.88 a barrel the last time Kenny looked. He had read about the previous day's OPEC meeting and how Saudi Arabia was refusing to cut oil production. Kenny projected that prices would drop sharply as the summer of 2015 approached, and he planned to buy futures at the bottom so he could profit when the market boomed again.

Later, a pickup came to deliver water, paint, and battery chargers, and the driver was one of those wistful fellows who still remembered the eighties bust. "Now they'll purty the girl up. Rigs, they're a beautiful piece of machinery. Stop and take a look," he said, and we did. "What's the difference between this and a ship? She got her mast up in the air, catching the wind. It's an artful dance when they got a good crew."

Two months passed.

Nevin went on a Harley ride through Colorado with his wife during his usual two weeks off. Afterward, he went to the Hi Way with a salesman friend who sold mud motors and drill bits. The call—the one everyone in the drilling business that year knew was coming—came just after he ordered a Bud Light. Oil prices, on the precipice of a rebound when I met Kenny, had been tumbling all summer. "You probably figured out when I called you on your days off it's not good," said the man from corporate. He explained: Nevin's rig was not performing as well as they wanted. Whiting wanted to stack the rig. Nevin retained his usual stoicism as he recounted the call. "They don't have the room to cut anybody slack. . . . If I can't do it, I shouldn't be here."

When I'd met Nevin the year before, Whiting was preparing to buy Kodiak Oil and Gas for $3.8 billion in stock and planning an ambitious drilling program with the newly acquired oil leases. Critics questioned the timing, as oil prices plummeted in the months leading up to the finalization of the deal. Nevin was on one of the rigs charged with drilling Kodiak's acreage. But North Dakota was still an extraordinarily expensive place to produce oil compared to Texas because of the high cost of labor, harsh climate, and remote terrain lacking enough pipelines to transport crude to refineries in the Gulf and on the East Coast. The number of rigs skidded: 200 . . . 180 . . . 150 . . . 130 . . . 100 . . . By the time Nevin got the call, it was in the seventies.

People in the oilfield watched the "rig count," as it was called, like stock traders watching the Dow. The *Williston Herald* printed the figure on the front page every day. But the falling rig count couldn't entirely be taken on its face. The industry used to need a lot more rigs because companies would drill one well to hold an oil lease before it expired in a couple of years, then race to the next, in helter-skelter fashion. Crews were far less experienced and efficient. Now workers were generally drilling multiple wells next to each other, using the walking rigs to save an extra four or five days of moving time. Oil production was holding steady at around one million barrels a day.

So that's what had eluded a lot of the quixotic types who'd rushed up here imagining a lifelong boom. There were so many jobs because the place had been disastrously inefficient. In the long run, the jobs would be less in drilling and fracking new wells than in maintaining existing ones. While each new rig supported 120 jobs, wells that were already producing oil required only a few workers to check on the crude and saltwater tanks and keep the pump jacks running.

Nevin joked he might just find himself looking for a job at the Walmart liquor store. With all the rigs shutting down, there were too many out-of-work company men and often no choice but to accept enormous demotions. Some took jobs manning the guard shacks at the entrance to rig sites, which was a bit like budget cuts forcing the school principal to become the janitor. But there was little time for recriminations. The rig had two last wells to drill.

There were all the usual hassles. As the crew drilled through the Dakota formation a mile underground, saltwater from a nearby disposal accidentally spilled into the well. The wastewater was diluting the muddy liquid they needed to ply the earth, and Nevin directed the men to increase the weight of the drilling mud to counter it. "We've got to play a game to see what Mother Nature will let us do," Nevin said. "We're pissing her off right now."

A salesman for a rig-moving firm stepped in. "How you doing?"

"I'm all right. We're going in the weeds." That was a common reference; they put idle rigs in a field where the weeds would grow around the equipment like cobwebs.

"Are you? No kiddin' . . . Well, come on, Nevin, this is a chance to use us. At least we can put you in the weeds." He paused. "I know you're going to another rig, though."

"I don't think so," Nevin said. "No . . . I believe I'm done."

Nevin answered the phone and the salesman began chattering to me about how he used to serve in Afghanistan. "I think I must smell bad or something, because he never goes with us." When Nevin hung up, the salesman said, "All right, Nevin, when can I give you a bid for this?"

Nevin was blasé.

"I'll be back, Nevin. Last chance, man, remember! We gotta do something. I gave you Christmas *dinner* last year!"

"Did you?"

"Remember? I brought you ham and all that shit!"

"I'm sorry, I don't remember."

After the door closed, Nevin lamented that he had given the man a shot on another job, and the man came in $100,000 higher than the competition. "He must not have wanted the work."

The weather turned cold and blustery enough to blow off hard hats. It was especially unforgiving as they cased a well. The older motor man helped out on the rig floor, hunched in a yellow jacket, and the driller and the others called him Big Bird as he straggled into the doghouse wet. "That old man's a tough sucker," the driller said. I struggled to steer my car to the rig through the currents and drizzle—a passing semi splashed mud all over the driver's-side window, making brown splatters over the white-gray rivulets. I disliked driving down the dirt rig road in the rain because everything turned to mud; it felt as though I was driving on a flat. A mechanic told me that was the mud clogging around the tires.

It seemed as though nothing could go right as the crew approached the end of the two-mile lateral. The crew accidentally drilled into the upper layer of shale rock and had to "trip out" a few stands of pipe before they resumed drilling along the correct trajectory. They only had four hundred more feet to finish the well when the electromechanical device on the bottom of the drilling apparatus failed.

Failures of the MWD (measurement-while-drilling) tool, as it was called, were routine on drilling rigs. But to have one come so close to the end was an enormous and costly hassle—it was almost as if the oil equipment was rebelling against the coming shutdown. They would have to trip out nearly four miles of pipe, replace the malfunctioning device, and trip the pipe all the way back in. Drilling the last well should have taken twelve and a half days, but with all the missteps and delays it would be nearly fifteen.

Directional drilling contractors sat in a separate trailer watching as sensors transmitted the steering of the drill pipe onto their screens. They appeared like a heartbeat monitor. When the tool failed, the image on the screen spluttered, prompting a torrent of profanity and phone calls. It was a chilly, drizzly day when they replaced the tool and began putting the drill pipe back into the ground. I walked into the directional drillers' trailer, where the malfunctioning probes were scattered on the floor. The workers inside were just as upset as the ones tripping out and flipping out on the rig floor.

"Not a good way to finish for us—or them," said Benji Rogers, who came to the oilfield from the air force.

I asked how much they made. Such an inquiry would be rude anywhere else; here, it was a get-to-know-you question.

Benji laughed. "That's a really sore subject right now. We're taking a pay cut tomorrow. I'm going from $24 to $17 an hour."

"That's what they make at the Williston Walmart," I said.

"Thank you," said Benji, "a very sore subject. And I'm one of the higher-paid men. I'm telling you, we've got guys all the way down to $14 an hour."

He believed it was only worth it because they could clock up to sixty hours of overtime a week. As an MWD hand, Benji stayed in the trailer for weeks at a time to see the drilling through. In just a year he had saved up to buy a house back in Montana. He thought of himself as a mountain man: on his days off he escaped to the woods to fish, trap, and hunt. But Benji questioned how loyal he could stay to his company. They had sixteen thousand feet of pipe to trip back in, so he went off to rest before drilling resumed. The crew finished their last well as the sun came up.

I met Nevin and the rig manager as they went out for beers and wings that evening in Williston. It was the only time Nevin invited me to join them in town, but a rig stack has a way of loosening formalities. The two swapped tales about the other company men working on North Dakota rigs—the one who got the job at the outrageous age of twenty-three, the other who was always with another woman.

"Most company men are on their fourth or fifth wife," the rig manager told me. "Now *that* would be a book I'd read!" He turned back to Nevin. "Steve was on five."

"Jesus Christ," said Nevin.

I asked how one could afford so many divorces.

"If I made your wage, I could pay off two wives and live pretty damn comfortably," the rig manager told Nevin.

The waitress brought out twenty wings for the rig manager alone and kept coming by to see if he was really going to finish it.

"Want me to put it in a box?" the waitress asked.

"No, I'll finish." He and Nevin high-fived.

"We close at midnight," she cracked.

"Only six left," the rig manager said. "When you eat once a day, you eat a lot."

Talk turned to the grim preparations for tomorrow. Nevin explained that they had to do it right, in the interest of attracting future customers. When I said something about a rig graveyard, a common phrase around here, Nevin corrected me. "Call it a stack yard," he said. The rig wasn't being hauled off to die, after all. It was merely going on hiatus.

The following morning, Nevin held a meeting to discuss the rig stacking while the crew laid down the drill pipe. The men moved the pipe from the rig floor to a hydraulic catwalk that lowered to the ground and rolled the pipe onto a rack. A forklift moved the pipe to a bigger rack on the periphery. We heard the clanging metal inside Nevin's trailer, where the supervisors of the rig moving and washing companies pulled up chairs.

Nevin wondered where they would set up the rig washers, the site being as crowded as it was. They would have to spread a liner over the ground to prevent environmental contamination.

"We're going to run out of room," said Nevin. "We do know that, right?"

"We'll get a crane out here to start," the rig mover said. "You going to lay over tomorrow?"

"That's the goal," the rig manager said.

"Don't bring the cavalry tomorrow," Nevin told the rig-washing supervisor, explaining that the busy time for cleaning the rig parts would come the day after.

A few phones started going off.

"The phones are ringing!" said the rig mover. "The price of oil is back up to $90! Boom's back on!"

It was Nevin's last day. He wouldn't be there to see the rig pulled apart—his two-week shift was ending, and another company man who worked the alternating two-week period was due at the rig. That supervisor preferred to school me on Led Zeppelin instead of the oil business. Nevin called around for somebody to take away the tank of invert—a fluid of diesel oil and mud—and monitored a contractor cleaning the mud pits.

"You ready for some four-inch? . . . How are we coming on the five-inch? . . . Okay, okay, do it, do it. There's going to be pipe and heavyweight headed your way tomorrow. . . ."

This could go away at any time.

I could hardly fathom that Nevin had recited those words to me fifteen months ago.

Nevin would have to miss the Old Settlers Day celebration in Alexander because of his work on the rig. He thought I should go, but I felt just as chained to the rig as he was, even if I wasn't on the payroll. It was going to be a momentous day in his hometown. The Alexander School, once in danger of closing, had so many children from around the country come for the oil rush that they could finally revive the Comets football team after twenty-seven years. They played six-man football, and nobody expected the ragtag team to win—some members barely knew how to play— but the community rallied around them like they were stars. The kids from Arkansas and California and Florida lived with their parents in trailer parks and they told me they loved it here, that the close-knit town got them away from trouble at their old schools.

I began stopping by the football practices later in the season. Coach Kevin Clausen rounded the players up on the field the day before their game against Savage, Montana, one of the best teams in the region. They were going to lose, of course, but on this cool fall afternoon the coach turned away from athletic advice and began berating the students for not turning in their homework. Didn't they know how important school was?

"Let me tell you guys something. I taught school for a *long* time. And I got out of it . . . because I *had* to. I couldn't afford to do it anymore. . . . So I got in the oilfield. Now, I got in the oil-field three years ago, but it was a different *time*. Basically anybody that had a *pulse* could get a job out there. It's not the same thing anymore, guys, and it's not going to be that way ever again. So if you've got these dreams, all of a sudden you're going to just get a job right after you graduate and make all this money, it's not going to happen unless you get extremely lucky." He told them he used to work on a rig sixteen hours a day, covered in crude oil, meeting guys who hadn't seen their families in years. "I wouldn't wish that on anybody."

"Dang," a boy said.

"The point I'm trying to make . . . you can change your *whole life* just by putting forth some effort right now." I was startled by the severity of his address, but came to understand that there were people working in the oilfield who had advanced and enjoyed the business—people like Nevin—and those who never really took to it but had been forced there because of financial considerations. And even some of the best couldn't ride out this slump.

I ran into Nevin at the Hi Way after the Comets lost their game and the parents and other locals had gathered for Friday night drinks, and he appeared to be in good spirits. Nevin had started up with Halcon Resources, doing the night shift supervising a rig on the Indian reservation. But the Texas operator was overleveraged and filed for Chapter 11 bankruptcy the following year. Nevin eventually lost that job, too. He didn't seem to have any regrets.

⋅⁘⋅   ⋅⁘⋅   ⋅⁘⋅

Have you ever seen a rig stack? The way the horizon goes blank? I was driving down the stretch of road where the rig always soared into view from the northwest when I saw that the derrick appeared to be gone. Another mile. I stopped. There it was: the long white derrick lying horizontally on a set of stands about twenty feet off the ground. A crane loomed overhead, its chain swinging like a threat. A worker was ensconced in the beams of the derrick while another maneuvered a hose from a man-lift—the medical team preparing for the patient's multiple amputations. *Diagnosis: drilled himself out of existence.*

I met lots of people who lost their job and their dreams, but the state of things never seemed as real as when a rig lay crippled, silhouetted against the sky. It must seem strange that a broken machine would be more moving than a person defeated, but weren't rigs supposed to be omnipotent? They lit up the fields like deities, drilling through dark skies and mad winds and blinding flurries, churning riches from the most inhospitable rock, always so noble in their endurance.

I parked on location and stepped into one of the last summer suns. A crane pulled one of the four sets of blue stairs from the base of the rig, letting it dangle a few feet off the ground: a dozen steps starting nowhere, leading to nothing. I watched as one man threw hoses onto a forklift loaded with a rig mat, nearly pitching forward from the weight before steadying himself.

A drilling superintendent for Patterson walked up. "This'll be the sixth one I stacked this last year," he told me, ticking off the other companies, "and now they want me to oversee this. . . . I've seen several ups and downs in this industry, but this one just don't look good. I don't see no end to this one."

The supervisor for the rig-moving contractor showed up and we watched the operations from his pickup. The cranes prepared to take down the doghouse. Workers carried away the stompers, the boxy feet that walked the rig to the next well. The supervisor, Troy Bakken, made a call to ask when the third crane would arrive.

A crane began rolling back toward the derrick. Much of the equipment sat on skids so it could be easily moved with trucks. A separate truck would load the parts up and take them away. The bigger loads would be the mud tanks, mud pumps, and generators. But the derrick was the giant. The crew unpinned the legs that stuck out at forty-five-degree angles near the base of the derrick and shuffled the cables around. The cranes maneuvered into position; the machinery groaned. The men tied the chains to the derrick. Slowly, slowly, the cranes lowered it to the dirt as though they were laying down the coffin of an esteemed statesman.

The following day, the rig-washers attacked the rig's entrails with a fury. Blasts and blasts of water—you could hear them from what seemed like a few hundred feet away, sitting in the car with the windows rolled up. The men came in neon-yellow Tychem suits over white uniforms, hoods tied around their necks. They set up six trailers, each equipped with two power-washing wands that shot out five gallons a minute. Supervisors reminded the crew of nearly a dozen not to hit another man or himself, as the high-pressure water stream would cut like a scythe. They were to start from the top of the equipment, allowing the dirty liquid to sop all the way down. When the muck stuck too hard to the metal, the crew applied a degreaser called Purple Power from a five-gallon bucket.

While the drilling crew was mostly white and had a lot of oil-field experience, the majority of the rig washers were black men who were newer to the business. Some were paid as little as $14 an hour. One was a skinny kid from Detroit who sometimes washed cars but hadn't worked a stable job in years. Detroit, as everybody called him, loved the long hours of the oilfield. Another rig washer was a teenager from Florida. Tired of struggling, he flew to North Dakota and pitched a tent in the woods. He found work three days later. "A big old blessing," he called the oilfield.

"I've never seen someone so dirty in my life," I joked. Dirt spattered his face like freckles, and soiled water ran down his uniform. But he took pride in being dirty; it meant he was earning his pay. He abandoned our conversation to power-wash a block of metal, leaning in close to scour off the grunge.

A rig washer from Los Angeles appeared to be wearing a black hard hat with white streaks, but upon closer inspection, it was a white hard hat coated in filth. He found the hardest part was removing the lingering oil from the equipment. He had to put degreaser on it and scrub, and it took a long time. One of the most diligent workers was a Liberian immigrant from Atlanta; I recognized him from the waiting room of the day labor office in Williston.

Power washing was more strenuous than it looked, as the wands were heavy and had to be wielded for long periods. When the men pushed the trigger and released the pressure, the wand kicked back with the recoil of a high-caliber gun. Water tinged with invert, or diesel-based mud, made their skin tingle and splashed in their mouths. They had to keep spitting it back out.

The movers traveled a wide berth as cranes dropped parts to the ground and a winch truck carried them to the washers. The winch truck was operated by a father-son team from New Mexico, Raymie and Raymie junior. The elder man drove it and the younger man acted as a swamper, walking along the back of the truck and making hand signals and communicating by radio to let his father know the path was clear. Raymie junior would climb all over the back of the truck, hooking equipment up and inspecting it. That day alone they moved the subs, mud pits, shaker skids, gas buster, choke house, and draw-works. The father told me he liked moving it all, the bigger the better. I was watching a few washers spray a mud tank when there was a clash of metal from the other side, and everyone came running. A tank tilted at a forty-five-degree angle off the end of the winch truck—the movers thought they'd secured the ropes on the side. I was rattled, having seen workers in the same spot only a minute before.

"That's what we call a near-miss," said the rig-washing boss, J.C. Christoph, shaking his head. He stooped down and wiped his hands on some dusty pickup tires—it was the only way to take the slime off after he grabbed a power washer from a man who wasn't supposed to have one, and forgot his gloves. J.C. was enthusiastic about their work, though the effect was hard to assess because of all the nicks of rust and paint chips on the metal. "I know it doesn't look like perfection, but . . . I'm sure you saw how dirty it was," he said. "It's shining!" And the top drive was all clean, he noted, resting on the pipe racks. Perhaps it all looked better now, gleaming in the sun, but I would much prefer an invert-crusted rig running hard. Cleanliness was a terrible sign in the oilfield.

So the rig washers finished the derrick by early afternoon. Men crawled around the crown of the derrick, sorting through all the cables so they could break the thing apart. Everything was so crowded, they were running into rig movers and Patterson workers. The crew used so much water they had to order more.

The Patterson superintendent approached J.C.

"This is going a lot quicker than I thought," J.C. told him.

"It don't look that way to me," the superintendent said. "It looks slow. That shaker skid, they said they'd move that around twelve o'clock yesterday. They set that shaker *tank* in there yesterday evening. They're both still there!"

Strange how the location felt even more alive than when the rig was running. Everybody rushed around like there was a dramatic deadline, even if the only thing at the end was the end.

The sun was setting. One side of the sky was streaks of purple, pink, and blue, and the other was yellow and white. A truck prepared to leave with a section of the derrick. I went back to the company man's trailer, where the man from Nova Scotia was lolling around; he usually worked the night shift, but they didn't need anybody to work nights when the rig was closing down. Through the

window, I watched as a truck came to collect the three rig generators nearby, each some of the heaviest loads at about seventy thousand pounds apiece. The company man checked the news on his
phone and halfheartedly remarked that some drilling company just
laid off half its workforce. I glanced up at Fox News to see the latest:
*Thirty percent of millennials would sell an organ to get rid of student loan
debt.* Soon the rig washers returned to their trailers in Williston,
where they stripped off their torn, soaked uniforms. Florida told
me that exhausted as he was, the motions he made with the power
washer carried into his sleep. Even in his dreams, he was blasting
invert off steel and forcing his arms to keep moving because if he
slowed he would stop and then he could not start again.

The last full day of rig wash and disassembly: the oil tract
seemed too big, as more and more parts departed up the highway.
The washers swilled energy drinks. Florida's usual energy was
flagging; he didn't even know what he was washing anymore. Detroit poured bottled water over his face, pausing to watch a truck
pick up the drillers' doghouse. Then he turned his attention to the
stompers. Dirty water had accumulated in the bottoms, and Detroit had to lean all the way in and twist his body to get the filth
off. The dirty water blew back into his mouth.

I followed J.C. off the location at eight in the evening, up Highway 1804 through the sunset. We turned right at Scenic Sports,
past the community college, Bubba Bubble's car wash, the lum-
ber store, MainStay Suites, Applebee's, down to the roundabout
by Racers gas station, and into a cul-de-sac of trailers. A former
member of the Vice Lord gang from Chicago had prepared the
last supper of chili with cheese and sour cream, cornbread, lettuce
with shredded carrots and cabbage, soup and oyster crackers. The
bosses kept wages a little lower in exchange for providing workers
two free meals a day. The workers trickled over to the table and
tore into the food, mostly wordless, as the football game blared
from the living room.

The chili was especially savory, and I asked how he made it.

"That's my recipe—c'mon, girl." The man surveyed the platters of food. "Nobody wants no salad?"

With his penchant for cooking, cleaning, and discipline, the former Vice Lord was the de facto den father. When the younger men in the trailer played their music too loud or ran their muddy boots too far past the door, he planted his imposing frame in front of them and hollered. He didn't let them forget that he was an ex-con. But he had gotten tired of shooting and getting shot at, figured he'd be back in prison if he hadn't left the drug trade in Chicago. The former Vice Lord went from over-the-road trucking to building oil tank batteries, and took up work as a rig washer when that dried up. He wasn't worried about the oil slump, a re-action he attributed to being black. "We've been in a recession all our lives," he said of African American workers. "It don't affect me. It affects white people."

He was distrustful of President Obama for being anti-oil and anti-guns. How else could they provide for their families, protect them from violence? "I just don't like Obama. . . . Yeah, my skin might be dark but I ain't with that. I'm a Republican—I believe in working, getting out there and getting it." The ex–Vice Lord was astonished that I'd come to the rig day after day with a notebook and pen. "You must be a gang member, too," he said suddenly. "What makes you so hard-core? What makes you say, 'I'ma do this'?" I laughed and reminded him that the mass of rigs shutting down across American oilfields was the biggest economic story of the year.

The bosses started talking among themselves. They only needed four workers for the next day—might call it by straws. By noon the following day, the scene was mostly scattered parts, rumpled liner, bored supervisors sitting in the trailer. Most of the rig parts were on the road to Wyoming. The rig count was around sixty-nine at the time; a year later it would be thirty-five. All the fallen rigs meant there were thousands fewer workers to eat at the restaurants, to support the apartments and man camps, to buy truck stop fuel, to go to Walmart. But Marcus Jundt, the top restaurateur in Williston, had a plan.

$100 Oil to $1 Beer

Many miners in America's nineteenth-century gold booms subsisted on beans, bacon, and sourdough bread, but more varied cuisine gradually spread. Chinese miners during the California Gold Rush established restaurants serving the food of their homeland, importing ingredients from Hong Kong. Patrons savored French cuisine at Le Poulet d'Or. A treat on the town was a jumble of oysters, bacon, and eggs called the Hangtown Fry. Though hordes of miners faced starvation during the Klondike Gold Rush, the well-off went to eateries for oyster cocktails, caviar sandwiches, fricandeau of veal, salade homard with artichoke hearts and capers, consommé imperial, and steak tartar. At the Arcade restaurant in Dawson, Alaska, patrons dined on canned oyster stew for an astonishing $12 a bowl.

Our modern victuals were largely meals from man camps, truck stops, and the microwave, but the North Dakota oilfield gradually blossomed with new restaurants after years of culinary deprivation. I'd arrange to meet with somebody for lunch and they'd suggest Basil Sushi Bar & Asian Fusion, a popular spot operated by a family from Wyoming. Or it was "Let's go to Sakura Japanese Steakhouse," where a statue of Buddha greeted diners at the door and New York–trained staff served sushi and offerings from hibachi grills. A new place called the Grand Buffet boasted "Italian, American, Japanese, Mexican, Seafood and King Crab, alongside traditional Asian fare," with a dozen buffet tables rotating more than two hundred items. "Prepare to dine like a king or queen," one ad said. The Hula Grill boasted that the aloha spirit was alive in North Dakota, though city hall briefly shut down the joint after complaints of the barbecue stench.

Yet business was slower than expected, as competition grew and thousands of workers left the region in 2015. The residents who remained were less inclined to dine like royalty than eat drive-through cheeseburgers as their fortunes became increasingly volatile. Marcus Jundt found the crowds fading from the Williston Brewing Company and his other establishments, as longtime patrons told him they were heading back to Idaho or California. He convened a staff meeting where he suggested giving away beer. "The place would be packed!"

Marcus knew he had to revive the atmosphere. Who wanted to come to an empty restaurant? A colleague questioned whether giving away beer was legal, so Marcus suggested they sell it for a dollar. There was no need for a Procter & Gamble–style analysis of the price elasticity of booze. The Bakken was such an inscrutable place that the most absurd ideas could succeed, and the wisest schemes could fail.

Even so, this one struck me as particularly preposterous—when a house-cleaning acquaintance invited me to Williston Brewing Company for a dollar beer one evening, I figured there was some catch. The place was rather upscale by Bakken standards, and I hadn't been back since around the time of Marcus's mayoral race more than a year earlier because it was too expensive, with beers there often running six or seven dollars. One imagined that even Budweisers in plastic cups at a rat-riddled dive bar off the freeway cost more than a dollar. But the bartender assured us that it was a dollar for any beer, anytime, any day.

Marcus came by. I told him I had stopped visiting the brewing company because it was overpriced—a piece of carrot cake cost $11, after all—but that the discounts had brought me back. He seemed annoyed, saying that more than enough people had been willing to eat here during the boom.

"How long will you keep beers a dollar?" I asked.

"Until oil prices go back up!" he said.

Back to what? A hundred a barrel? Marcus didn't say.

Dollar beers at Williston Brewing Company. Dollar beers at
Doc Holliday's. Dollar beers at J Dub's. All of Marcus's restaurants
were swarming again, and it was sometimes as hard to find a seat
these days as it had been when oil was at its peak. I liked to order a
pale ale called the Badlands, though I'm not sure how many people
in the oil business would have appreciated it, as they didn't seem
to like hops. The experiment had entirely transformed the town's
social life, even as Marcus was taking an enormous hit. This, from
the receipt a bartender gave an acquaintance and me for our two
beers:

```
1 l*m badlands . . . . . . . . . 1.00
1 l*m coors lt . . . . . . . . . . 1.00
beer total . . . . . . . . . . . . 14.25
discounts . . . . . . . . . . . . 12.25–
tax total . . . . . . . . . . . . . 0.22
total due . . . . . . . . . . . . . 2.22
```

The conversations over dollar beers were reflections on the
town's future. A young couple bound for Alaska: "To raise a family here is damn near impossible." They could overlook North Dakota's flaws only when the money was abundant.

A man gossiping about local pols: "There were these French
businessmen with $5,000 or $6,000 suits. The guy who paid for
those suits versus the mayor and company—come on." He believed that, if not Marcus, another outsider should take over. "We
need a political upheaval. . . . This is colonization. You can't leave
the aboriginals in charge!"

A real estate broker from Colorado: "These first ten years
could be boom, crash, mini boom, mini crash, littler boom, littler
crash, until it all stabilizes out."

One day I saw a familiar figure walking up to the bar. I was
struck to see him in real life: Pastor Jay Reinke, the protagonist
of the hit documentary film *The Overnighters*, which followed his
controversial efforts to open his Lutheran church to the desperate job-seekers who flooded Williston when there was hardly

anywhere to live. The media attention toward the Bakken had grown so over-the-top in recent years that it was becoming increasingly common to recognize a person one had never met. Another time, I had spotted a woman sitting at the bar who had starred in a TV show about the Bakken called *Boomtowners*, on the Smithsonian Channel.

Jay told me he missed the old El Rancho—the banquet rooms, the dining hall, the Friday night specials—and I got the sense it was odd for him, by comparison, to be drinking dollar beers at a brewing company that didn't brew its own beer. He thought Marcus had a vision but disliked his campaign, the way he plastered signs everywhere. "You have to appeal to the stable and voting populace," he said. The area was governed by a cultural modesty that favored the familiar. One didn't just put himself out there—which was, in a way, Jay's own downfall. The documentary showed how city hall had forced him to close his program for homeless migrants—some who were sex offenders or had other problems in their past—and the church ultimately ousted him in disgrace. A truck driver from California whom he allowed to stay with his family was later arrested for sex trafficking.

Jay lamented that the area had not approached its housing shortage more creatively. He was as conservative as they came, and still believed that Williston should have done more for the have-nots. Jay had great sympathy for the ones who had found themselves vulnerable and alone up here. "If I was by myself, I'd be doing this all the time." He held up his dollar beer. "I'd drink myself to sleep, and I'm not a beer drinker."

Three months into the experiment, Marcus and a few cohorts met me for lunch at the brewing company. I ordered a citrus salad, and Marcus took a double serving of gyro meat, nothing else—he wasn't the first person I knew around here who was on the Atkins diet. A photographer with him said she was dying to stand at the end of the bar and take a picture, because it was all men today. We still saw that periodically, even though the lopsided gender ratio had greatly improved. "All guys drinking a beer, see that?" Marcus said excitedly. He was willing to bet that they wouldn't be here without his special deal, and they were ordering food, too. "It's worked!"

He found himself annoyed by a column in the local newspaper that derided the experiment at "Jundt's joints" and likened it to the Saudis flooding the market with cheap oil. Bargain-basement beer, cut-rate crude. Marcus told me everybody seemed to be happy. "We don't put a gun to customers' heads and say, 'You have to come in and you have to drink beer.' It's freedom of choice. It's America. It's *capitalism!*"

It was almost a replication of his ideas from the mayoral campaign: give the town a real atmosphere, try something new. I asked Marcus if he felt relieved to have lost. The election happened at the pinnacle of the boom, and we had fallen well into the nadir. But he discouraged this suggestion. Marcus still believed he could have done something; he felt that city hall had not made Williston a real hometown. There were no assurances that if somebody bought a home, a warehouse wouldn't be permitted next door. As he saw it, the region had blown a gift bestowed upon few communities in the world, making it a case study in municipal dysfunction. Marcus began going back and forth with his business partner about John Maynard Keynes, the famed British economist. Something about how Marcus had a few aging investors, and, as the economist put it, in the long run we're all dead.

"I think he's a *brilliant* man!" Marcus insisted.

But it was Keynes's philosophy that the "animal spirits" drive our economy that I found most apt—the theory that much investment relies on spontaneous urges rather than cold calculation. Would the brewing company have been built—would the Bakken itself have ascended—were it not for the exuberant passions of so many? Marcus himself had used the word *fever*, and people often talked about an emotional pull that the oilfield held over them. A mathematical rationale underlay the great feats of oil development, but logic was hardly enough to build a society like this. Then again, perhaps we could have used a good deal more of it.

Marcus had dozens of restaurant competitors in the oilfield now—too many, in his opinion—and I saw that at least one of them, Sakura Japanese Steakhouse, started offering dollar beers, too. He began spending much of his time in the Houston area on his dozens of Überrito restaurants, which were Mexican-themed competitors of Chipotle that his Williston Holding Company had acquired in a deal worth about $20 million. I am usually loath to cede much to our southern rival, but Texas simply had a more attractive climate for many investors in the long run.

After four months of dollar beers, a bartender handed me a glass of Badlands and a tab for three dollars one evening. It was over. Oil prices hadn't risen (in fact, they were about to go off a cliff), and Marcus could only give away so much booze.

"How's the three-dollar beer going versus the one-dollar?" Marcus asked the bartender.

"I like it," she said. "A lot of people said it changed."

"It's a good deal. I mean, a dollar was free."

I took a sip. "I'm starting to forget what's normal and what's not," I said suddenly, reflecting upon how strange this town was.

"Then you're a real Willistonian!" Marcus said with glee. He and a colleague began chattering about playing poker back at the house, where Marcus lived with a pile of his employees, and they invited me. "Just bring $200 to $300."

"And a lighter to set it on fire," added his associate.

On the way out, I noticed that a revolver-shaped door handle was missing and asked if somebody had stolen it again. But Marcus said that this time the gun had simply broken off. I approached the passenger's side of his F350 Platinum pickup truck, which had a six-inch lift kit. He got it just for the oilfield. It wasn't the first time in the Bakken that a pickup was so high off the ground I almost tipped backward trying to climb inside. The difference was that none of the other pickup owners had an MBA from Northwestern University. I asked him if this was really necessary.

"Ego, testosterone, for the hell of it," he said. "This can go anywhere—it is the beast." Marcus turned right on Route 2 and we began our way to the outskirts of town. The walls of his sprawling house were adorned with posters from *Goodfellas*, *Pulp Fiction*, *Casablanca*, and *Saving Private Ryan*; a *Scarface* poster above the fireplace said, "This is paradise, I'm tellin' ya," over an image of Al Pacino in a white suit and sunglasses. An enormous globe sat nearby. The garage had two Harleys; Marcus had been to the seventy-fifth anniversary of the Sturgis motorcycle rally that year. The basement had a sign that said MAN CAVE, along with a foosball table, a bar, an enormous TV, and a poker table. He'd posted a picture of the floor plan of "Condo 16 at the Four Seasons," the project whose failure had pushed him to North Dakota.

"Are you going to file for bankruptcy again?" I joked.

"I've heard that comment before."

There were also photos of Marcus with George W. Bush—the president had attended a fundraiser in 2006 at his parents' legendary mansion on Lake Minnetonka, Minnesota, a house that would later go on the market for more than $50 million. I asked about the ferocious sentiment against Obama in the oilfield. "He's hated here. . . . He has this naive idea that he can eliminate these greenhouse gases by killing a pipeline," Marcus said. "We are very capitalistic and patriotic people."

He poured a can of Fresca soda into a glass of Tito's Handmade Vodka. Four of his employees gathered around the poker table. While they doled out the cards, I told him I'd stop coming to the Williston Brewing Company if the price increased again. "How am I going to pay for these guys' gambling habits if you don't come to the restaurant?" he asked.

Marcus bought in for $200. He won an early round. "Thank you for the pile, gentlemen," he said. "I was bluffing the whole time; I had two eights." He asked somebody to turn on *Scarface*, but nobody obliged. Marcus agreed to let me take some turns on his dime. I got a ten, a jack, and a king, a favorable hand given that the cards on the table were a six, a ten, and a king. The next few cards were a nine and a four. I upped my bet ten bucks and won. "You got me," one of the employees said.

Marcus began inquiring about his workers' relationships. "You don't have a woman here?" he asked one employee.

"I don't want one," the man said quietly.

"Too many problems," somebody piped up.

Marcus's early luck fell off. He got a four and a six and immediately folded, a pattern that began to repeat itself.

"You get a lot of lousy hands," I told him after he'd folded a few more times.

"Have you *seen* the hands I've been getting?" he said, taking a sip of vodka.

He announced this would be his last round. He got a nine and a queen and said he was done, ending the game having won back only $129. "I'm a net loser," he joked. On the drive back, one of his colleagues asked the other how much the population of Williston had fallen. Marcus's restaurants were so embedded in oilfield life that the associate guessed it was whatever percentage they were down in sales.

So there was the caveat to what the engineer had told me as we sat near the Abe Lincoln head the year before. The suppliers would surely profit more than the workers if they sold out at the peak, like the owners of the Wild Bison. But those who planned a long future faced a greater risk, despite their admirable motives. Marcus quietly put his properties up for sale, the engineer's truck stop never came to pass, and I noticed that Abe mysteriously vanished during the summer of 2015, when the dollar beer experiment began.

Nat Geo's in Town

*H*istorically, word of the next boom traveled by newspaper. In 1897, an extra edition of the *Seattle Post-Intelligencer* hyped the arrival of a steamer from Alaska loaded with more than a ton of solid gold:

GOLD! GOLD! GOLD! GOLD!
Sixty-Eight Rich Men on the Steamer Portland.
STACKS OF YELLOW METAL!

The article celebrated the steamer's cargo, worth $700,000. Thousands rushed to see the boat dock. Soon Seattle was mad with Klondike fever—fortune-seekers quit their jobs and began the journey north. Newspapers around the country printed stories, spurring a stampede to Alaska by way of Seattle. Print continued its influence during the Alaskan pipeline rush in the 1970s. A New York *Daily News* article about the boom resulted in 6,576 letters and 1,370 phone calls to the pipeline company in one month.

But starting in 2011, it was the screen that propelled people all over America to the North Dakota oilfield. One viewer in Olympia, Washington, saw a news feature on the oil boom during a blur of *Jersey Shore* episodes. He was struggling to find work after being laid off as a graphic artist at a sign shop, and had been melting for weeks into a tattered couch in front of the TV, spending his unemployment checks on booze, pizza, and ice cream. The marijuana was running out; he scraped the resin out of his pipe in desperation. Gregg Thompson taped the episode and watched it several more times, feeling his excitement build.

He packed his belongings and rode the Amtrak eleven hundred miles east. When the train finally stopped in Williston, he stepped eagerly into the dark of winter and walked north down Main Street, past the day labor office, the strip clubs, the biker bar across from a wall with the Ten Commandments, the Chamber of Commerce, and JCPenney, and into the lights of the main thoroughfare, 2nd Avenue West. Gregg called hotel after hotel to book a room, but they were all full. Weary of the foreboding night ahead, Gregg went to the lounge of the Vegas Motel and ordered a Jack and coke. He played pool and met a man who gave him a lead for a job doing wireline, which involved handling explosives on frack jobs. It must have been midnight when he rolled his suitcase down the road again. Gregg spotted a mattress store and walked around the back.

Gregg climbed into a Dumpster filled with discarded mattresses and built himself a fort that would guard against the icy winds. He created a bed out of an old recliner and burrowed himself in bubble wrap. Gregg smoked a bowl and began filming himself: blue eyes peering from a pale face shining from the darkness, tilted as though he were being filmed at gunpoint in a hostage video. "Color me crazy . . . I did what I had to do. . . . Got a $19-an-hour job offer, pending my clearances because we work with *explosives*."

His rest was fitful, perhaps from the thrill of it all. Early in the morning, the shriek of a garbage truck awoke him. Gregg panicked, scrambling over the mattresses and hurling himself onto the asphalt. He was determined to find a room for the following night as soon as he could, so he walked to a hotel and made a reservation. Gregg followed up on the lead about the wireline job, using the barfly as a reference on his application. Then he applied to work at Walmart, the hotels, a tire shop, even Applebee's. He sent the video of the dumpster fortress to his brother, who loved it and told him he should post it on YouTube. Thus were the beginnings of a small-time Internet star: 6,466 hits.

·:· ·:· ·:·

Gregg knew he couldn't count on finding an apartment in Williston. So he took out the bench seats of an Aerostar van, put in a mattress, and stacked totes to the ceiling filled with utensils, food, clothes, towels, and documents. Gregg stashed the van in the parking lot of a hotel by Walmart. His third day in the van, the story went, Walmart called him for an interview and he landed a job managing the housewares section for $17 an hour. A coworker sold him an RV that he parked in somebody's yard for $800 a month.

Gregg had always considered himself an artist and often went by a stage name, Gregg Zart. It was a play on words—Gregg's *art*—that he had invented to ensure his name ran at the end of the program during a local art festival. Gregg had been taking pictures and filming since high school. How strange it was that his economic misfortunes had led him to the capital of documentary fodder. Reporters, filmmakers, and TV crews flocked to the North Dakota oilfield from all over. Many of their reports were either sensational or generic because they were only in town for a few days or weeks. Remarkably, Reuters was the only out-of-state news organization to establish a full-time bureau in the Bakken, in a sign of how substantially the media—particularly newspapers—had declined in coverage of important stories beyond New York and Washington.

So Gregg had the advantage because he lived there. He turned his lens to his landlord, who he said resembled an Elvis impersonator. Gregg affectionately dubbed him "the Williston slumlord." In one video, he panned his camera to a dismal row of RVs, where a neighbor was erecting a wooden shell around his camper to protect it from the elements. "He's . . . entombed himself in a Plywood Palace!"

Gregg's video-making took him to Boomtown Babes Espresso, the bowling alley Million Dollar Lanes, and the tattoo parlor Skinful Pleasures. He went to crack jokes at the Lincoln and

Roosevelt heads. "I've become the Northern Plains version of Sein-feld," he said in one video caption. He enlisted a woman to cohost an episode on tumbleweeds. "Did you even know it was real?" she asked on the video, holding up a tumbleweed like a game show host posing with a prize. The video cut to Gregg in front of a line of tumbleweeds blown against the front of Walmart. "It's like an alien invasion here," he said.

Gregg moved into an apartment but returned to his old trailer yard when he learned that the city would ban people from parking RVs there. Standing on the snow-covered lot in sunglasses and a short-sleeved jersey, he interviewed a man who said that he and his pregnant girlfriend would be forced onto the streets. Gregg turned the camera to a woman rooting through a dumpster. "It's not moldy," the woman said when she found a bag of clothes. "There's no bugs. There's no lice. Just ghetto-wash the shit." She shrugged. "You know, I don't care. It's survival of the fittest."

Other boomtowners posted a flurry of videos on YouTube, describing their journeys, giving advice for finding housing, and showing the intricacies of drilling. ("WARNING!" said one visi-tor's headline. "Watch this before you head to North Dakota to get rich!!") It is amusing to contemplate how we would have imagined the Klondike Gold Rush or Trans-Alaska Pipeline construction had YouTube been around then—the medium is particularly suited to the individualist, unfiltered nature of a boomtown. What if Mark Twain had been roaming the silver-mining town of Virginia City, Nevada, in the 1860s making online videos, instead of penning tall tales as a reporter for the *Territorial Enterprise* newspaper?

Gregg became a quirky, unofficial spokesperson for Wil-liston. Reporters from New York to Germany came calling. He appeared on *CBS This Morning*. He even drew the attention of Ty Pennington, who was best known as host of *Extreme Makeover: Home Edition* and featured Gregg for the series *American Journey* on the HLN network. On the feel-good segment, Gregg said the boom could last twenty years. It ended with the statement that Gregg was planning to run for mayor. A Walmart executive sent Gregg a message saying she was proud he was part of the Walmart team. "Wow! What a story of survival and willingness to do what it takes to make it," she wrote. But Gregg believed that even his toughest day in Williston surpassed his best in prison.

I was shocked when Gregg confessed, after at least a half dozen interviews, that he had been convicted of sexual exploitation of minors in 2002. On two occasions already, I had discovered that men I knew had had their mug shots in the paper for felony sex offenses and were out on bail. My problem was that I assumed once I'd met a certain number of such characters I was unlikely to meet more. But the laws of probability didn't apply in the Bakken.

Sex offenders stampeded to North Dakota as news reports circulated that it was a place to start life anew. Mug shots of the worst offenders lined the wall of the Williston Community Library as a warning to residents, who were terrified of the predators in their midst. The rise in sex offenders was depicted in the popular documentary *The Overnighters*, which followed the lives of broken men who came to Williston for work and the Lutheran pastor who allowed them to stay in his church. (The pastor was Jay Reinke, whom I met over dollar beers at the Williston Brewing Company the year after the film aired.) In the film, a *Williston Herald* reporter chases the pastor down the street to interrogate him over his housing of sex offenders.

That same reporter wrote up a glowing profile of Gregg that began, "Most struggling artists searching for their fame and fortune head to big cities with thriving art scenes like New York, Los Angeles or Venice. But Gregg . . . caught his big break when he moved to the artistic middle of nowhere—Williston." Gregg wondered if the reporter would find out that he was a sex offender, as his registration was on file with the local authorities. But no one did. Months later, the *Williston Herald* listed every sex offender in town, including Gregg under his official name. It was a common name—too generic, perhaps, to notice. Gregg wondered whether he would have received so much adulation from the press had they known the truth.

Authorities claimed that Gregg had taken nude photos of several teenage women during a night of drinking and was involved in activity of a sexual nature. In his statement to the police, Gregg said that he and a friend went out with two young ladies who wanted Gregg to buy them beer. They all went back to the friend's place, where the women showed interest in his vocation as a photographer and asked him to take pictures of them. Gregg said they assured him they were legal adults. Eventually, one guest made a drunken commotion, and he told them to leave when he realized they had been stealing—a pilfered DVD of *Dude, Where's My Car?* fell out of a teen's coat.

"I didn't go looking for trouble, it found me," Gregg told cops after his arrest. He claimed he received poor legal counsel, and his defense attorney was soon disbarred for unrelated misconduct. But Gregg served three years in prison. He said he falsified the paperwork showing his judgment and sentence to trick the other inmates into believing he was there for grand theft auto, worried that admitting his offense would have made him a target for violent retaliation. When he got out, Gregg had to register as a sex offender wherever he went.

At Walmart, Gregg said, he was promoted to a job as assistant manager at another location on the southern edge of the Bakken. While I wasn't aware of Gregg having a criminal record since his prison term, he claimed that Walmart eventually fired him after uncovering his past. He left the oilfield and tried to get by as a medical marijuana farmer back in Washington, scoring nearly 880,000 hits for two YouTube videos on how to grow pot in your backyard.

Then a TV show came calling with his big break: a chance to find interview subjects for *Underworld, Inc.*, which ran on the National Geographic channel. "From illegal weapons to the underground sex trade, nothing is off limits and everything is for sale in illegal, often brutal, underground markets," the show advertised. *Underworld, Inc.* touted unprecedented access to the "inner workings of the last bastion of 'free' enterprise." Producers planned a segment that would take viewers into the real underbelly of the North Dakota oilfield. They had seen Gregg's videos and wanted to hire him as their fixer, the man who would help them locate the prostitutes, pimps, thieves, and gamblers for the episode. Gregg had always loved National Geographic. He immediately agreed. "To attach my name to that little yellow rectangle was really exciting," he recalled.

Because the oil boom happened in the most remote place imaginable, it was mainly known to the world through media depictions. The townsfolk had been so oversaturated with TV crews that they grew arrogant when they met *another* member of the media unless they heard a big name. Citizens walked around like jaded celebrities, name-dropping the reporters they had spoken to from the *New York Times* and CNBC. I ran into film school students from Columbia University and sociology students from Princeton and UC Berkeley. A journalist and I met a Norwegian TV crew for dinner at the restaurant in the Williston Boutique Hotel, where they asked us for advice on reporting in the oilfield. "I would say this is a banana republic," the journalist warned the crew, "but a banana republic is governed better." The crew offered me a chance to be a fixer to help them find interview subjects, though I wound up declining because of a lack of time.

Thus the sheriff, a gruff man with a prominent mustache, seemed mildly annoyed when he sat down with me one spring morning in Williston to talk about how crime had transitioned from attacks against people to attacks against property. Desperate people stealing from oil sites, that sort of thing. He had more important reporters to attend to.

"Nat Geo's in town," the sheriff boasted.

Underworld, Inc. was produced by a company called Wall to Wall Media, based in London. After producers flew in and began their ride-alongs with the sheriff's officers, Gregg received his instructions. *Underworld, Inc.* appeared to want characters ripped from an old frontier novel: a laid-off oil worker who stole to maintain a meth or alcohol addiction, a biker who collected debts, a former working girl, perhaps a preacher. Did he know any charismatic bounty hunters?

Gregg started out at the day labor center by the Amtrak station, where shiftless men lined up every morning to receive assignments as flaggers or construction workers in exchange for cash payment at the day's end. He trawled seedy bars and inquired around the Salvation Army. Then he saw a downtrodden couple outside a gas station—used up from hard drugs, greasy and colorless. A woman needed a ride home to a trailer park north of the Love's truck stop, where she assured him he would meet the characters he needed. Gregg drove her home, picking up a bottle of vodka she favored along the way. Wild dogs roamed the trailer park yard, ready to accost uninvited visitors. The cops had the place under surveillance. Gregg felt as though he had stepped into a ring of thieves. He met two meth heads who stole copper to get by, hoping to pay their way out of Williston.

But they were paranoid that he was a policeman. He won them over when one of the thieves said he wished he had some weed, and Gregg pulled a joint out of his pocket. The man looked especially excited when he offered $100 gas vouchers and Walmart gift cards for their participation. Gregg petted the dogs and said all the right things, promising he would protect them from the law. With assurances that they would appear on camera wearing masks, the men finally agreed to star on *Underworld, Inc.* He allowed them to choose their stage names: Cowboy and Hoo Doo Brown.

Gregg realized that his calling was working as a fixer for TV shows. He could schmooze; he could be a social chameleon. "You're part bounty hunter, part detective," he said. He was so skilled at being a fixer, in large part, because of his time in prison. "Why I'm a great fixer," Gregg reflected, "is that I can speak the language. I lived among criminals for a couple years. . . . I know what the bad guys look like, how they think, how they talk, and how to talk to them." The producers agreed to film the meth-head copper thieves. They all went riding around together as Cowboy reminisced about his old heists. They filmed Hoo Doo Brown smoking meth.

Gregg was less successful in his other attempts at exposing the underworld. He said the producers wanted him to find a sports bookie, figuring one must be taking bets on the upcoming wrestling match where Vanilla Ice was to perform. Gregg questioned people playing pickup basketball at the gym, went to the bars and the bowling alley, and even asked his old friends at Walmart. During the wrestling match, Gregg shot with a GoPro through the spaces in the mesh of the fighting cage, wincing as he was flecked with the wrestlers' flying blood and sweat. He even interviewed Vanilla Ice for ten minutes. I remember that concert: Vanilla Ice was dressed in all red, holding a shiny red microphone, and he lingered with his fans long after the performance ended, enjoying being a B-lister in a C-list town. But the footage didn't make the show. There was no underground gambling ring to be found.

Gregg couldn't resist scoping out the two strip clubs next to each other on Main Street. During the boom, a patron was shot and killed outside Heartbreakers by an ex-con from California. Another man was beaten to death the following year. The city had compiled a binder of every cop call at the clubs during the last few years in an effort to force the venues out. One could open that binder, skim the headings of dozens of police reports, and watch them blur and coalesce into a jailhouse poem:

vandals—stalking—trespassing
unwanted male—fake money—won't pay—trouble
threatened by gun—urinal shot—dispute/detox/border patrol
fight/stabbing—assault
man bleeding from head—ambulance

It had calmed down lately, of course, though Gregg figured he could find trouble if he looked hard enough. Gregg went in to see if a dancer would proposition him for prostitution, figuring that would be a big scoop for the show. He wore his best outfit: an Affliction shirt, Revival pants, gaudy Gucci shoes, and a fancy-looking watch that came from a supermall kiosk. He sprayed on Versace cologne. Gregg met an attractive brunette at one of the clubs who he thought was surely in the business, as she was drinking alone and dressed elaborately. But she wasn't, or at least he wasn't her type. Gregg nursed his drinks and went to the bathroom frequently, trying to catch the dancers' eyes. He realized that if there had been any prostitution activity at the strip clubs in the early boom days, it was harder to find it now, after so much media and police scrutiny.

The most perplexing task was finding an outlaw biker. Gregg found a man who wasn't in organized crime but was passionate about biker culture and had put a lot of money into fixing up his Harley. Gregg suggested him as a character, he told me, but the producers had apparently found another, more gangster biker. The problem, Gregg said, was that this gangster biker didn't have a bike—or, for that matter, a leather jacket. "He didn't even have a damn bike," Gregg said. "It just seemed ridiculous." He convinced the legit biker he found to supply his bike and leather jacket. The legit biker, who didn't want me to print his name, later recounted the experience with some amusement. He agreed to let the show use his bike because he wanted it seen on national TV, and they were going to pay him a few hundred dollars.

To establish the dark mood, *Underworld, Inc.* had drones fly over the oilfield. Gregg studied the sad-sack list of drone shots. Silhouettes of trucks against a sunset, trailers, soulless man camps. The "hooker hotels." Flares at night. Bikers. Neon lights along 2nd Avenue. They sent the drones whirring like lawnmowers in the sky, as startled residents craned to see where the noise was coming from.

It wasn't the only exaggerated media portrayal in the works. ABC's *Blood and Oil* was about to premiere. Inspired by *Dallas*, the show was a fictional depiction that featured former *Miami Vice* star Don Johnson as a North Dakota oil baron, a character loosely based on fracking executive Harold Hamm. But Hamm lived in Oklahoma, and the region wasn't dominated by any one tycoon— rather, the oil wells were usually operated by publicly traded corporations headquartered out of state.

Because of such inaccuracies, or perhaps the general media fatigue, the show advertised on New York subway billboards was so locally irrelevant that we couldn't find a bar in Williston that planned to play the series premiere. Deano Vass, a real estate broker from Illinois, had no luck calling around. The Williston

Brewing Company and Applebee's were playing sports. The lady at Big Willy's Saloon hadn't heard of the show but said they *had* to play sports—it was the rule. "But this is about the Bakken," Deano told her, to no avail.

At last he convinced a bartender at the Grand Williston Hotel to change the channel. It was the night of the blood moon eclipse when we found seats at the far end of the bar. I sat to the right of a water hauler from Florida and an oil rig electrician from Delaware eating pizza and drinking a Corona. We saw something amiss right away. They had filmed *Blood and Oil* in Park City, Utah, to land millions in tax credits, and the show had a landscape of snowy mountains instead of the grasslands and buttes of western North Dakota.

"It definitely ain't like that here," said the water hauler.

"Where are the snowcapped mountains?" Deano piped up.

"That's definitely not Williston," the water hauler said as the show depicted a bustling downtown.

The show focused on a young couple who set out for the oilfield to start a laundry service, but lost their washers and dryers when an eighteen-wheeler slammed into their pickup. They made their way to a tent city and a rollicking bar, and a skirmish broke out when some young fool shot a moose on the street.

"People think it's 1849 in the California Gold Rush, dancing around with a freakin' gold nugget," said the electrician.

"I carry a vial of oil around my neck," cracked the water hauler.

"Gee, all the oil workers are gorgeous!" the bartender said sarcastically.

"Everything I've seen of this show so far is BS," the electrician announced. "I've never seen oil workers work without flame-resistant clothing, or seen a shooting of an albino moose, and I'd like to find the bar in the opening [of the show] because that was a happening place!"

People stopped watching, bored. Some of us stepped out briefly in hopes of seeing the blood moon lunar eclipse. I got to talking to the hotel chef, who was wearing a Yankees hoodie. He was working his way through a mound of pull tabs piled on the bar (they were tickets that gamblers could pull open to reveal matching numbers and symbols for a prize). "I like the process of opening up pieces of paper and throwing them in the trash for three dollars," said the chef, who was from Detroit. He set down his Heineken. "There's no other way to pass the time."

He resented the media madness, saying that Lisa Ling's TV feature depicting prostitution at the Grand Williston and other hotels the year before was a ridiculous exaggeration. And now this. The actual mood in town was a wild swing from the bustle on *Blood and Oil*. The Grand Williston held corporate events, and there was one company, as he recalled, that paid him to cook for 250 people. The boss was laying everybody off and tried to temper the bad news by offering a lavish spread. "But nobody ate a thing, so I was stuck with a hundred pounds of pulled pork."

Fracking Hell

Behemoth oil trucks blared, whistled, and honked down a highway. Pump jacks nodded. Grain elevators soared. Traffic lights flashed. "Williston, North Dakota," said a narrator in the opening scene of Season 2, Episode 5 of *Underworld, Inc.* Tens of thousands of workers had come to make their fortune, "but the cash pouring in from fracking also funds a black market economy in extortion."

"We run the town, we don't have no rivals," said the bogus biker, his face concealed by sunglasses and a skeleton mask. "Now the oil boom is going BUST," the narrator said. Footage cut to Hoo Doo Brown in a black top hat, sunglasses, and a green handkerchief over his face as he lit a meth pipe. "Laid-off workers are turning to drugs—and theft," the narrator said. Sirens flashed. "The cops are stretched to their LIMITS—and organized crime is muscling in. . . . Welcome to Williston, Boomtown USA." Lightning flashed. "Where for SOME, life is a FRACKING HELL."

The fake biker called himself Rick and rode up Main Street, past the biker bar across from a wall that displayed the Ten Commandments. "Rick's gang makes most of its money off a good old-fashioned protection racket," the narrator said. "Every morning, he rumbles down Main Street to collect his street taxes."

"I run extortion. Bars, clubs, strip joints. Places of ill repute, you would call it," Rick said with a vaguely southern accent. "If you don't do what you're told, you get BLEEP-BLEEP! I've seen guys get their arms broke, their head bashed in."

"But loyalty like this comes at a price," said the narrator.

"The only way you can retire," Rick said, "is you die or you go to prison."

Now Rick was supposedly making $100,000 a month from cooking meth for addicts desperate in an imploding economy.

This part of the show produced the most scorn in Williston. "That was totally faked," said a woman who ran with bikers, rolling her eyes. While it was plausible to people far away who imagined Williston as a Wild West stereotype, the biker story raised too many questions for those of us in the know. Main Street could be seedy during the height of the boom, but if there had ever been a protection racket, intense police scrutiny and an oil crash guaranteed that nobody needed to pay off a blowhard like Rick. I regularly went to Main Street while the "Fracking Hell" episode of *Underworld, Inc.* was in production, and it was eerily dead—an image far distant from my first trip there three years earlier, when a former roommate recounted how the police were too busy to respond to his call of a meth head yelling threats out his pickup window. Gregg was alarmed by what he had seen so far. "I didn't know you could invent a character out of whole cloth," he said.

The narrator said bars often got violent at closing time, though the show featured outdated statistics showing that violent crime in the region had increased 121 percent from 2005 to 2011, a period that was mostly before the boom. Reports came in of trouble at a biker bar, and cops showed up to the scene to talk down a few drunks on the sidewalk.

"Fracking Hell" interviewed a pimp named Wild Bill who had come from California to expand his business—the show dubbed him boomtown's biggest criminal. Wild Bill claimed to make over $3 million a year off his girls from as far away as New York and New Jersey. This, too, gave me pause. A lot of the young, single men who paid for prostitutes during the boom had gone home when the oil industry crashed. Oil companies usually laid off people according to seniority, and the masses of solo, twentysomething, troublemaking men we saw so much of during the heyday had thinned out. As more women and families moved in, the sex trade slowed.

But the farce continued. A haunting echo sounded as the scene switched to an array of RVs in a weedy lot. "With unemployment rising, former oil workers are stuck in Williston with no cash. And SOME turn to crime!" the narrator said. The camera cut to meth head Cowboy getting in a truck wearing a white mask. "I hate to call myself a criminal, but I guess I am," Cowboy said. He scoped out spools of copper wire sitting in industrial yards, which could fetch $4,000 on the black market.

"COWBOY'S got some trouble," the narrator said, as the thief looked startled and swiveled his head to the window. A sheriff car was on the road. "A police patrol scares him off."

"Son of a BLEEP!" said Cowboy.

He had lost his oil job after failing a drug test. Cowboy needed more than copper; he needed meth. "Meth has changed me to the point where I don't even like myself."

"Williston is a hellhole," said Hoo Doo Brown inside the trailer, his voice eerily sonorous. He had to get high to even summon the courage to steal copper.

Cowboy walked out of his trailer. "I want to leave Williston so bad that every morning, when I come outside my door, I make a plan on how I can leave that day." All he needed was five grand.

"One final haul of stolen copper could be his ticket out of town," the narrator said. "And he knows where to find it . . . He and his partner Hoo Doo will try it tonight."

Hoo Doo would have to prepare the getaway vehicle by changing the tags and the tires; they would dress up like the workers, then go in and grab their haul.

"It's MAKE OR BREAK TIME," the narrator said as Cowboy cruised down the road. But the next morning, Cowboy was slumping in sadness outside his RV.

Their scheme had folded. "They got double-crossed by their crew," the narrator said.

"They got greedy and went back without me," said Cowboy, his voice shaking. "They violated the rules of the game and took a lot of money from me."

"The two meth addicts are still where they started," the narrator said. "Small-time thieves trapped in a BOOM-BUST town."

But somebody offered Cowboy a job dealing meth, and he seemed heartened by his turn of fate. "Sky's the limit."

I watched this part with the greatest interest, having interviewed some meth heads several months earlier. One was stealing diesel tanks left at idle oil sites. His friend, a prostitute named Stephanie, complained to me that the man had blown his newfound cache on a Harley instead of getting caught up on child support. "Still broke as a damn convict," she said. She rode up on a Greyhound bus after getting out of prison for meth manufacturing in Georgia, hopeful to find work after a truck-driving friend from down south said he had a house for her to stay here. (One temp agency administrator claimed she encountered ex-cons who said they were, upon release, given bus tickets to North Dakota straight from the prison.) But when Stephanie refused his sexual propositions as they drove along in his semi, he tossed her onto the roadside and drove off. She hitched a ride with a stranger, found a place of her own, and soon landed jobs waitressing and house cleaning. She stayed clean for six months, until a man at a bar offered her meth, and she'd been back on drugs ever since. Stephanie eventually turned to prostitution, a line of work she favored because it allowed her to be an independent operator. "I always like working for myself—I'm not the kind of person that can be under somebody," she said. Stephanie dealt meth on the side, and sent some of her prostitution and drug clients to her friend's diesel tank scheme.

So many people in the oilfield were addicts, whether or not they were sticking themselves up with needles in a hotel room. Addicted to escape . . . addicted to money . . . addicted to adrenaline . . . addicted to oil . . . it was all *now! now! now!* as fast as they could get it, forget next year, forget next month, forget tomorrow.

The oilfield itself was a ravenous junkie who had just come off an epic, years-long bender that drew partiers from around the world and now the money was all gone, the room was strewn with beer bottles and shattered meth pipes and overturned furniture, loan sharks were coming to collect, and he was convulsing from the withdrawals of his voracious indulgences. People like those meth fiends were one of the biggest stories during the oil crash— emblematic—desperate, strung-out people on the margins who could no longer work out their dysfunctions under the cover of boom-time money. Then there were all the folks robbing this place senseless. Laid-off workers helped themselves to tools worth a few grand on their way back south, in one final act of vengeance aimed at an oilfield that had jilted them. I knew a trucker who was so angry at his boss for reducing his work hours that he was prowling the man's property for tools to steal before going back to Texarkana. By the time anybody noticed the items were missing, the thieves would be pawning them a few states away.

The idea that these criminals would have let me, as a journalist, accompany them on law-breaking escapades was absurd, but I wondered if I should have pressed harder to find the quality of material that "Fracking Hell" had landed. Gregg disabused me of this impression. He said the film crew had never been out with Cowboy when he was on his way to a copper heist. They had driven around with him while he showed them sites he had targeted in the past. There was no make-or-break time; there was no double-crossing crew. Gregg said they never saw a cop car on the way, and that the footage of Cowboy appearing startled was really of him spotting a friend he didn't want to recognize him. Gregg was ashamed that he had deceived people about the project. It seemed a desperate attempt, he believed, to spice up an already interesting story.

"Fracking Hell" enraged the residents of Williston. This was right after ABC's *Blood and Oil* debacle, and it was yet another example of the oilfield losing its own story to outsiders with an agenda. Tom Rolfstad, the town's former economic development director, was dismayed over "Fracking Hell," especially since he had grown up reading *National Geographic* magazine. "If that's the way they report Williston," he said, crossing his arms, "maybe all the stuff they've reported my whole life was wrong."

He had thrived on the early media hullabaloo, fondly recalling how officials had met a reporter from the *New Yorker* at Trapper's Kettle. Tom enjoyed visiting oilfield types in Manhattan and having a car pick him up to take him to CNBC's studio. But as time wore on, he was aghast at the journalistic tendency to write about mayhem in the Walmart parking lot and prostitutes.

He told me that Williston began to feel as if it was O.J. Simpson ("Get us off the headlines!"), a notable comparison given a comment by one tour operator in the old Klondike town of Skagway during the gold rush centennial in 1997. "The Gold Rush was one big O.J. trial," said the tour operator, Dave McClelland. "The coverage was so sensational." During the Alaskan pipeline rush, an article ran in the *Pioneer All-Alaska Weekly* about prostitution increasing 5,000 percent. "Fairbanks Becomes Wild City . . . Chamber Ponders Damage to City's Image by Articles 'Outside,'" a headline went. So it went: criticizing out-of-state journalists reporting on North Dakota was almost becoming a sport. The *Williston Herald's* crime reporter sensed something was amiss with "Fracking Hell" and tracked down Cowboy, who told her his account had been distorted. "They just did it for the damn money, the publicity," he said. "They had me believing they cared." The reporter, who would later cover Mama's drug bust, agreed to accompany me to Cowboy's trailer park and make an introduction, as it was not the sort of place one wandered into cold. She had moved here from the East Coast after her husband, an FBI agent, was transferred to the bureau's new Williston office.

When we arrived, a herd of psychotic dogs roared up in the snow, and a half-blind man shuffled out of his trailer and said Cowboy wasn't around. (Hoo Doo Brown was beaten to death shortly after the show aired, for unrelated reasons.) Later, Cowboy's wife told me they were done talking to the media—they felt exploited. A month later, an acquaintance asked if I wanted to visit the biker bar portrayed unflatteringly by *Underworld, Inc.* A crew—*another*

film crew!—had arrived to shoot a movie called *Boomtown* about
a man who left his family behind to pursue a job in the oilfield,
drawing on an array of locals to complement several professional
actors. They were shooting a scene at a biker bar that was still skit-
tish about the bad publicity it had gotten from "Fracking Hell,"
and the bar allowed us inside under the condition that we wouldn't
take photos. We stood near the door for a few minutes, waiting
until they finished filming the blonde, blue-eyed bartender giving
her number to a roughneck.

"Who is that woman?" I asked. "I've seen her somewhere."

My acquaintance thought she was one of the locals. During
a lull in filming, I walked over to the bar. "I'd like a Heineken,
please," I said.

She laughed and told me she wasn't a real bartender. I stared at
her for a few moments, and then it struck me. She was the actress
Rachel Brosnahan, who played the prostitute killed off by political operative Doug Stamper on *House of Cards*. The last season of
the Netflix show had ended with him burying her in the desert—
now she had risen from the dead in Williston. Before we could say
more, a producer scurried up. "You're in the movie now," she told
my friend and me. She directed us to order drinks from Rachel
again.

"What can I get you folks?" Rachel asked as the cameras
turned toward us.

"I'll take a Bud Light and Heineken," my friend said.

"That'll be seven bucks." Rachel took the wad of cash and
walked to the refrigerator. "There you go," she said, plunking the
bottles down. As the crew shot a series of retakes, Rachel took the
drinks and brought them back and took the drinks again. We began drinking the beers after we thought the shooting was done,
but a producer ran up. "Don't drink the beer!" We set the drinks
down. "We may need to order another round for continuity of the
props," my friend joked to Rachel.

A producer whisked away the half-drunk beers we set on the
table. "Hey, you guys are in it," she said, waving release forms.
She turned to me. "Actually, you're not really in it—your hair is in

it—but even to put your hair in there we have to have you sign a release."

Afterward, Rachel said the director's mother was Laray May-field, who had been casting director for *House of Cards*. I had my friend take a photo of Rachel and me, prompting a manager to storm up and berate me for violating their policy against taking pictures. Rachel apologized to the woman, trying to take the blame. I was as impressed with her graciousness as I was baffled by the manager's outsized reaction. But I came to understand that the bar felt betrayed by *Underworld, Inc.*, and as another member of the media, I was automatically suspect.

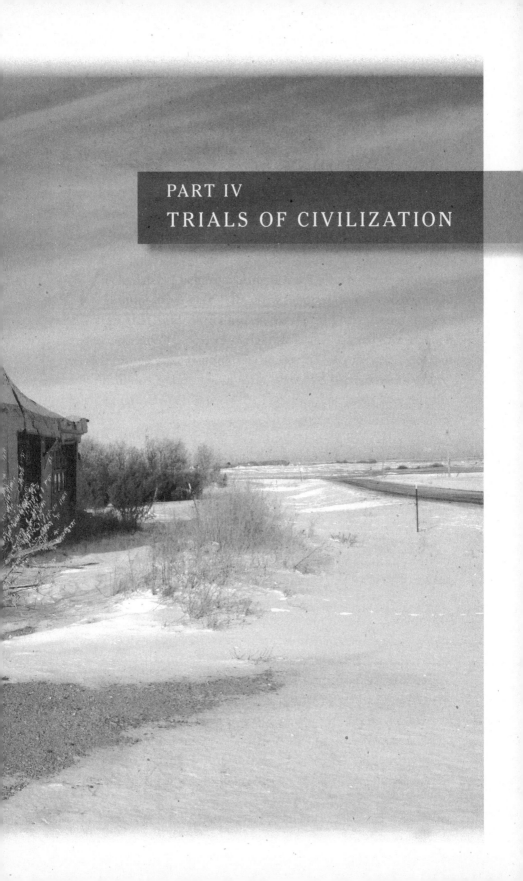

PART IV
TRIALS OF CIVILIZATION

Wasteland

I rang ex-banker Dave Noack's doorbell, huddling in my winter coat. It was Sunday, and I hoped he would have time to talk about the financial crisis. But when he opened the door, I saw waste disposal entrepreneur Jack Johnston sitting on the living room couch watching football. Noack ushered me inside, and I sat awkwardly next to Jack with my notebook, shivering from a freeze that even the fireplace could not dispel. Lasagna with jalapeños was in the kitchen for dinner in a few hours. The men sipped glasses of red wine and flipped back and forth on the TV between Noack's team (the Green Bay Packers) and Jack's (the Denver Broncos).

"I don't know why you really want to watch the Green Bay game anyway," Jack said. It was all the more grating because they were killing Dallas, while his own team was falling behind. "Denver's defense is really falling apart."

"If you guys lose to Oakland, something's wrong," Noack said.

"I'm having a bad day. Don't pick on me! . . . Son of a bitch," Jack said, staring at the 15–12 score. It was the fourth quarter. The Raiders were on their way to triumph. "This is sad, and especially if the Packers won." Then came the point of no return. "Son of ten thousand bitches!"

"There's still four minutes left, big guy," Noack said.

The neighbor walked in and plopped onto the recliner. He was a scruffy, broad-shouldered man of thirty who didn't seem to say much. In two months, the *Williston Herald* would report that he'd been busted for possession of a controlled substance with intent to

238 ·ŀ· GREAT AMERICAN OUTPOST

deliver, as part of Mama's $1.3 million drug ring. Records showed he was on her lease. The FBI raided their condo and found scales, heroin, and nearly $13,000 in cash. Noack's jalapeño-studded lasagna might be one of the last gourmet meals that the neighbor would enjoy before going to prison. But on this afternoon, before his criminal travails had come to light, it was the neighbor's turn to offer condolences. "You can switch and become a Packers fan," he told Jack.

I saw this was a rare chance to talk to Jack about what had happened at the Berg saltwater disposal, so I shifted my attention from collateralized debt obligations to another kind of radioactive toxin: TENORM. That was oilfield jargon for technologically enhanced naturally occurring radioactive material, the rancid stuff of oil waste. I don't suppose he wanted to be quizzed while watching football, but he seemed to indulge me out of mannerly obligation. Jack was a portly man of nearly eighty at the time, with a genial southern disposition.

He told me he'd gone to school in Baton Rouge for geology, worked on the rigs, and moved to Colorado. He went out on his own in the drilling business at age twenty-six. Few people were making money in it then, he recalled: "I was one of the ones on the ragged edge." They explored for oil hours east of the Bakken, an area that everyone now knew was a dead zone, traveling around on snowmobiles and drinking rum at the bar to stay warm. During the infancy of the latest oil rush, Jack learned of opportunities to buy and flip oil leases with other investors. "We didn't do as well as a lot of the big boys who had the nerve to hang in there—we turned over ours as fast as we could." The major players could get returns of up to fifteen times their original investment. Jack and his cohorts figured they had won if they made any sort of profit; if they got returns of 300 percent, they were fabulously lucky.

The authorities came calling when the filter socks from the Berg were discovered at the abandoned gas station, and Jack said he didn't even recognize the fugitive when they showed him a picture. By Jack's reckoning, the guy in the photo had been wearing some sort of muscle shirt and looked as though he'd just broken out of jail. "It was bullshit! . . . He [presented as] a well-connected, well-dressed, nice guy. I saw a picture of him later and he looked like leftover lunch."

A year had passed since I sat near the lunch counter on the Canadian border where the authorities were griping about regulators knocking down Jack's waste-dumping fine. But Jack said that the word from one government official was that the fugitive had turned up south of the border again. "They told us the other day that he was dead . . . in Mexico."

∴ ∴ ∴

Some months earlier, I had watched two jumbled heaps of filter socks drying in the sun. I was standing at the waste disposal complex of Secure Energy Services, near the Pilot truck stop at the intersection where Highway 85 rolled an hour to the Canadian border. "This is where we make our money, is over here," the plant manager said. From a distance the piles of filter socks resembled a mélange of fish decaying on a wharf, brown and gray and blotted with sediment—but no, they were ghouls, macabre spirits, the plastic rings on the open ends of the mesh tubes peering out from the piles like hollowed faces. They were becoming crumbly, and a worker would have to flip them. Soon somebody would come to transport the filter socks out of state. Secure Energy was one of the Bakken's biggest players in waste disposal, and its expert Kurt Rhea had overseen the cleanup of filter socks at the Noonan gas station. He was determined to set the record straight following the bad press over North Dakota's oil-waste-dumping scandals—the turning point had been when MSNBC host Rachel Maddow went ballistic over the fugitive's dumping case and flashed his mug shot on the screen. Kurt lamented that filter socks had become the symbol of oilfield radioactivity (a term, he believed, that needlessly scared people), even though he was more concerned about the toxic sludge that accumulated in saltwater disposal tanks. Those "tank bottoms" carried far more radioactivity than a filter sock, he told me, sometimes as high as 1,000 picocuries per gram.

North Dakota required waste with a radioactivity level higher than 5 picocuries per gram to be trucked out of the state, a standard that Kurt called "over-conservative." (By contrast, Colorado allowed waste up to 2,000 picocuries a gram to be disposed of within its borders, and Idaho permitted 1,500, though neither state had North Dakota's intensity of oil activity.) With the input of Secure, the state was developing new rules allowing twenty-five thousand tons a year of low-level radioactive waste (up to 50 picocuries per gram) to be disposed of in North Dakota's landfills. The changes would spare oil companies the enormous expense of transporting filter socks and other waste out of state. Illegal filter sock dumping was already becoming rare as rogue haulers left the state and requirements for more convenient disposal took effect.

But critics charged that oil companies and regulators hadn't properly handled waste at its current limits, so why allow more? A sampling of public comments that North Dakotans submitted to the state:

"We ask: WHAT ARE YOU THINKING? We have a big enough mess in our state with all the oil leaks, oil spills, saltwater spills, etc., etc., etc., etc."

"So what if it costs the oil companies more? They can certainly afford it. They will be long gone when this is done and our children will be stuck with this mess."

"What took place in the wake of the discovery in Noonan was a total disaster. . . . The industrial commission's handling of this as if it was a little extra garbage on someone's curb and [the state] reducing the fines levied are all just ludicrous examples of how increased levels of waste will be handled in the future." Western North Dakota is "being systematically and methodically turned into an industrial wasteland."

Despite residents' pleas, the regulations passed.

The debate unfolded as business at the Berg saltwater disposal dropped dramatically. The number of saltwater disposals in the oilfield had risen from 185 to 435 in the last decade—there was a glut of disposals, just as there was a glut of apartments and restaurants. By this point, however, the Berg had seen traffic slow to a few trucks a day dropping off wastewater, and Jack was open to selling it. I drove up one morning to meet Josh Velo, a longtime operator at the disposal.

"You can hang with the Norwegian mafia any day," he told me.

"I'm a quarter Norwegian," I said.

"That's not enough to join the club, ma'am," said Josh. He was *half* Norwegian, and this apparently made all the difference. When I protested, he said, "Fine, you can come in."

So on to the border: a hundred miles from Williston, edge of the world. This was nearly the distance from Philadelphia to New York, but by Northern Plains standards, it was the psychological equivalent of a short trip down the road. I found the border to have an especially melancholic resonance after it claimed one of the first victims of the oil collapse: a Denver company that had extensive holdings here, American Eagle Energy, cited crashing oil prices as it filed for bankruptcy. Then a pipeline owned by Tulsa-based Samson Resources leaked 179,000 gallons of saltwater for days before somebody discovered the breach. It was the largest brine spill this part of the border had seen during the Bakken boom. Soon afterward, that company, too, filed for bankruptcy. Darwinian wreckage . . .

My GPS led me astray to a narrow path rimmed in ice—impassable. I looked around the hibernal terrain uneasily. It was below 22 degrees with windchill, so cold my check-engine light turned on. My repeated calls to Josh failed with sparse reception, and I could only send text messages. I watched the wind blow a fog of settled snow across the pastures, and then Josh came by in his Toyota Tundra. He urged me to leave my car by some oil wells down the way. We drove through the raw winds, past frozen sloughs that flanked the side of the road like angel's wings. He showed me the Berg saltwater disposal, with its two rows of tanks, just a blot in a frosty outland that rambled without bounds. Josh told me he had found old filter socks when he dug up a flow line once, that people found them all over the countryside out here, buried from way back when environmental regulations weren't as strict.

After leaving the Berg, we found ourselves on a slight hill with an enormous white maw beyond and then, as I held my breath, Josh sped across until the Toyota Tundra was just a fly gliding into the snowy corpus. I feared those great wide-open spaces, and had grown accustomed to them only out of the necessity of being in North Dakota. We were supposed to shoot his AK-47 for a while—everybody kept big guns around here—but the wind was too searing to fire off more than a few rounds. He gestured to the sky and asked if I saw the sun dog. "It's so cold that the ice crystals in the air freeze and it creates a rainbow. . . . You've never seen that?" We stopped to look at the mirage of blue-yellow-red in the glare of the sun, then carried on to Josh's father's farmhouse, past a thicket of bony trees, and settled around the kitchen table. The old man was driving a garbage truck after being laid off from the Berg disposal. I was surprised to hear him say he hated the oilfield. "There was people in the oilfield that were terrible—they didn't care about our state and this is our home." They had never seen so much trash everywhere, and Josh's father had taken to picking up all the bags of garbage and jugs of urine dumped by outsiders along the highways. And that fugitive . . .

"They found him dead," Josh assured his father. "They found him dead in Mexico." Sometimes they had to scare off the culprits at gunpoint. Josh used to see truck drivers pick up saltwater loads from the Berg, drive a short distance, and dump the toxic liquid on the ground. He chased one driver down at dusk and held him up with a 9 mm until the sheriff's department responded. "You don't dump shit in our backyard!" Josh barked at the man, who was from Illinois. You had to be careful whom you screwed over around there, Josh joked to me—might get tossed down an old mine shaft.

The Velo family hoped the new owners would revive the Berg. Months before, several businessmen from Minneapolis had stopped by the Williston Brewing Company. One used to work for the restaurant owner, Marcus Jundt; the other was convicted securities fraudster Todd Duckson. (Did you think, for a moment, that our Ponzi schemer from England had popped in for another shot of luxury cognac? Alas, his whereabouts were still unknown.) The pair was interested in waste disposal deals. Marcus liked to pass on business tips culled from his flagship restaurant, so he told his ex-banker friend Dave Noack, who helped arrange a sale of the Berg for the Minneapolis men and agreed to be a sales consultant for a time. "That's all it was, word of mouth over a bar," said Josh.

The new owners planned to upgrade the disposal into a treatment plant to accept specialty oil waste: sludge from the bottom of oil and saltwater tanks, buildup in pipes, flowback fluids, frack gel, spilled oil, and various drilling and production waste. That was more profitable than straight brine; the nastier it was, the more you could charge to get rid of it. The Velos told me the Berg had charged 75 cents a barrel to dispose of regular production water, but that specialty fluids would cost between $16 and $32. Regulatory records indicated that the trucks would unload the fluids into pods. The fluids would then move to a system separating out the solids using screens and hydrocones. The solids would be transported to special landfills, and the remaining liquids would be pumped into tanks before being injected into the earth.

The Securities and Exchange Commission won its suit against Todd in 2013, when a civil jury found that he was part of a fraudulent scheme that raised more than $21 million by misleading investors about the deteriorating condition of a real estate fund where Todd served as an attorney and later manager. Authorities said the fraud occurred as the fund was losing money during the financial crisis. The Minnesota Supreme Court suspended Todd's law license. But a past with the SEC wasn't a legal barrier to doing business in most cases, and Todd appeared before the North Dakota Industrial Commission during fall 2015 to obtain regulatory approvals.

The Berg waste disposal crew met at the bar of the Brooks Hotel, that old hub for deal junkies built by the wealthy Turks. Noack was there, along with the disposal workers. Todd was a bald man with an affable comportment. He showed me a phone video he'd shot inside a dumpy bar on the drive up Highway 85—supposedly run by an ex-stripper from Pittsburgh—where Todd and his business partner had stopped for shots of Jäger ("Jäg," as he put it). The footage resembled the opening of a horror movie, the camera trailing through the dark bar as the eyes of dogs glowed from the floor.

"Do you think that place has been cleaned in fifteen years?" Todd asked his business partner. The bar had mousetraps in the bathroom—he even found the skeleton of a rodent in one of them.

I asked how Todd ended up investing in North Dakota. "I was a little boy, four years old, and said I really want to grow up and dispose of oilfield waste," he joked. Everybody laughed. "I was involved in a big hedge fund that didn't do well in the real estate crisis." Todd explained that he had started coming up several years before because there was a lot of money to be made, and reminisced that it had been a place for real deals. He had served as the organizer and manager of a Bakken wastewater firm, getting into sewage treatment (one of his co-defendants had also been involved in the operation).

Todd and his business partner warned me about the pull of the oilfield. "We'll be happy to be out, but then we'll get Bakken fever," said the business partner. "You just miss it; [you think] *I've got to come back.*"

"Here's one thing you miss," Todd said. It was hearing stories from Josh and Mickey, another waste disposal worker at our table. The workers had spied a cottontail rabbit while driving near the international border and struck the animal with their vehicle, figuring it would be an instant kill. When it wasn't, they stomped the rabbit to death and marinated it in buttermilk.

Mickey stood to leave, speaking with a heavy Louisiana accent, and Todd shook his hand. "We're going to rule the world," Todd said. "Next time you get a rabbit, man, we can be here in twelve hours [from the Twin Cities]. You keep that buttermilk on hand." He turned to me after Mickey left. "He's tougher than shit—you couldn't kill him if you wanted to."

The men lamented the filter sock fiasco. "It's a big disposal problem," Todd said of the filter socks. "The biggest environmental scandal in Bakken history was at that gas station in Noonan." But he believed this was the right time to invest. "History is full of people who buy at the top, when the press is good, and what they do is they sell at the bottom. It's 100 percent the opposite of what you should do." I met Josh four months later in spring 2016 at the Williston Hardee's, where he ate a Frisco Burger as we caught up on the oilfield. He had recently left the Berg to work at Jack's pipe repair shop full-time. Josh agreed when I asked if he thought it seemed strange that one remote waste disposal was linked to so many people with a background. He got quite a surprise when he Googled everybody recently—running Internet searches on one's acquaintances could be a frightful ordeal in the Bakken. He complained that Noack hadn't brought in the disposal clients they had hired him to do—Josh believed he was better at making connections than closing deals—and suggested that he was on his way out, though I couldn't confirm the particulars because nobody would speak with me.

The disposal injected 141,703 barrels of waste that year. By December, Noack would reach a settlement with the SEC agreeing to pay a $100,000 civil penalty and join with the bank Stifel, Nicolaus & Co. to forgo $2.5 million in ill-gotten gains with interest. (The bank paid an additional penalty of $22 million.) Both parties admitted to violating federal securities laws and steering Wisconsin school districts into unsuitably risky investments, in a classic case of what went wrong during the financial crisis.

Lawsuits added up against companies associated with ownership of the Berg. A trucking company sued, alleging it was never paid $5,000 it was owed for hauling waste disposal tanks from Wyoming. "They just don't want to pay their bills," said the owner, Pat LaJoie. He was so furious when I spoke to him that he wanted to drive to the Canadian border and yank those tanks out of the ground. Then the court issued a $75,000 judgment against the ownership of the Berg for unpaid waste-hauling services. Oil services conglomerate Baker Hughes sued for unpaid rental fees for the Triplex Injection Pump Package, and a sheriff seized the equipment under court order. A lawsuit even claimed that the Berg had stiffed a contractor for $2,694 in rental costs for a portable toilet. The state's agency for workforce safety and insurance won a judgment of more than $15,000.

As for the fugitive—I called his mother in Montana to confirm his death, but she hastily got off the phone. Jack told me he didn't really believe the guy was dead, and I figured he was right. A deputy US marshal in Wyoming who'd worked the case over the years said their office fielded tips once in a while that the fugitive was deceased, but said he wouldn't really believe it until he saw an autopsy. It was too easy to fake a death in Mexico, and the fellow had a way of . . . resurfacing.

He was eventually indicted on charges of wire fraud for cheating Jack's company on the filter sock disposal contract by improperly dumping the waste, and the Environmental Protection Agency issued a WANTED poster with the fugitive's mug shot, warning that he was considered violent and dangerous.

The Perils at Twenty Feet

G ray clouds sulked as Danny and I drove just south of the Canadian border in a drizzle. He had agreed to accompany me on a ramble up here during his day off, as there was little else to do, and we meandered down the route that ran parallel to the international line. An enormous white house with a battered roof glided toward us on the back of a truck, jutting into our lane, and I swerved. We took a wayward route over a narrow dirt road between two sloughs and came upon a battery of oil tanks he used to service. They were filled with toxic black crude, not the light, sweet variety Danny favored. We paused at a loading station, staring at the long black oil train stalled on the grass like a flammable, fat-bellied centipede lying in waiting. Black birds skittered in the distance. I remarked that it was all so eerie, and he said, "Every day I feel like that. Starting to get to you, too, I see."

He wanted to go to the 109 Club later to have a little rum, and soon enough the drink would ease his escape from these ashen hollows of isolation. But it was too early for that just yet, and I drove past the abandoned gas station where the fugitive had dumped the filter socks in Noonan, down Main Street, past Bootlegger's Bar, Traveler's Hotel, a tire shop, a hardware store, the post office, the Crashpad Bunkpad with its sign touting A GREAT PLACE TO REST! LAUNDRY—SHOWERS—RV PARKING. We stopped at a bright yellow Mexican restaurant called Uno Mas. I hardly ever saw anyone in that restaurant, or even traveling down Main Street. If it weren't for the waste scandal, I wouldn't have known that Noonan, population 123, was a living town.

"*¿Como estas? Tengo hambre,*" Danny said to the owner as we sat down at a table. He asked why there was no music playing, and the man turned up a lively Mexican tune. We ordered a burrito and enchiladas. Danny chattered on about the money he was making selling items on eBay while the oil was loading. He wished he could be more entrepreneurial—perhaps start his own trucking business, or get into aquaponics—but wasn't sure he was much of a businessman. Danny was reading more spiritual self-help books nowadays. They said he could have anything he wanted, but he had to live as if it were already true—it seemed profound while he read it, but Danny felt himself revert back to the usual mind-set after a week. Lately he was reading a book called *The Circle Maker* about making prayer circles around one's dreams. *What impossibly big dream is God calling you to draw a prayer circle around?*

Get out of here—but how?

"I'm a seasoned Bakken driver now," he often said, and wasn't always sure if that was something to take pride in or regret. He never felt as though he belonged—he didn't care for other truck drivers. Not very intellectual, and some of them scared him. One time he noticed a semi had parked on an oil site for three days and knocked on the door, wondering if the driver had died. The man came out wielding a gun. "These guys from Texas and Arkansas and Arizona, they shoot," Danny said.

But he could always avoid them. The real threat was inescapable. The effluvium from the oil tanks nearly knocked him onto the catwalk the other day, and he had to wait on a folding chair for a while before his mind was clear enough to drive. His tongue went numb for hours. Danny wore a monitor that was supposed to beep warnings of potentially fatal levels of gases such as hydrogen sulfide, and all oil workers received safety training instructing them to run crosswind and up if the concentrations got too high.

Danny feared that if he rejected a load, his boss would find another worker who wouldn't complain. He had begun to feel pangs in his chest now that he was hauling oil again, strains that he had never felt hauling freshwater. He had been asking the other drivers if the fumes bothered them, but they mumbled the question away. "It's dangerous stuff and they're not talking about it."

"They probably don't have the luxury of worrying about it," I said.

He swiftly corrected me. "It's not a luxury if it's going to kill you."

·:· ·:· ·:·

The first death happened near Mandaree, the Indian reservation town where Danny had taken me to transport oil. A Montana worker named Dustin Bergsing had gone to check the level of oil in a tank. A coworker found him passed out on the catwalk just after midnight, the hatch of the tank left open. He was pronounced dead at the hospital hours later. Poisonous hydrocarbons were found in his blood. Dustin was twenty-one years old.

Then: a thirty-nine-year-old truck driver was found slumped over the catwalk railing, his body already cold; a fifty-two-year-old truck driver lost consciousness while taking an oil sample and fell backward on the corner of the catwalk guardrail, hooking his clothing in such a way that he was hanged to death by his sweatshirt hood; a fifty-nine-year-old trucker died while taking samples from an oil tank, weeks after he was found disoriented and lightheaded and went to a clinic for a checkup; a man who had just gauged an oil tank collapsed at the bottom of the catwalk stairs. By the time Danny returned to crude hauling in 2015, the National Institute for Occupational Safety and Health had identified nine cases of workers who died after opening the hatches of oil tanks. All were men. All were working alone. Three were in North Dakota.

Researchers at the institute, as well as the Occupational Safety and Health Administration, found that workers faced significant health and safety risks when they gauged oil tanks. In addition to the already well-known hazard of hydrogen sulfide, the internal pressure in the tank could rapidly release a plume of butane, benzene, propane, and other toxic vapors that displaced oxygen and caused asphyxiation, explosions, dizziness, cardiac arrhythmia, hypoxia, and respiratory depression.

In one survey, OSHA researchers found that all workers who gauged tanks had reported light-headedness and weakness of knees that forced them to sit down until the feeling passed. Federal safety officials wanted more training for employees who had to go to the top of the tanks, along with more respiratory protection when remote tank gauging wasn't possible. The following year, OSHA and the National Institute for Occupational Safety and Health issued a hazard alert recommending that workers not perform the job alone and that alternative procedures be found to replace manual tank gauging.

Danny usually worked by himself, as most oil haulers did, and he was too busy hauling crude to know about the growing federal scrutiny. Dispatch began sending him to a site west of the Indian reservation where the oil was flowing out of control. So much pressure was blasting through the tanks that they seemed to rock back and forth, whistling. It sounded like an explosion when he opened the top of one. The twenty-foot-high tank appeared to have nineteen feet of oil—it was never supposed to be that full. Oil companies assigned an employee called a pumper to monitor the level of fluid in the tanks so that dispatch would know to call truckers to take it away, but the pumper had been a no-show, leaving the tanks unattended.

Danny felt the pressure from the gases blow his hair straight up. He opened another tank to equalize the force. Danny felt nauseous and dizzy when he came down off the catwalk to the ground. He saw a box stuffed with the paperwork of other truck drivers, indicating that nobody had checked on anything for a few days. His eyes burned. He filled his truck with as much crude as he could and left the oil tank on the site open. This was forbidden, because the tank could overflow, but he feared that if he didn't, the next man would encounter a terrible surprise when he opened the tank. *Well, which of the evils do you want?* he thought. *Let the bitch flow over.*

A few days later, Danny invited me to follow him to the wells. This way, if a supervisor appeared he could always say he didn't know me; having me in the truck would have been a firing offense, and he was increasingly afraid of risking it. We traveled west on Highway 23 and took a fork on the right, ending up on a dirt road carved with deep ruts that unleashed clouds of dust. It was one of those roads, like the tribal BIA-12, that appeared destined for nowhere, until one drove far enough in and saw the land open into a sprawling cosmos of oil wells. I took note of the Patterson rig far off on the horizon, knowing I would have to rely upon it later as a guidepost.

The windshield was dusty and dry and streaked, nearly impossible to see out of with the hard glare of sunlight. The wipers were broken and I stepped out to empty a water bottle over the glass, causing a semi behind me to stall out. We turned left at a dead end. I came up a hill, and as I crested it, a magnificent view unfolded all around—the Missouri River, surrounded by soaring buttes, crystal blue and far and away in the distance. A large scoria pad had been cut out of the lowlands.

I followed Danny there and idled at the edge, watching as he walked along the catwalk to open one of the olive-hued oil tanks. The site was leased by a Texas operator from the US Bureau of Land Management, which required manual oil tank gauging because it considered this the most accurate way to measure crude and ensure the accurate payment of royalties. That year, the agency was considering updating regulations to allow automated measurement. But the petroleum industry expressed concern about the cost of retrofitting oil tanks with measurement devices. "In an era of rising economic challenges and increasingly important domestic energy security, BLM should not add unnecessary costs on oil and gas development," the American Petroleum Institute and several other industry groups wrote to the agency. Notably, Enerplus Resources—the Canadian company whose oil Danny and I had loaded on the reservation—wrote to BLM in support of switching to an automated system, saying that manual methods exposed workers to unnecessary health and safety risks. Remote oil measurement technology was common in Canada. (By fall 2016, the agency moved to *allow* automated systems, but it didn't require them.) After a few minutes I walked over and struck up a conversation with an old man who was loading oil in the truck in front of Danny. There was a blast of noise. The man hooked up a hose, saying something about how a well can go sour at any time . . . numb your nose . . .

I caught a whiff off the trucker's vent pipe and an acrid burn seared my nose and chest. I hurried back to the car, weaving around the unpaved roads until I found the Patterson rig on the horizon, my beacon. I pulled over and steadied my breathing . . . think, don't think, inhale . . . Danny told me over the phone to calm down—it was nothing serious. The truckers, after all, were standing there just fine. He thought I must have gotten overcome with panic. Danny convinced me to come back and we talked as he waited for the oil to load—the gases had calmed down over the last few days. "Hauling oil isn't for sissies," Danny lectured. "It's not for boys. It's for *grown men*! You're all right. *Years* of this, you may not be."

We agreed to meet back at the Van Hook truck stop for lunch, and as I walked back to my car a truck driver who had just arrived thrust a sheaf of papers at me. "You're getting a correction ticket," he said. "They screwed up yesterday by 10H and then they said I did 2H. I let dispatch know." I looked at him in bewilderment, and realized he had mistaken me for the no-show pumper. I was often mistaken for an oil worker because I always wore the required steel-toed boots, hard hat, and (rather ill-fitting) FRs on location, and knew the basic jargon. "I don't work here," I said.

I hastened to the car. Some twenty minutes later, that tall yellow sign by the truck stop appeared, warmth on another far-out stretch. As I stepped out of the car, I heard someone call out, "Hey! Oilfield trash!" as he rounded the corner of the Van Hook truck stop. It was a truck-driving acquaintance dressed in the same mismatched T-shirt and shorts I'd seen him wear to the Aerosmith concert at the state fair recently. He'd gotten divorced, done a lot of meth, and wound up in a Tampa trailer park; then he came to North Dakota to pay off $20,000 in back child support, though he was working off the books so his ex-wife wouldn't know his real income. While he was on ecstasy, he'd told me at the concert that he was so bored he went on a three-week meth binge while delivering dirt for road construction projects on the reservation. People could go to North Dakota for a better life, but their natural tendencies didn't change upon crossing the state line.

Inside the truck stop, I found Danny at a back table by the TV. We each bought the special of turkey and gravy, green beans, and macaroni and cheese. "You'd have never been able to get up top—it's just overwhelming," Danny told me of gauging oil on that site. He thought the requirement that they stand over the tanks was Jurassic. Danny said the site was a monster before the wells calmed down over the last day. He made a guttural noise to imitate the hiss of the flare. "You see the gas coming out of the flare? Add that by seven in your face." It wasn't the only conversation I had about these matters—one of my housemates, who worked as a pumper for an Exxon subsidiary, confided in me during a night out at Doc Holliday's about her chest pains from the fumes. But she was young and educated and not as desperate as Danny and a lot of them were—she knew she could leave if she ever feared for her life.

I asked why he could get on the catwalk and I couldn't—I wondered if his body acclimated to the fumes over time. But he told me it never did. "I've got to do my job," he said.

Danny and all the others were performing some of the most dangerous work in America, and out in the oilfield, many abided by the truism that it was better to risk your life for more money than take a safer job for less. But even Danny had his limits. He had finally reported the perils to his superior the other day. "It's out of hand, it's dangerous," he'd told his boss. "I'm getting dizzy and headaches. We shouldn't have to handle our own load like that." He'd described the problem on the routine job safety analysis sheet that workers turned in to the boss. Danny showed me a picture of it. "Very dangerous site drivers are doing pumper's job on a federal site," he'd written. "HAZARD PAY!!!"

"I don't think anyone reads them," he told me. "They don't care. 'Just get in the truck and drive.' So today I just put it like it is."

Pipelining Blues

O nly a wild place inflicts the violent apparatus of industrialization on the masses. Pipelines, then, were the arteries
of the Bakken's civilization. Rod by rod, they displaced the clunk
of trucks and flares from the landscape so that one might come
to believe we occupied a natural state—even as the oil and gas
and brine coursed just below the ground we trod on—even if every farmer could show you the scars that pipelines wrought. This
hiding away of things, dissociating industry and workaday living,
was what they had done in building the bypasses on Highway 85
that looped around small-town Main Streets, skirting Theodore
Roosevelt's plaster-eyed watch. It was all aimed at making western
North Dakota a less dangerous and costly place to produce oil.

So as the ranks of frackers and drillers receded, pipeliners
emerged as the final architects of society. Among them were
the young cousins Raymond Pennington and Steve Bass, who
had traveled from Texas and found themselves in a park of beige
shipping containers called Bakken Acres. The name conjured a
country estate, though the park occupied the same cluster of developments that Doc, my Iraqi acquaintance, compared to Baghdad. Raymond said it reminded him of serving in the armed forces
in Afghanistan. "The rocky parking lot, the Conex containers . . .
if it was a bunch of hajis and soldiers it'd be the same."

The shipping containers were divided into units of two, so
the Texans crammed themselves into a unit the size of a studio
and slept in a bunk bed. Every time they ran the water it stank up
their living quarters—what came out of the tap was so laden with

sulfur that they dared not drink it. Red bumps grew over Raymond's skin when he showered. They paid $800 a month to live here and tried to send most of their earnings home to their kids. "It's a dog-eat-dog world out here," Raymond said. "You've got to fight for your own."

The pipeliners were building lines for a natural gas processing plant just west of the Indian reservation in McKenzie County, eating dirt all day and blowing black mucus out of their nose. Steve was a welder's helper, and Raymond was a swamper for the heavy machinery, ensuring that the rest of the crew didn't accidentally hit an existing pipeline and cause a blowup. He also monitored dozers that cleared the right-of-way so that no dirt fell over the boundary. The right-of-way, or easement, was usually a fifty-foot swath of ground where landowners permitted the pipeliners to work. As landowners became increasingly antagonistic toward pipelines, the right-of-way came to be seen much as the fragile border of a geopolitical dispute. Raymond told me that spilling even a small amount of dirt over the line was something a worker could get fired for; the foreman reminded them every morning to not so much as *walk* off their allotted land.

They whiled away the evenings singing country songs and drinking beer. One Sunday, I listened as Raymond sang his best song while strumming his guitar on the bottom bunk.

> *I'm a pipelining man, and I've traveled this whole land,*
> *Pipe jobs keep me out on the road,*
> *I'm getting paid to pipe black gold,*
> *It's not an easy life, being gone day and night,*
> *But I'm here till I finish the line,*
> *Don't worry baby we'll be fine.*

I was struck by Raymond's melodic tune, even as his cousin made distracting, futile attempts to fix the broken hot plate so they could cook chili. The cousins had bought a cajón, a percussion instrument, in Williston and wanted to record their songs in a studio, or at least find a decent open-mic night around here. They had gone carousing at the American Legion the other night, where McKenzie County GIS coordinator Aaron Chisholm worked on the weekends to help pay off his student loans. There Raymond's little brother made the mistake of flirting with a married woman who already had a boyfriend, and they barely dodged a fight. If it wasn't the men looking to throw a punch at the bars, they feared, it was the women who serially seduced pipeliners because they had money—"line chasers." So they entertained themselves at home, if one could call Bakken Acres that.

The job got rained out the day after Raymond practiced his pipelining blues, and even when the skies cleared they were not permitted to work because of muddy conditions. I accompanied the cousins across the street to a gathering of their fellow workers at a development called Telluride Lodge. They had lived here upon first arriving in the oilfield, but came to fear the gang of drunken welders who roamed the camp looking for a fight. The Telluride pipeliners gathered outside the door of an older, deadpan Texan and joined in cooking a pork roast and sharing cheap beer. They mocked the cousins' shipping container across the highway, where rent was nearly half that of Telluride. "I go there and sleep," Raymond said. "I ain't trying to live like a king." He began singing his pipeline song as his cousin drummed on the cajón. He experimented with some more verses.

"We're going to write music, pipeline for five years, and go to Nashville and get famous," Raymond told everybody.

A cheerful pregnant woman came by to say hello—she was married to a pipeliner—and told me about her struggles to get decent prenatal care in the oilfield. As the afternoon waned, I noticed that a ruffian had wandered over, lingering at the periphery. He got to swapping prison stories with the deadpan Texan. "I stabbed the foreman on my last pipeline job," back in Pennsylvania, he said.

The deadpan Texan said he'd shot a man. "I did four calendar years."

"I just got aggravated assault. I lost one tooth, moved back to Pennsylvania, lost two more teeth in a bar fight. I fought six

Mexicans in Crosby, North Dakota . . . went back to Pennsylvania . . . knocked two more teeth out in a fight . . . fought the Ku Klux Klan one time in Pennsylvania . . . went to prison and ended up with the grand wizard and all that in the same cell block . . . did a year in county, it sucks. Then state. Then in Wyoming, I only did sixty-six days. . . . When I was nineteen I tried—I had a felony already—to go to the army . . . they denied me . . . Who would you rather have on the front line, a pansy?" So he got into the pipelining business, where criminal records were tolerated as long as you weren't a thief. "I mean, I don't look like a criminal, but I am."

"You do," somebody said, snickering.

They began debating where to hold their next gathering.

"We ain't doing it in that box," the deadpan Texan told Raymond and Steve.

And as the ground dried they went back to the right-of-way the next day, working furiously to meet a state-mandated deadline to reduce flaring. The year before, in spring 2014, a hearing to restrict the waste of natural gas spanned more than five hours. Remarking on the twenty-foot flame outside his window, one farmer questioned why they didn't slow drilling. "What is the rush? Unless it is a truly callous and cynical thought that oil and gas might not be so valuable in the future and we need to get our money out now." The industry argued that restricting drilling permits would make oil operations less efficient, increase the costs of operating wells, and discourage outside investment. Midstream companies were already investing billions of dollars in the region. Regulators voted to require the industry to capture 90 percent of the gas from oil wells by 2020, which would necessitate far more pipelines and gas processing plants.

But around the time I met the pipeliners, the industry had come to the North Dakota Industrial Commission to plead for leniency on meeting its first annual benchmark. Not only was the market down, creating unfavorable conditions for such ambitious investments, but companies were drilling more gaseous wells as they moved to the "core" of the Bakken in McKenzie County and the surrounding areas. Oilmen in suits gathered in a small room at the state capitol and stepped forward one by one to make their case that the commission should extend the intermediate deadline to cut back on flaring. Ron Ness, the state's top oil lobbyist, sounded alarms about planning for five years into the future when they had seen such an enormous drop in rigs over the last year. Who could say what the market would do? "This is not west Texas," he told regulators. "This is not a huge market . . . we're going to need help."

The commission voted in favor of the industry's requests. This was a trying time and place to manage North Dakota's surfeit of natural gas. The gas from oil wells here produced more natural gas liquids, or NGLs, than in other shale plays, and required enhanced equipment at gas treatment plants. Workers had to constantly pig the pipelines, or clean them out, in frigid weather. The craggy terrain made it harder to lay the lines through steep hills and valleys, and large rises and falls affected how much gas could be moved. The pipelining business in North Dakota relied more on contractors, like the Texas cousins and their associates, because it was so hard to find qualified pipeliners for the job.

And it simply wasn't possible to put in pipelines everywhere. Around remote oil wells, companies installed gas compression mechanisms and trucked the gas to processing plants, which could be rather uneconomical. XTO Energy, which was owned by ExxonMobil, reported struggling to fit the mobile units in the badlands, where the harsh topography limited the size of oil well pads. It was granted exemptions for more than a hundred oil wells in the first year that the flaring reduction law took effect, largely after a gas processing plant was delayed. Companies told regulators that key plants were held up because of difficulties in securing rights-of-way from landowners, sometimes finding agreements stalled over spans as small as a quarter mile.

A fracking supervisor for a Texas operator put it to me this way: North Dakota landowners were eager for oil companies to drill on their land at first, but then they saw the hassles, and some were starting to hire lawyers and demand more pay. The rich ones were the worst. "They don't want the trucks but they don't want the pipelines—they don't know why they don't want the pipelines!" he said, aghast. Indeed, landowner complaints seemed to stymie the oil industry in every direction. Ron, the oil lobbyist, brought an entourage of industry representatives to the McKenzie County courthouse to meet with commissioners the following month. The meeting was ostensibly about workforce housing, but members of the oil industry began accusing officials of enforcing overly bureaucratic procedures for permitting overland pipes to transport freshwater to the fracks.

"We're taking [hundreds of] trucks off the road for every well, and you're making us jump through extraneous hoops!" a stern-faced oilman said, referring to the very advancements that had cost Danny and so many other truckers their water-hauling jobs over the past year. But local farmers had been complaining of fracking contractors sucking water out of their creeks and dams without state permits. "One hundred percent noncompliance and 100 percent theft," county commissioner Vawnita Best told the oilmen. She wasn't against oil development, but later described the meeting as an ambush by the industry. Locals feared that cattle and various wildlife downstream might not have enough water, especially if a drought came to pass. Some found the pipes leaking water that drowned their crops.

"We're overregulating," complained the stern-faced oilman.

The Northern Plains, historically, had little use for heavy-handed government. The pioneers who migrated there in the late nineteenth century were uncommonly industrious because survival was never guaranteed. The weather was violent; farming cycles were unpredictable. The land was so sparsely populated, especially on the western edge, that there was little to regulate. Lynn Helms, the director of the Department of Mineral Resources, told me after one meeting on flaring that the North Dakota concept of regulation was to give the market time to work. If that couldn't handle the situation, the government would intervene. Even years into the oil rush, regulators tended to wait for unfortunate events and bad press to establish tougher rules. While sitting in on government debates during the boom's wane, I was struck by a sense of missed opportunity. Regulators hadn't come down on flaring until most of the oil development had taken place. That year I attended meetings of tribal members in Mandaree who organized a new government entity to crack down on illegally heavy truckloads and environmental spills, though the worst of the problems had passed. Then there was the meeting I attended at Williston city hall, where they were talking about shuttering the Heartbreakers and Whispers strip clubs. People crammed every row of the council chambers and more stood in the back, as a cop discussed the hundreds of criminal incidents: a man shot and killed, another beaten to death, several officers assaulted after responding to a call at the clubs. The establishments were taking time away from an already busy department. One by one, members of the public stepped up to speak about how the strip joints had once hosted twenty-two-year-olds making six figures who acted like they ran the town. Still, many of the young male troublemakers had gone back south by now—it was late. "In all the years I've been here, three or four years," said one man, "this has been okay and now all of a sudden it's not. . . . Why now? Why not before?"

But sensible government action often takes a while—and a boom, by its very nature, runs as quickly as it can—so I sat in on a series of ill-timed public debates.

"You'll find people that think you can regulate everything," said agriculture commissioner Doug Goehring, who was also a member of the Industrial Commission and had voted for the flaring rules. "Quite frankly, you can't." The commissioner knew that so much pipe had been jammed in the ground that farmers felt bowled over. But he and other state leaders maintained that people were legally permitted to develop their minerals, and that what happened in western North Dakota was merely the trajectory of a free market. The Agriculture Department had begun an ombudsman program that would allow landowners to call with pipeline problems. Only twenty-two people had complained by November 2015, the same month that the commissioner found himself standing before dozens of landowners who had taken an afternoon off from working the fields to report their discontent.

You Chose Oil over Us

S ay your ancestors settled in western North Dakota, fash-
ioning lives from a landscape forsaken by so many others—
forefathers and -mothers who learned to see the grace in rugged
winds and stark skies and solitary terrain. They married and had
children and harvested crops and built churches here, died here,
got buried here, and their progeny and the next generation and the
next did the same, and now it was all yours. You were caring for
the land as the family always had, accepting of the struggles and
grateful that this was forever home. Then they said there was a
lot of oil and the Texan land men came calling. You invited them
in for coffee because that was the polite thing to do, and they just
wanted the right to put a pipeline on your property. You said yes
because you didn't see the harm, and they'd pay you a little for the
trouble. They said the land would return to its old state after the
pipeline went in the ground.

Then you saw the soil slumping. Topsoil misplaced. Vegetation not restored right. Noxious weeds sprouting. They said they'd
fix it. More land men came with more promises, and you believed
them because the North Dakota way was to take a person at his
word. They said they'd pay you more money, but the farm equipment could no longer run over masses of compacted dirt. The land
could no longer grow the same kind of crop. Scars crossed once
unsullied fields, marking the presence of pipelines years after the
disruption. Cattle escaped as surveyors left open the gates. You
were calling some pipeline number every day to get somebody
to help, and they kept transferring you around or ignoring the

messages or sending out more subcontractors, each one shoddier than the last, and then a new round of land men were ringing the bell . . .

"And then you wonder why we're frustrated?" farmer Richard Johnson demanded of the commissioner. He turned toward the rest of the farmers. "We just get so fed—so tired of it!" He suggested having a landowner association negotiate one easement across all their properties, perhaps lessening the individual headaches.

The farmers and ranchers had filed into a civic center in Watford City and filled rows of folding chairs as agriculture commissioner Doug Goehring perched on the back of a seat, dressed in blue jeans and a black blazer. He was skeptical of the suggestion, given North Dakota's strong tradition of personal property rights. If those were infringed upon—well, then he'd really hear the phone ring! He tried to be understanding, he wanted to help, but he didn't know how to please everybody. The commissioner acknowledged that plenty of companies had come along that didn't understand their state's culture, but advised the farmers against threatening land men with hiring an attorney. They should call the state ombudsman's program first to attempt mediation.

"We shouldn't have to babysit you guys. . . . It's a nightmare out there and that's why a lot of us are just fed up," said another. Companies were even careless about leaving their tiny plastic flags in the ground—useful for marking pipelines, but a bane for livestock. One man said he had a picture in his pocket of plastic being pulled out of a dead cow.

Relations grew more embittered given that the pipelines for oil, gas, and brine seemed to snake so erratically. A farmer in a leather jacket wanted to know if it was too late to approve more orderly construction that would lessen the effects on landowners. Regulators planned on building twenty-five hundred miles of gathering pipelines annually until 2020, when the state expected to have a total of thirty-six thousand miles. "You look at that spiderweb that's out there . . . it's going to be worse and worse, and North Dakota dropped the ball at the start of this thing." But the commissioner conceded that it would be difficult to coordinate the building of pipelines, given that antitrust regulations prevented companies from working so closely together.

There in the front row was Kyle Hartel, whose family went back five generations in McKenzie County. "So the phone rings and they want to meet and you want to be Scandinavian and hospitable," he began. It was a plight most people in the room understood. They wanted to try to reach agreements over the kitchen table, and trusted more, perhaps, than they should. Kyle said they'd beg pipeline companies to use a more established corridor on a less sensitive strip of the ranchland, and talks would break down as officials accused them of being poor compromisers. But the Hartels had not asked for any of this development.

Here was the crux of everything: the clash of North Dakotan tendencies with the culture of Texans and other outsiders who controlled the pipelines. It almost seemed as if the South had colonized them, bringing a brash way of doing business that just didn't sit well. "Quite frankly," the commissioner said, "if you look at . . . our culture, we're trusting. We're hospitable, we're humble . . . and that's looked at as a weakness. People take advantage of that. . . . We become cynical and skeptical, and that's unfortunate."

·:·　·:·　·:·

The dirt road to the Hartel ranch curved past a billboard promoting the new Buffalo Hills subdivision, then rose over a hillside that sloped down and left behind the shops and highway and advertisements as it approached a verdant idyll. An early pioneer in McKenzie County built a log cabin here in the late 1800s, hauling the wood up a hill with a horse and wagon. More settlers arrived and a town grew around it. They built a stone jail nearby. Its most notorious prisoner was a man who killed six members of the Haven family, who'd hired him as a farmhand. In 1931 a mob broke in, strung a noose around the murderer's neck, and hanged him off a bridge over Cherry Creek in what was known as the state's last lynching. The Hartels moved onto the land following the Great Depression.

Kyle's father had struggled as a dairy farmer and began building houses and barns for extra money. His mother worked part-time as a church secretary and sold homemade pies. The Hartels were broke, like a lot of their neighbors, but theirs was a life of honest contentment. Kyle and his siblings would clean out the parlor where dozens of cows were milked morning and evening, bottle-feed the calves, lay out the feed and hay, build fences, help neighbors run cows through the chutes, and tend to sick animals. Fun was pheasant hunting and fishing in the creek—bullheads, junk fish, nothing to keep. Their world was small: school, church, neighbors. By the time Kyle finished high school in the 1980s, the Hartels had switched to ranching beef cattle. They weaned the calves from their mothers in the fall and took them to the stockyard, where buyers transported them to large feedlots and sent them for slaughter.

Kyle moved away in the late eighties, like a lot of the younger generation. His job with the US Department of Agriculture took him all over the state, but Kyle and his wife ultimately decided the ranch would be the best place to raise their children. His elders had fought so dearly for this land, losing cattle to the droughts, surviving blizzards, and negotiating with bankers—it would always be in the family. "You've got this piece of property that's all you identify with," he said. "It defines who you are." The oil boom arrived a few years later. The Hartels did not own minerals, but God blessed them with abundant water. One of the largest freshwater springs in McKenzie County flowed near the historic jail on their land. They piped a portion to the feedlots to keep the cattle from the creek bottom, as too many animals there would erode the soils.

Oil companies, of course, were desperate for water, relying on millions of gallons to frack a well. The Hartels tore down the rotting one-room schoolhouse that Kyle's father had attended—it had been empty for decades—to build a freshwater depot. They installed two tanks that could store forty thousand and twenty thousand barrels of water—Poseidon tanks, as everyone in the oilfield called them, even after the Calgary company that made them went belly-up and a former North Dakota executive settled securities fraud charges. In any case, the Hartels' water depot could load six semis at a time. What the ranch didn't use went to the water depot, and if the water depot was full it went back to the creek, and thus the water never stopped flowing.

In the early days, the ranchers served land men coffee and arranged business deals with handshakes. The Hartels didn't mind the first pipeline transporting natural gas—they figured they might as well profit off what the company paid for the right-of-way. The compensation per rod (sixteen and a half feet) was modest in these parts at first, perhaps $50. But the land men could be rude. A land man once approached Kyle's father and, when he didn't immediately sign papers for a pipeline easement, threatened him with eminent domain.

At first neighbors didn't ask one another about the sums they received. But as more pipelines went in, stories of their trouble quietly spread. The land men would ask the Hartels if they had heard about all the trucking accidents, all but suggesting that their reticence to allow pipelines had caused the record increase in traffic deaths. "We've got to make our roads safer," Kyle would reply, "but you can't put that on us." The price advanced to $350 a rod, as ranchers jacked up their rates to offset the cost of poor pipeline management—and, if they were being honest, to retaliate. Make them pay. But Kyle's family hadn't grown up with money—what was the point of getting any now?

So they had at least a half dozen oil and gas pipelines running beneath their land. Their holdings had become rather valuable, being near Watford City in the fastest-growing rural county in America. But the Hartels rejected the offers of purchase. Kyle had talked to just about every sizable landowner in McKenzie County as a district conservationist for the USDA, and he was starting to feel more like a counselor than anything else. At least a quarter of them, by his estimate, would never allow a pipeline on their land again. The stresses some farmers bore made them ill. A neighbor had accidentally ridden a horse into a hole created by a pipeline and now could hardly get around anymore. Some were all but ready to take shotguns to ward off further intrusions.

Kyle and I drove one morning into the family's pastures, past the pipeline sticks poking out like lawn ornaments. Northern mallards waddled in Cherry Creek, filling up on corn before their southern migration. He rounded the curve and waited for a cow to retreat, then kept on a few hundred feet until the field's dips and peaks came into view, dancing away from us beyond the creek. We walked down the creek bank. Kyle and I looked upon a hillside beset by a wide scar. Now a broad swath of cropland had such compacted soil that it would hurt their yields for years to come. You could usually tell where a pipeline had gone in because that strip of grass was a discolored green or brown.

Then another pipeline was proposed. His father relented, after some hesitation. The laborers were to come over the slope and bore under the creek to the other side, leaving the banks unmarred. The crew agreed to move their equipment over the crossing the Hartels had made especially for the pipeliners. But when Kyle and his father came by later, they saw the workers had bulldozed straight through the creek, opening scars and disrupting the soil. The Hartels were shocked.

The culprit was a subcontractor of Kinder Morgan, based in Texas and the largest pipeline company in North America. The next day Kyle's father came out and saw they had dozed the creek banks down and put in their own bridge. It seemed as though he had talked to them ten times—what were they *doing*? It would devastate the bank in the spring, leading to years of erosion. After the snow melted, he anticipated the bank would collapse. "They got greedy and just kept cutting," Kyle said.

We stood on a mat of grass tinged with beige, slate, and purple. In the other direction lay cropland that they hadn't tilled in twenty years. Pipelining crews worked on a faraway hillside. The neighbors' pump jacks nodded in the distance. Then: the sight of a flare. It was baffling. We were standing above a labyrinth of pipelines and they were still burning off natural gas? But Kyle reminded me that the oil companies didn't work in concert, so a line would go to one well and not another nearby.

We walked over to the group of men huddled in the morning chill: Kyle's father, whose name was LeMoine Hartel, along with a land man and a representative from Kinder Morgan. LeMoine wanted to take somebody in his ATV and show them what the land looked like a little ways up, where laborers had poorly seeded the grass and made big gouges in the topsoil. As for the creek, he wanted them to fix the crossing. "Kinder Morgan just pushed it in the [water]," he told them.

"It's all 'We're going to do this, going to do this, going to do this,' and none of it gets done," said LeMoine. He would pass his message on to the land man, who passed it on to Kinder Morgan, who passed it on to a contractor, who passed it on to a subcontractor, who told some third-party inspector . . . Kyle told the pipeline representatives that quality was disappearing in the chain of subcontractors.

The man from Kinder Morgan nodded. "I'm not going to lie—we get a contractor that goes rogue every once in a while."

We walked to the four-wheeler, the stiff, dry grass crunching under our boots. I climbed in with the man from Kinder Morgan, and LeMoine assumed the wheel. We rode a little way through the field and then the wheels began struggling over a swath of chunky dirt. We stepped out and LeMoine pointed.

"They seeded this grass and you can see the dirt . . . this stuff down that hill is going to go on deep," he said. "In my field, they leave cracks like this, these are rocks. You get ridges like this in my field. It should be smooth. . . . I ain't going to run equipment on this. When you seed and hay, I come across with a mower conditioner and baler."

We got back into the ATV. "We don't mind it if people do it right," he said of pipelines. LeMoine paused so the pipeline official could step out to pick up a fallen yellow flag. We drove further and stopped again, as the official plucked another. We returned to where we'd left and LeMoine found a third flag in the grass and handed it to someone. "I got a whole pile of 'em," he said.

The land man told them once the water receded they would come out again and check the condition of the creek.

"What ticked me off more than anything is somebody says, 'Yes, we'll do it right now,' and they lie to you right in the face and don't mean it," LeMoine said, but he agreed they could visit the creek again in the spring. "I think for the hassle I'll want $5,000."

"I passed that on to the guys with the checkbook," said the man from Kinder Morgan.

"*And I don't negotiate,*" LeMoine added quickly. His face was stern.

The land man told me that when contractors ruined the property, it was far more difficult for land men to obtain rights-of-way the next time they came to make a deal. He was on the landowners' side, but a lot was beyond his control.

As Kyle and I walked back to the truck, he told me his father was usually a laid-back fellow, but he had grown tired of the damage. LeMoine came and sat with us for a while. He explained it wasn't only the work that he had put into the ranch, or his boys. It was the labor of his elders. His great-grandfather had come from Norway to homestead in Iowa before moving west. Over the years, the family had raised cows, chickens, and pigs, and sold cream and eggs. LeMoine's only time away was being stationed with the army in Taiwan and going back to Iowa to work for an electronics company for a few years. Once the oil came he didn't go to town much to catch up with the other farmers the way he used to, and when he did, the landowners talked about pipelines the way they used to talk about the weather.

The Hartels were skeptical of the state's response. The agriculture commissioner hadn't told them anything new, and they wouldn't trust anybody, much less a government program, to look out for their land better than they would. "That's just a PR thing," LeMoine said. "Now the TV will show it; it'll be in the newspaper."

⊹ ⊹ ⊹

On Halloween 2015, shortly before I met the Hartels, I went to a house party near downtown Williston with a few thirtysomething professionals. I didn't have time to come up with a clever costume, so I wore jeans, steel-toed boots, a DRILL, BABY, DRILL T-shirt from the Wild Bison truck stop, and a Halliburton hard hat. As I walked into the kitchen where everyone was drinking beer, a young man thrust a clipboard and pen into my hands.

I looked down at a piece of notebook paper that said, "Petition to save the planet from the badness of fracking and stuff," and looked back up quizzically, wondering why he would give this to someone dressed as a Halliburton worker. Then I realized—it was his costume. He was dressed as an anti-fracking activist, one of those liberal, coastal, out-of-touch environmentalists. Those types were so unheard of in western North Dakota that the costume was intended as an ironic joke. He offered the clipboard to everyone who walked into the kitchen, to see who fell for it. One woman said she tried to avoid "those people" before someone clued her in on the ruse. "Think about the grandchildren, at least," the man quipped. "At least I'll be rich by then!" somebody crowed. If you were in the oilfield long enough, absorbing those attitudes was inevitable. After the Obama administration rejected the Keystone XL oil pipeline around this time, my first instinct upon watching a video of protesters was to roll my eyes. *Those people!*

So the complaints of Kyle and many other North Dakotans didn't come from the perspective of a liberal environmentalist; their position was far more nuanced. Indeed, Kyle had me assure him during our first meeting that I didn't have an anti-fracking agenda (I didn't). It would financially ruin him to be associated with a book like that, given all his family's work supplying freshwater for oil companies. This dichotomy was apparent when I was sitting with him later and he fielded a call about supplying freshwater to XTO Energy, which was owned by ExxonMobil, for a frack job.

The Hartels wanted to put some of the profits from the water depot into their longtime Wesleyan church, which was overflowing from new arrivals because of the oil. Kyle's wife, Kela, headed the women's outreach program and had befriended a lot of the younger stay-at-home mothers who were eager to meet people. They dreamed of making it a church that served the community seven days a week, with Wi-Fi, a coffee shop, a fireplace, and a playground set. He wanted to create a man cave for the single men in town, some alternative to the bars. The church sought to be more modern to appeal to the new young families, jettisoning the organ in favor of a band. Kyle missed the old ways but wanted to expand the church's reach. "We believe the government should take care of basic human rights. The church should take care of the rest."

We went to the ranch for lunch after one Sunday service. Fourteen Hartels lived in four houses spread over the land, and the meal was served at the home of Kyle's parents. His mother, Clarice, was delighted that the grandchildren had come over to set up the Christmas tree with golden lights and hang the wreaths and snowman decorations. Stockings lined the corner mantle. The window looked out onto slopes, sparse trees, and hay bales dusted with snow, a rig far afield. In the Norwegian tradition, the Hartels took their coffee black. I mentioned that I had recently been to a social gathering where an official with Statoil, the Norwegian-owned oil giant, questioned the farmers' criticisms of pipelines. "They're getting paid!" said the official, confounded.

"That right there!" Kyle said. "That's precisely our point." It dismayed him—this idea that everything was okay as long as you wrote a check. The farmers' soul was their land, and they weren't going to sell their soul.

And what of the place they would leave for their descendants?

You may recall my discussion of fatherhood in the oilfield often being reduced to a check, and I should say that there was a broader symbolism to all of this, given that America's fracking boom spurred so many debates about social responsibility. I was amused to come across a blog post on the liberal *Daily Kos* website that compared the fracking industry to irresponsible fathers after oil companies denied culpability for their role in the earthquakes shaking Oklahoma and elsewhere. These quakes appeared to stem from the underground injection of saltwater, the unwanted by-product of oil production. Texas activist Sharon Wilson claimed that the industry was narrowly defining fracking to mean only the time they sent their fluids down-hole but not after they pulled out—dodging responsibility for all the attendant problems. "This industry is like deadbeat dads who, in this case, inject toxic fluids into a hole in the ground and walk away from responsibility for the consequences," Wilson wrote. "The public end up paying."

The Hartels wouldn't have shared this activist's anti-fracking beliefs, but I found the metaphor to have some resonance when contemplating attitudes toward the land. A segment of outsiders had come to North Dakota to plunge things into Mother Earth for their own benefit, then take off and leave others to deal with the consequences. Some figured they could pay their way out of it; others just split.

Kyle's son worked at a nearby natural gas processing plant owned by Oneok Inc., a major midstream company from Oklahoma, so the Hartel family was invested in the industry. They just wanted it to work the way it should. Their grievances were so strong that Kyle had voted for the agriculture commissioner's opponent in last year's election. The candidate, Ryan Taylor, was known for his signature white cowboy hat and newspaper column called "Cowboy Logic" and campaigned on stronger protections for landowners in oil country. Kyle was thoroughly conservative but felt the state's Republicans had been too friendly to the petroleum industry, so he did the unthinkable: vote for a Democrat. The cowboy sage lost to the commissioner, who was flush with contributions from oil companies.

Even so, there was a growing sense that minerals were a volatile means of wealth and that agriculture was enduring. This tension harkened to the days of John Sutter, whose discovery of gold in 1848 unleashed the California Gold Rush. But the pioneer claimed prospecting for gold was a lottery after he went broke in the end. "Most people prefer a safe investment; farming is the best of all," Sutter concluded.

"They'll ride this oil for another few years and they'll come back and kiss the farmers' butts," said Kyle. "They'll come back to a very jilted ex-girlfriend, and we'll say, 'You chose oil over us and you can't make amends so quickly.'"

Exodus

*A*round the time I moved into my basement room near Walmart, I read a story about a glamorous open house to be hosted by Eagle Crest Apartments. The complex boasted high ceilings, bay windows, and luxury living on the west end of Williston, perched on a slight hill overlooking a long ribbon of green punctuated with pump jacks. Guests would enjoy free burgers, a jazz quartet was flying in from Seattle, and visitors could win a trip to a lodge in Wyoming and a golf outing at The Links in Williston. The developers were still cheery about the real estate market. "We've gone from white to merely red hot," one of the principals, John Sessions, told the *Williston Herald*.

So I drove over on a Sunday afternoon and saw a hubbub of families wandering around a lawn with barbecue areas, picnic tables, and a playground. The façade was slate blue, white, and brick. The lobby of Eagle Crest featured a painting of three boats on a lake as the sun set. A genial Seattle resident with a trim gray beard, John brimmed with enthusiasm as we talked in the clubhouse. Every entrepreneur seemed to remember that moment that convinced him to invest in the Bakken. John recalled fist-bumping his business partner in triumph as they sat in the left lane from West Dakota Parkway to Route 2—waiting three stoplight cycles to turn because the roads were so crammed with fortune-seekers.

Building their dream was less inspiring. Construction took one and a half times as long as scheduled. Skilled subcontractors were difficult to find, and many made larger commitments than they could fill, finagling multiple jobs at once. He used bonds underwritten by Wall Street to fund the next project, a 160-acre development called Hawkeye Village. The underwriter attended a VIP thank-you that John had recently organized. After a few drinks, the underwriter said, "You know, we got this done with about two days to spare." Oil prices had been on the cusp of plunging, which would have deterred bond buyers. John fielded calls from investors soon enough, however—largely New Yorkers and Floridians—who saw TV reports about oil workers losing their jobs and panicked. "Oh my God, my bonds!" they'd exclaim, and John would reassure them to think about the long game. Nobody knew then how deep the slump would become, and at first he said 2015 would be a prime year to catch up on a backlog of building projects—channeling the old frontier optimism.

A *Williston Herald* reporter stepped into the clubhouse to inquire about the rental market. John noted that companies were dropping housing allowances for oil workers and pressing them to live in the region full-time. "By the time all the dominoes fall, it could be a good thing for an apartment project," he told her. Some of the early apartments were simply for people who needed a bed, but developers were adding game rooms, parks, and fitness centers to suit a growing influx of families. The new developments were scattered everywhere, from downtown to the college, north of Walmart, and all through Harvest Hills and behind the new Menards. At one mass of new homes, rectangles of siding had already blown off to reveal HomeGuard Housewrap, as though puzzle pieces had gone missing. Those wide streets with their charming names—Sleepy Ridge Avenue!—and plastic orange fencing and heaps of dirt and wood frames waiting for windows . . . They were building, building, all of it planned several years earlier, and by the time they got their permits and financing and construction, the market was taking a wild turn. Builders included high rents in their pro forma documents—not solely out of greed, as their critics accused them, but because it was an expensive place to buy land, hire laborers, and transport materials. The dwindling market was forcing them to drop prices a little, but not nearly enough to account for people's swooning fortunes.

Three months later, I was driving in that direction, near the apartment I had lived in for a month the previous summer. I passed a yellow sign that read MOVING SALE and followed the directions to a beige townhouse. A man in sunglasses was leaning against the side of the house with his arms crossed. He had little good to say about how everyone had gouged the newcomers. The locals had been hostile to change and mismanaged development. "Their greed is biting them real hard," he said bitterly.

Greed—a word everybody used all the time. The old mayor who presided over most of the boom, Ward Koeser, later told me his biggest disappointment was the greed that overcame too many people. He was a free enterprise type, but even he was troubled by the exorbitant rents, though he noted that state laws forbade rent control.

"It's an exodus," said the man's brother-in-law, who was overseeing the garage sale. The offerings included one FR jacket, two raincoats, three pairs of steel-toed boots, and eleven pairs of FR jeans. He turned to a customer walking up the driveway. "Ten bucks for the FRs . . . 30-inch waist and you have to fix the legs." The brother-in-law turned back to us. "They blew it," he said of Williston. He'd come after the short sale of their house in California, where he'd struggled to compete against undocumented immigrants as a house painter. But his wife disliked the Bakken, and they finally had enough money to return home. North Dakota hadn't made it comfortable for them; why should they be loyal? "You can't fix something when there's an exodus."

∴   ∴   ∴

"All the money we made out here plus the money I've saved and what he has saved is gone—everything's gone, you know?" Cindy had never been homeless before, and the realization jarred her to tears as her long black hair tumbled over her face. We sat on church pews in the Salvation Army as her boyfriend, Johnny, lamented the state of the oilfield with another man. "We just kept getting false hopes . . . but there's been layoffs and layoffs," Johnny told him.

Cindy used to run a Mexican restaurant and boutique in Idaho and traveled to North Dakota for better prospects. She considered it too expensive to start another here, but found work as a sous chef making $18 an hour with a free room and meals at a man camp. And then, love. Cindy met Johnny at a wedding reception at the Midway bar, where he had come to drop off his brother to play blackjack. He hadn't had a drink since 1989 ("I was a bad boy," as he put it), but they enjoyed themselves. The man camps forbade tenants from having guests, so Cindy would sneak Johnny in through the side door where there were no security cameras—a common practice for staff and their paramours.

Then the camp closed down. Cindy went to cook at the Ramada Inn, but lost that job as the economic decline deepened. Johnny skipped between trucking jobs as bosses promised hours that never materialized. Then he thought he'd landed a promising one. It came with a two-bedroom apartment for $2,700 a month at Dakota Ridge, a new complex developed by a Colorado outfit a little north of Love's truck stop. The buildings were tan and slate blue with balconies, and there was a dog park. Cindy and Johnny thought the place was beautiful, and it was so full that they could scarcely find a parking spot. But when work slowed, the company fired Johnny, telling him he had forty-eight hours to vacate.

For much of the oil boom there were too many jobs and not enough places to live, so firms gave their employees housing because it was difficult to keep them without it. Now there were too many apartments and not enough jobs. People were losing their jobs and homes all at once and were being forced onto the streets as the war with OPEC raged.

Cindy and Johnny scouted for places to park their Dodge Ram at night: Walmart? The truck stop? They settled on the lot behind the Atco man camp. It had no lights, shielding them from the scrutiny of drivers on the highway. Their savings dwindling, Cindy and Johnny soon walked into the Salvation Army for help. It was known for giving out one-way bus tickets to stragglers who showed up during the oil boom and found it was not the mecca of wealth they had seen on TV. As the industry faltered, the charity gave away more tickets than ever, along with housing and gas vouchers. The Salvation Army covered Cindy and Johnny's stay in various hotels, then put them in an empty man camp in eastern Montana.

The couple arrived to find a grouping of trailers so filthy they were unlivable, so they washed sheets, made beds, cleaned rugs and toilets, and mopped the floor. The owner was somewhere in Nevada. Guests came sporadically, sometimes prompting the furious barks of their pet Yorkie. Once the couple heard a commotion and found a stranger from Virginia wandering the hallway. The owner's nephew and his friends, fresh out of high school, showed up from Idaho thinking they'd get oil jobs; they left after a few weeks, cursing the uncle's exaggerations. Cindy and Johnny hoped to leave soon. A senior apartment complex had tentatively approved them—they were in their fifties—and Johnny had a promising job lead with a trucking company hauling dirt and gravel. Man camp cooking jobs had dwindled, but a woman offered Cindy a temporary gig bartending at the seventy-fifth anniversary of the Sturgis motorcycle rally, coming up later that summer.

Curious to see their new home, I accompanied them on their ride back to Montana. Signs adorned the roadside:

MAN CAVE BASEMENT!

MINUTES FROM WILLISTON . . . A WORLD APART! HOME/LAND PACKAGES

FROM $255,900

AFFORDABLE ACREAGE

LOTS AVAILABLE

ROLLING HILLS SUBDIVISION

Near the border, we came upon the sign erected by the owner of their man camp proposing a 150-acre development. We followed a dirt road south until it abruptly curved to the right and ended before a cluster of white trailers with blue trim. The rooms were furnished as sparely as hospital wards. We sat at the kitchen table, where I picked up a *Williston Herald* that was a few days old. A front-page story chronicled the controversy among McKenzie County commissioners about approving oil storage tanks for the Dakota Access Pipeline.

The twelve-hundred-mile pipeline from North Dakota to Illinois was a remarkable innovation that would make the Bakken a more efficient place to do business and prevent dangerous oil train explosions. But the project had already stirred resentment among landowners fatigued from the mishandlings of the smaller gathering pipelines. "They came in like the schoolyard bully and they learned this isn't Texas," farmer Lynn Hovde told me—the same fellow who'd presided over the hearing on the encampment by the McKenzie County landfill. The Hartel family, for their part, had been fiercely negotiating that year with the Texas company's pipeline representatives, dismayed at yet another intrusion on their property.

But Johnny was quick to remark that the pipeline would bring in the high-paying jobs they needed. Everybody was desperate for jobs, perhaps even more desperate than before because they knew what prosperity tasted like and had seen it abruptly taken from them. Union pipeline laborers were coming to community meetings in bright orange shirts, handing out burgers and sodas on the lawn to foster goodwill.

The three of us rooted around in the refrigerator, and I asked if they had anything to eat with the fried chicken.

"I've got chili beans," said Cindy, "I have chicken salad, I have pudding, I have—"

"Strawberry shortcake," Johnny interjected.

We ate, and they retired to their room to nap. I walked outside, stepped over a collapsing wire fence, and began approaching two pump jacks on a hill gilding the horizon. I came upon a ribbon of water and walked along it a quarter mile until I found a crossing. I felt a chill looking around and hurried back when lightning flashed. It was all eerily remote, but then again, there was a lot of empty space, meaning there were a lot of places to squat undisturbed. A mud contractor on Nevin's rig told me that when the oilfield went south he knew a man who swiped a hotel house-keeper's key card and bounced from room to room. Then he took refuge at a site where they stored rig trailers.

Cindy and I watched TV while Johnny cooked barbecue chicken and spare ribs. Sometime after six we gathered in the kitchen, holding hands as Johnny said grace. We ate heaps of dinner rolls, green beans, and potatoes. Then Johnny began telling oilfield stories. His trucking company used to house its workers in trailers by the shops, but after Williston outlawed the practice he had to move into a house with four stinking men. One young roughneck would come home covered in filth and crawl straight into bed without a shower. "You could wring oil out of his sheets," said Johnny. "It was all over the wall where he rubbed his head." The man spent much of his money on prostitutes. One night, he raced upstairs to ask Johnny for Viagra. Johnny was horrified.

"Well, you're old," the roughneck retorted.

"I should have gone down there and showed him how to do it," Johnny told us.

The next morning, I awoke to the bounty of the Montana sun and a startling quietude. Johnny and Cindy reflected over breakfast on their hopes that the oilfield would have been their chance to make it later in life. Cindy still held warm memories of watching Fourth of July fireworks with the man camp tenants and sharing camaraderie with the kitchen staff. They wanted so dearly to stay. . . .

Months later, the same company hired to move the parts of the stacking Patterson rig began taking apart Cindy's old man camp. Troy Bakken, the rig-moving official I'd met in Nevin's trailer, showed me around the empty halls. He worked for Black Gold, a company that had a man camp next door and made a bid to move the trailers to their own site because they had to be worth something. The owners had taken off and left everything inside—TVs, beds, microwaves. I thought of Cindy and called to tell her about what I'd seen, but she and Johnny had given up on North Dakota and were back in Idaho.

Mark Twain wrote of the California Gold Rush in *Roughing It*, his account of traveling the West in the 1860s. His exaggerated musings on that society's fall were suffused with the dead ends of defeat that echoed in a later century. "And where are they now?" Twain asked of the old fortune-seekers. "Scattered to the ends of the earth—or prematurely aged and decrepit—or shot or stabbed in street affrays—or dead of disappointed hopes and broken hearts—all gone, or nearly all—victims devoted upon the altar of the golden calf—the noblest holocaust that ever wafted its sacrificial incense heavenward."

Twain described the disfigured remnants of old gold mining towns where not a soul breathed, where the houses and shops had vanished, where the laughter and swearing and music went silent. "In no other land, in modern times, have towns so absolutely died and disappeared, as in the old milling regions of California," he wrote.

I did not foresee the same fate for North Dakota's oilfield towns. Unlike California, North Dakota hadn't been *settled* by its boomtowners; the region had a populace long before they came. Many of the old-timers were still here. Schools burst with the enrollment of more permanent newcomers, and hospitals recorded increasing numbers of births. Oil companies were continuing to drill and frack wells at lower and lower costs. The oil was still in the ground and the industry knew how to get it—money in the bank, as some put it. So the word "bust" did not seem especially apt.

But the hype had deflated.

We were hurtling through a wild market correction, and the psychological affront was almost as dark as the losses of jobs and people. To accept it: North Dakota was no longer an unstoppable engine of prosperity. To admit it: our boundless optimism had shrunk to a square of reality, with all its hindrances and indignities and mundane excuses. A surplus of buildings remained, testaments to the grand civilization that we always believed this place would become—that perhaps it might be still. As oil prices kept sliding, apartment owners grew desperate for tenants. They lobbied to oust man camps, their cheaply built competitors.

I wrote earlier about an industrial encampment by the landfill forty minutes south of Williston, in McKenzie County, which was notorious for its madcap zoning. These are not the sorts of living quarters I am describing in Williston. The largest man camp Williston was moving to outlaw was an early landmark when travelers approached the oilfield from the northeast. Walk into the main building, the Bear Paw Lodge, and you'd find a half dozen mud rooms for workers to remove dirty work boots and hang FR coveralls before washing up in deep sinks. Narrow hallways opened to dormitory-style rooms, each with twin beds, desk, microwave, and TV. The rec room had foosball and pool tables. Posters whimsically promoted the lodge's offerings:

AFTER A SHIFT AT THE WELL, OUR SAUNA'S SURE SWELL.

AFTER YOUR FRACKIN', COME ON IN AND RACK 'EM

Workers' long, irregular hours prompted Bear Paw Lodge and its counterparts to act as hotels, with regular housekeeping. Big employers like Halliburton assigned workers there under lengthy contracts, preferring to house them all in one complex with strict rules: no visitors unless authorized by management, and no drinking, pets, violence, gambling, guns, or dirty boots. Bear Paw Lodge, part of a broader complex of a thousand beds, was owned by Target Logistics, a Boston company that billed itself as the largest provider of remote workforce housing in the nation. Drive west into Williston and one of the parade of billboards touted HOME FOR YOUR WORKFORCE IN 9 BAKKEN LOCATIONS.

"We're housing one percent of the state of North Dakota," the chief executive boasted at the height of the boom. The company maintained the bulk of its operations in the Bakken, even after adding man camps in Texas. But local leaders assured investors that the man camps were a temporary solution to a severe shortage of housing, that as soon as they built enough apartments they'd phase out the trailers. As the rest of the country emerged shaken from the housing bust, western North Dakota went on a house- and apartment-building spree, the sort of chaotic, terrifying frenzy of bricks and Tyvek wrap and plywood and granite that suggested a bubble was inevitable. And it was all the more absurd because it was the real estate crisis that had sent so many broke, desperate people to the oilfield in the first place.

By fall 2015, Williston city hall moved to oust the man camps. It was one of those rare times that city leaders stood up to the oil industry, which had erstwhile played the benevolent colonizer. The city argued that man camps, unlike the hotels and apartments, had always known they were temporary operations. The industry's main oil lobbyist, Ron Ness, continued backing Target Logistics, concerned about workers being forced into hotels and apartments that did not align with the rotational nature of many jobs. The company launched an offensive. During a government meeting in Watford City, I heard Ron advocate for the company to be allowed to remain in North Dakota, and later I mentioned it to Williston's former economic development chief, Tom Rolfstad, as we ate lunch at Sakura Japanese Steakhouse.

"I know the guy with Target—he's worked Ron," said Tom, taking a sip of his tea. He told me that Brian Lash, the former chief executive of Target Logistics, had called him a couple of weeks earlier asking if he would be their lobbyist to keep the man camps in Williston. "He's working everybody," Tom quickly added. The executive, he said, had met with the *Williston Herald*, too.

Tom said he didn't want to get in the middle of the debate, but he would come out in favor of the apartment constituency months later. He had been "Mr. Williston" for years, traveling across the country to convince people to do business there, going on TV, and meeting Wall Street types, and the time had come to back up the apartment developers.

The general push to oust man camps in a shaky economy also meant that investors in the Great American Lodge scheme were even less likely to recoup their money: the following year, a receiver in the case notified financiers that the Securities and Exchange Commission had hoped to sell the properties that had already been built as a going concern, but the need for such housing had "drastically declined" and local governments were now resisting such facilities. Even if the British developers hadn't been accused of running a Ponzi scheme, their investors would likely have faced losses soon enough.

·⫶·   ·⫶·   ·⫶·

"Do you think we overbuilt?"

I posed this question to Travis Kelly, a vice president of Target Logistics, as we reflected on the debate in a conference room at the Bear Paw Lodge.

He paused, then said, "I think at this point in time it's fairly obvious there was some overbuilding that happened here." Travis sighed. "I honestly don't know how you wouldn't overbuild. I don't know how anybody would know when to stop until it was almost too late." Travis believed that man camps could help mitigate the overbuilding and high housing costs. Perhaps the debate would have been more evenhanded if it hadn't unfolded against crashing oil prices. Developers' anxieties were tipping into desperation. He admitted he was nervous about next week's meeting before the city commissioners.

That Tuesday evening, people crowded into all eleven rows in the Williston City Council chambers and stood in a line out the door. Seattle developer John Sessions stepped up to speak. He was far more circumspect than he'd been when we spoke that spring day at the open house for Eagle Crest Apartments. John said that when he and his business partner financed Eagle Crest two years earlier with the city's help, they assumed a two-bedroom, two-bath apartment would rent for $2,700 a month. They had since dropped the price to $1,500. Current rental rates required almost full occupancy to pay debt and operating expenses, but the average occupancy among the apartment builders he knew was less than two-thirds. "This is not what the investment community expected," he told officials.

The sole female commissioner suggested that too many developers came in hopes of making a quick return on their investments. John paused. His financing was written over more than two decades. Of course they expected supply and demand to rise and fall. But he'd assumed units would lease out far more quickly.

Travis stepped up. He began to argue that the government should listen to the voices that had built the community—those of the energy industry. He'd rather the government simply raise standards for the type of man camps it allowed, instead of banning them altogether. The company feared losing the trust of longtime clients and claimed its reputation would suffer.

A representative of the Confluence Apartments read a statement from the chairman that he had been assured by the last mayor and several other municipal officials that the man camp permits would not be renewed. "My point is," the man from Confluence continued, "to some degree this debate here tonight is a debate between short-term interests and long-term interests."

Halliburton was the biggest employer in the Williston area. Over the last decade, the global oil services firm had invested $450 million in Williston's infrastructure, including fifty homes, forty-eight townhomes, and two apartment complexes. Halliburton had encouraged its employees to move to North Dakota, but that wasn't to say that it wanted the higher-end camps to go. "You're going to lead sheep to the slaughter if you close the man camps," a manager from Halliburton told the commissioners. "Give it enough time—the market plays itself out." I found this curious, having heard several city officials and Ron, the oil lobbyist, recount how Halliburton CEO David Lesar had urged them many years before to get rid of man camps; I imagine that the oil industry nevertheless saw a distinction between high-quality operators like Target Logistics and slipshod trailer parks.

I sat down with Williston mayor Howard Klug later to understand why he was sticking so strongly to his position. "The thing that I've said and that I'll always say is I don't want a temporary town," he said. The mayor wanted companies to train employees who lived in North Dakota. This struck me as grandiose given the historic collapse in the oil markets—indeed, the cyclical nature of the industry itself. By late that year, a city survey of apartment buildings found they were two-thirds full and that rents had dropped by nearly half. Apartment owners gathered privately to discuss their future at Renaissance Heights, a luxury complex that featured an indoor swimming pool and spa. Somebody on staff told me it was at 48 percent occupancy at the time, on the market for scarcely a year.

The new generation of apartments was embodied in Prairie Pines, with an exterior of decorative rocks, a beige and green color scheme, tidy balconies, and furnished one-bedroom units that went for $1,200. The building was two-thirds full. The first-floor common area featured a dining table decorated with a centerpiece of glass cylinders filled with pinecones, framed photos of farming country and dramatic sunsets, orange couches with checkered pillows, and granite countertops—a modern, trendy place.

"If you had the option, why wouldn't you want to live in that?" asked a representative of Greystar, the large property management company that oversaw Prairie Pines and many of the area's new developments. We walked across the snowy grime to his car and began driving around. "They all look sort of similar," he noted, and it was true that everything had a pleasantly generic facade. We stopped at Vue 28, where one-bedrooms were going for a thousand dollars. The entryway was decorated with Christmas lights draped among five pictures on the wall, each depicting different sections of the building: Pikes, Teton, Kilimanjaro, Rushmore, and Everest. Large corporate leases were dwindling, and oil workers were increasingly expected to find housing on their own. The best apartment complexes had to compete ferociously for tenants. One developer put it to me in three words: "Things matter now." A year or two earlier, even the most slapdash lodgings had had more interest from residents than they could accommodate. Today apartment complexes had to be run like a proper business. Some developers began giving away a free month's rent to anyone who signed a lease and agreeing to shorter terms. Even so, researchers at North Dakota State University found that 80 percent of out-of-state oil workers didn't want to move here permanently, concerned that housing was too expensive or that if they purchased a home the value would later drop.

As the city proceeded with closing the man camps, Target Logistics sued. The company said such a move would hand the apartment owners an unearned windfall in pumped-up, unearned market share. Developers wrote letters of alarm to city hall. Dakota Ridge, where Cindy and Johnny had been forced out after a layoff, told the city that apartment owners couldn't pay their mortgages. Another developer from Minneapolis complained it had had to readjust the terms of bank loans after achieving an occupancy rate of less than one-third. "We know what happened to many cities in the most recent real estate bubble . . . what Williston is about to go through will be ten times worse."

The region, yet again, was confronting the reality of a so-called free market. During boom times, landowners and investors jacked up rents to rival those in New York and San Francisco, forcing elderly residents out of Williston. When occupancies and rental prices were still very high in 2014, the editorial page of *The Forum* of Fargo-Moorhead wrote that players in this market couldn't justify hiding behind the amorality of the free market, or excuse the harm they had caused in gouging oilfield residents. Didn't they have an obligation to uphold the high ethical standards that had set North Dakota apart for generations? Two years later, the newspaper's editorial page crowed at the hypocrisy of Williston leaders' "rescue mission" for apartment developers. "If they worshipped the free market when times were good," *The Forum* wrote, "they should not throw their religion under the bus when times are bad." During these debates, I often drove up a hill off West Dakota Parkway past the new Menard's, a major construction store that had been in the works for years. It had been held up in part over concerns about how to find enough people to work the lower-paid retail jobs, and finally opened just as the construction boom was waning. The new road beyond it continued all the way across the fields to the lavish, just-opening apartments on the west side of town—an artery allowing residents to reach their destinations more quickly by circumventing the crowded main roads. It was all so impressive, and in many ways too late, but this was the way of a frontier that had always fought time.

Bile of the Subterranean

The oil barrel counter on Danny's semi stopped working. He was loading crude on that dangerous site where the tanks were nearly overflowing, and he figured he could wing it by counting the time. But six gallons of crude spilled out of the vent pipe onto the ground. It was common for truckers to have little spills, and Danny's boss always told the drivers they wouldn't be fired as long as they reported their errors. Danny reported the spill. The boss fired him.

Companies scrambled for any reason to dismiss workers as the market plummeted. They began testing people's hair for drug use and raided oil workers' lodgings for illicit alcohol (tipping off favored employees ahead of time, of course). One of the unlucky roughnecks came crawling to the truck wash next to the Wild Bison for a job, felled by his beer cans. A roughneck reduced to power-washing semis was one of the biggest indignities to be suffered. "If you're not on your game at all times they'll cut you loose," an oil worker told me. "You blink your eye the wrong way, you're gone."

So Danny began trucking saltwater. Oil flowing from the earth produced the unwanted by-product of brine trapped in geological formations, and the rows of tanks on oil sites had at least one designated for wastewater. Trucks picked up the fluids to transport them to saltwater disposals. "All the BS they're putting in that frack-hole . . . that's being puked out from the earth," he said. "They shove it into a tank and I go get it." This was a common sentiment that was somewhat misleading, since saltwater flowed out of all oil wells, not simply those that were hydraulically fractured. But the ones that had been fracked produced wastewater mixed with extra chemicals, metals, and toxic additives. I often heard workers describe it as earthen vomit. How strange it was to Danny to have spent most of his life in saltwater and then haul waste labeled with this absurd euphemism. "Saltwater," as though it were almost natural.

Much later, Danny laughed when I told him that Lynn Helms, the director of the Department of Mineral Resources, used a surfing metaphor to describe the oil downturn. He had told reporters that you had to take a longboard and balance perfectly. "That allows you to hang ten. And that really looks like what the [oil] industry is doing right now." "That's ridiculous," Danny said. "Surfing is the farthest thing from the oilfield you can get. Hang ten? Give me a break, man." As a Christian, he saw the spirit of the Lord in the ocean and the devil in the oilfield, and little was viler to him than the brine in his truck. Danny took a job on the night shift but nearly drove into a ditch his first time because he struggled to stay awake after dark. He found another saltwater-hauling job, but it was cheaper these days to leave the oil in the ground and there was less of the attendant saltwater to transport.

He considered hauling crude in Saskatchewan and got a proposition to truck grain to California. But nothing came of any of it, and he was losing his will to try. Danny began hanging around more at the Pilot truck stop north of Williston. It was a few miles from the biggest saltwater spill in Bakken history, and one of the largest environmental disasters of America's modern fracking boom. The trouble began around the time I met Danny, in summer 2014, as laborers rushed to install a four-inch pipeline from forty-four oil wells to two saltwater disposals. Oil production had just hit a record million barrels a day and the industry was working fast, as usual, to keep up.

∴ ∴ ∴

The chocolate chip cookies were almost done when Joanne Njos heard a rap at the door. A stranger stood in the snow, saying something about a pipeline. She told him to talk to her husband, Larry, in the shop. "I don't want my cookies to burn," she said.

A saltwater pipeline had breached just west of the creek, they said. The owner swiftly shut the system down, but there was no telling how long it had been seeping into the soil and the waterway. Laborers excavated the earth until the pipe emerged, revealing a two-inch hole ringed with sediment. The brine had flowed north and east through a low-lying area and run all the way to the Missouri River, as oil leaked over a slate of ice and stained the vegetation. Parts of the waterway had turned a thick rusty maroon, as though the ground beneath it had bled. As the sky darkened, hordes of men arrived in her yard to trawl the banks of Blacktail Creek. They began pumping out the toxic liquids as the winds blew up to thirty miles an hour. Days flowed into nights that flowed into weeks.

So that's why the creek had not fully frozen that fall. The Njos family had wondered about the scum percolating for months. Joanne told their four grandchildren visiting for Christmas not to ice-skate or even touch the water. "Something's wrong with the creek," she said. Blacktail Creek! That stream of water rushing through the farm was the joy of Joanne's life, and the rhythms of the creek wove themselves into her family's traditions so deeply that they were like an heirloom shared between generations. In the summers she and her grandchildren walked the banks looking for the turtles and carp as the dogs paddled away. They watched for the frogs and muskrats and beavers. They squeezed into canoes and floated down, picking off the bloodsuckers. The children threw sticks and watched them float downstream. The family sat by the fire in the yard those evenings, dwelling in the comfort that the creek was in the distance. When the creek froze, it was narrow and shallow and perfect for sledding. They would ice-skate and return to the farmhouse, huddling around the pellet stove to drink hot chocolate and laugh about who had fallen down. They listened to the bursts of cascading water when the ice melted. That was the sound she forever treasured, the sound she would long for when everything died.

An inspector for the pipeline owner, Summit Midstream Partners, discovered the spill while on foot in January 2015, even though the Texas company's last flyover inspection had revealed nothing amiss a week earlier. The initial assessment was underwhelming: "Some saltwater entered the Blacktail Creek," a state health inspector reported after visiting the site. Crews worked fervently to stop the brine and residual oil from escaping further down the creek.

Workers tested chloride levels and set out devices in the soil to create electrical currents that attracted salt, enhancing the recovery of contaminants. They built an underground barrier to stem the migration of groundwater tainted with chloride. Along the creek, crews stationed floating, absorbent barriers to stem the spread of oil. That January was unseasonably warm, and the ice was too thin to cross. Mild temperatures increased the water in the creeks, overtopping the underflow dams. They hauled away truckloads of ice, but what to do about the rest? They tried unsuccessfully to remove some of it with hand mops. At other points, the absorbent barriers froze into the creek and had to be reset after breaking up the ice. As the snow melted, oil was released from the icy vegetation by the banks.

Responders soon discovered the magnitude of the spill was far greater than they expected. It was the most massive spill the oilfield had ever seen: *three million gallons.*

So there the pollution leached, more than a dozen miles north of Williston at the turnoff on Highway 85 that began the hourlong journey to the Canadian border. They pumped four million gallons of freshwater, brine, and oil in the first few weeks alone. By August, Summit said it had set up seventy interceptor trenches and sumps along the creek to capture contaminated fluids and provide hydraulic control to protect the creek and waterways downstream. Workers noticed that in their rush to pump up wastewater from the trenches, they were taking away too much freshwater, and so they switched to pumping lower levels over a longer period. In just those seven months, Summit erected an eight-hundred-foot-long hydraulic control wall with a series of extraction wells to isolate tainted groundwater. It put in twenty-four monitoring wells and thirteen piezometers to better understand the hydrology of the groundwater. Summit also installed a handful of dams to raise the level of the creek so that it flowed into the ground, in an effort to prevent the saltwater in the soils from leaching into the waterway. The pipeline company claimed there would be no long-term effects to public health or wildlife.

Joanne listened for the sound of melting water rushing down the creek as the seasons changed, but it never came. All she heard was the blare of fifty or sixty semis driving over the yard seeded with winter wheat, and the whir of super-suckers vacuuming waste. "The *noise* of the creek!" she said. "And this summer . . . it was all dried up. . . . The creek was dead."

Summit initially estimated that the pipeline had been leaking for only two weeks. But a state regulatory investigation found that brine had been seeping out for more than three months, as nobody noticed that the disposals were taking in far less saltwater than what the wells would have been sending out. Struggling with a shortage of pipeline inspectors, the state hadn't even inspected the pipeline when it went in the ground. The company had installed a remote, real-time monitoring system but hadn't turned it on, according to Lynn Helms, director of the Department of Mineral Resources. Summit instead relied on visual inspections, sending people out to the pipeline to read meters. The state required the firm to use the more sophisticated system when the pipeline resumed service.

I was surprised that the disaster didn't draw more detailed coverage from the national media, given that it was one of the largest onshore pipeline spills in American history. Searching the archives of the *New York Times*, I only found several briefs from the Associated Press. Had the Blacktail Creek catastrophe eluded broader attention because we often think of oil when we talk about pipeline breaches? Large saltwater spills were a relatively recent phenomenon, following the surge in domestic oil production over the last decade. Saltwater scorched the ground, so nothing would grow again. Near the Wild Bison truck stop, crews were still cleaning up a million-gallon brine pipeline spill from a decade earlier. Saltwater was the bane of the industry. Companies had to pay to transport it, but unlike crude or natural gas, it was pure refuse.

Lawmakers approved stricter pipeline monitoring and inspection requirements and set aside $1.5 million for researchers at North Dakota State University to examine pipeline spills. The university's study concluded that such leaks tended to be discovered by people who stumbled upon them rather than by high-tech detection systems. Researchers ascertained that operators of saltwater disposals connected to the Blacktail Creek spill weren't aware of the flow in the pipeline, while operators of the pipeline weren't aware of how much fluid came into the disposal. This helped explain why the leak lasted so long.

When should the government punish those responsible for such disasters, and how? What role should regulators take? North Dakotans, most of them wary of such intrusion, were finally confronting these questions, sometimes finding themselves in contradictory territory. When I asked agriculture commissioner Doug Goehring if the oilfield was sufficiently regulated, he said it was. After the pipeline spill of 840,000 gallons of oil on a wheat field several years before, he objected to the press fixating on how large the fine should be—the wrong question, according to the commissioner. He believed that too often politicians tried to appease the public by approving a big fine instead of really trying to correct the problem.

Farmer Ron Sylte lived a few miles south of Joanne. The brine had spilled on his land, too, though it was far enough from his residence that he had not suffered as considerably as the Njos family. We sat in his kitchen, which offered a view of the road spanning miles, the lights of the Pilot truck stop shining near the horizon—lonely iridescence in the wintry gray. Ron said he'd heard the mess cost $40 million to clean up that first year (the company didn't answer my questions on this matter). He was normally loath to suggest bureaucratic interference, but the spill prompted conflicted feelings. "I don't agree with more government regulations, but . . . somebody's got to be held responsible for this."

The Njoses' land had been in the family for nearly seventy years, and Joanne and Larry had been husband and wife for more than half that time. They anticipated their final decades of enjoying the land with their children and grandchildren in retirement. But it would not be so. The pipeline could not unburst. Joanne feared their heirs could never treasure the land as she and her family had. It was as though their own property no longer belonged to them. State regulators proposed fining Summit $2.4 million, though at the time they often reduced penalties by 90 percent. Joanne didn't like to cause a fuss, but she was so upset that she sat down to type out a letter to the governor, pleading with him to enforce the full penalty. When I saw her, she wasn't sure if she would send it. In that letter Joanne wrote that their life had become a nightmare. "This spill has invaded our lives to the point we can no longer enjoy life. . . . We cannot use our land the way it was supposed to be, it has all been taken away from us."

Joanne was reluctant to speak with a reporter because she didn't want to publicly criticize the pipeline company or draw extra attention. Nearly a year after the spill, we climbed into a four-wheeler and drove out onto the snow, passing a wood shop fringed with icicles. She showed me where the creek was still running, a tiny sliver through grass several feet tall. Chloride-pumping equipment was stationed at sporadic intervals.

That winter, her grandchildren looked up to where she kept the decorations and said, "Grandma, there's your Christmas decorations up there." But Joanne couldn't bring herself to put up a tree; there was nothing to celebrate. They attended Christmas Eve services at the Lutheran church down the road, and they went caroling, but there was no joy in their hearts. December 25 came and it was not Christmas. Every time Joanne looked out the window above the kitchen sink, the mess was always there. Her family could find no respite from monitoring the remediation, the emails, the calls.

"The trust that we had with the state to make our water safe is broken," she said.

Joanne depended on the Lord to carry them through this. She only wanted a sign to make sense of their loss, but there was none she could find. "And for some *reason*, some *odd* reason," she said, her voice rising, "the spill happened kind of where the church is . . . So you tell me *why* it flowed down here and it stopped and it just contaminated our land." She ruminated over this, reaching for an answer that never came. "What plan does God have for us?"

The following month, 7,584 gallons of brine spilled from a new breach in the same pipeline, a mile and a half north of the first leak.

Despite the mess at Blacktail Creek, the industry was still installing saltwater pipelines across the oilfield. Danny had less and less cargo to haul, as trucks were being displaced. He caught a break when one of the pipelines failed a pressure test and they called in an army of semis to deliver the saltwater to disposals. But that job just lasted a few days. As the Njos family pondered their future and another wave of toxins spread over the glacial fields, Danny found himself in the vise of a vengeful winter.

Frigid Despair

*B*y Christmas night, a lamina of ice spanned the road that ran east of Love's truck stop and abruptly twisted north, rolling past the farms and a frack and a frozen lake—no lights, of course, and the sky and the ice were the same shade of black. It was a few degrees below zero. I was searching for Danny, shot up with dread as the car slid an inch this way and the next. He said he was at some oil wells down an embankment to the left, and finally I made out the lights of his semi. Where to park? I eased down the hill and stopped somewhere in the snow. A slate of white ran from my car to the truck for a hundred yards. I didn't want to get out. I didn't want to walk across the snow through that craw of dark. I called Danny, asking if he would come so I wouldn't have to do it alone. He refused. It was too cold. I gathered my laptop and bag and hurried to the semi, frightened by the rumbling of the engine and growl of the flare. I was too afraid to confront that sinister luster of gas in the distance—couldn't so much as look at it—just pulled open the passenger's door and fell over my heap of belongings, relieved to escape the apparitions of night. I scrambled upright and pulled the door closed, squinting into the truck's dim interior. Danny was on page 221 of the mystery novel *Bad Luck and Trouble*. "I almost died this week," was the first thing he said.

The fuel line had frozen, necessitating a call to the mechanic. The only thing that saved him during the long wait in those sub-zero temperatures was a phone signal, which one could never take for granted in western North Dakota. Then he was hauling a massively overweight load late at night, as desperate for money as he was, going over a bridge where heavy trucks were prohibited. A cop made him back up. The officer looked at his bulging tires and said, "I know you're heavy. If I weigh you right now you're going to jail!" But he showed Danny a route around and let him go.

It was a struggle to keep the truck warm, and he relied on thick blankets and thermal underwear, breathing in dry, stale air. He'd wear the same dirty clothes; Danny didn't have the will to take them to the Laundromat in this weather. That afternoon, his boss took him and three other truckers to Sakura Japanese Steakhouse for Christmas dinner, a gift on top of their promised $1,000 holiday bonus. He was waiting this evening for the saltwater in the tank to rise high enough for him to pull a load to take to the disposal. *Bad Luck and Trouble* was part of the series about Jack Reacher, an ex-military man who defies danger as he wanders America meting out justice. Danny felt the books conveyed what it was to be tough and lonely in a way that few other writings could match. He had been on this latest job for one week and was miserable. I confessed that I, too, felt battered by North Dakota, desperate to get out.

Hearing the drag in my voice, Danny suggested that I had done as well as I could have during my time as a journalist in the oilfield. "You could be doing meth," he said. "You could hook yourself out for extra money, making $200 an hour—not that you would, but these are things that people with a lesser mind would do. You've interviewed them. . . . You're going to places that are scaring you. I made you walk across the ice because I wanted you to conquer your fear." He asked if I was sure I wanted to come to the disposal. "Anything could happen along the way at these temperatures. *Anything.*"

Finally, at 9:37 p.m., the load of production water was ready to pull. He put on his black and white plaid flannel FR jacket and his white hard hat and stepped out of the Peterbilt, letting in a wicked blast of air. He dreaded the smell of the saltwater. "Nasty, stinky shit." We drove off the site twenty minutes later, jerking unevenly over the bed of snow. He sped up when approaching the slope on the way out, knowing he would stall if he moved with any hesitation. Danny turned onto the narrow road. The lights shined far away from some blot of a town called Epping, home to a large oil loading terminal, and I counted three flares ahead—no, four—all too distant to guide our path. It had recently made the news as the site of a crime that was vicious even by oilfield standards: a man hit a woman with a car jack and another man sexually assaulted her on a dirt road in below-zero temperatures.

Danny turned on the radio. Queen. He jacked up the volume. *I just gotta get out of this prison cell, someday I'm gonna be free, Lord!*

The oilfield itself had become a prison cell from which there seemed no escape. I wanted to bang down the truck doors, but there was nowhere to run; I wanted to bang down Williston and that basement room across from Walmart. But we cruised along wordlessly as the music crashed against the walls of the truck.

The music faded.

Danny cranked the brakes.

He warned that we would move to a dirt road soon. Then he swung left, and we rumbled over deeper ruts, rolling down a hill and struggling up again. We crossed railroad tracks. A semi approached from the opposite direction. Danny shielded the side of his face with his hand. The headlights blinded him; then it was the cloud of snow lingering after the semi blew past. He pulled the Jake brake hard and the truck pitched back and forth.

It must have been midnight when I drove home on a snake of black ice. Danny crashed into an electrical pole four hours later. He saw too late that he would miss a left turn and curved his truck a few miles an hour faster than he should have. Danny scrambled to the floor as the pole snapped and crashed onto the hood, taking out some of the lights and shooting sparks. The pole felt flimsy, but it made a large dent. For weeks afterward, he turned over the memory of it every time he drove. Hitting that pole, calling 911, waiting. His biggest pride had been writing "None" on that line in trucking job applications that asked how many accidents and tickets he had. Now he was tainted by error.

The boss had just repaired the truck and was angry that he'd have to fix it again. He revoked Danny's Christmas bonus and assigned him the worst semi in the fleet. It was old, with faulty brakes. Work over the next three weeks was dangerous and sporadic. Dispatch sent them to unload from saltwater tanks over several icy hills and down a ravine. He ramped up the RPMs, accelerated to third gear, locked the wheels, but let up for a moment and slid backward. Somehow he regained control. But the water in the radiator couldn't stay warm. He knew if the truck broke down he could die.

"Look," he said when I met him at the Pilot truck stop just north of Williston. "I'm not doing well right now spiritually, mentally. I'm very unstable. I'm on my last legs. . . . I'm up here all alone. My wife is [far away]. I can't speak to my kid. Can I have made any more of a mess of my life?" The truck stop sign loomed across the snowy grime of the pavement.

PILOT TRAVEL CENTER

SUBWAY

UNLEADED 1.93

#2 DIESEL 2.15

The other night the company had sent three trucks to a tank that had just four feet of water in it; that wasn't even enough for *one* truck to haul. So he was risking his life for nothing. *If you don't have work, leave me alone,* he thought. This demotion truck didn't even have a passenger's seat, and it was filthy, cold, and wet. His feet were freezing. "They put in the pipelines and the trucks are done. I can feel it. I can see it. That was the plan all along." All he looked forward to these days was sleeping. God was fading. Even the spiritual self-help books didn't have answers anymore. A man at the Tiger Discount Truck Stop off Interstate 94 had told him the other day that we were all on the back side of life at fifty, a threshold Danny had recently crossed, and he turned this over and again in his head until he was convinced that by this age you'd either taken the chances you had in life or screwed them up, and you would get no more, and he had no more, and there was nothing left for him. A series of blue frack tanks had been dumped just north of the Pilot, reminders of the prosperous days he longed for. I told him to call me any time of day or night if he ran into trouble—I'd pick him up or find help—but as I lay awake at night, staring nervously at my phone, it never rang. The oilfield was a slowly deadening grind for many workers—lives yielded to that great master unseen, the laborers' accounts blurring like phantoms of dust and fog. *Four o'clock in the morning when you're sixty feet in the air in the man basket and the horizontal rain's coming and that North Dakota wind hits you to the side and you think,* I'm glad it's not snow this time . . . *You fall, you're dead. If that well blows up, you're dead, or relatively dismembered. I get a lot of family saying, "You make good money." You don't do what I do. You don't sacrifice what I sacrifice.*

Those voices played as I lay in that basement room near Walmart, checking the price of oil on my phone—was it still low, or had it gone even lower?—and turning up *The Big Bang Theory*, not to watch but as a reliable droning over the *hawk-hawk-hawk* of diesel pickups outside the window. Feeling aloneness warp the heart—seeing so many dreams forsaken, the shadows that disillusions cast. One Saturday afternoon I walked out the back of my house and saw that police cars had the neighbor's place surrounded. A cop was leading a man out in handcuffs. "Everybody get the hell out!" the officer said as he herded a handful of other men through a side door. They'd come to arrest a man from Washington State on warrants for drug and theft charges, and while searching his room they found meth, prescription pills, and the keys to a stolen pickup that was parked outside. Cops also spied a box by the front door with cylinders wrapped in electrical tape and what appeared to be wires coming out. Police feared he was trying to build a bomb with fireworks and smoke grenades.

As a mass of law enforcement cars blocked the street off all afternoon, I found some of the inhabitants of the house being investigated down the street at Champs Place, in a squat building that advertised CASINO LIQUOR. One of the dispossessed tenants was still sitting in his plaid bathrobe and flip-flops; he and a housemate had been running up a bar tab on credit because the police hadn't given them time to grab their wallets. The housemate was a brickmason from Florida, James Williams, who had repeatedly pleaded with me to wash the exterior of my sea-green Toyota—it had turned an odd shade after all the time driving dirt roads to the rigs—but I didn't wash anything, or fix the cracked windshield, or replace the fallen-off hubcaps, because of course it was only a matter of time before the vehicle would revert back to the old state on these roads. I interviewed them, filed a short dispatch for the *Williston Herald*, and bought their next round. "The amount of police—it would make you think somebody got shot or killed," said James, as Metallica blasted from the jukebox.

So many lives gone to foul ends. I thought about a few of the oil workers I had met: one was back on drugs, one had gone to prison for theft and forgery, and one had left a note on my windshield trying to lure me to the Wild Bison—it was so frightening that I reported him to the police. Another, Cali, hadn't answered my last few texts, and I saw that his Facebook page had been deactivated, so I Googled him and found his mug shot in a recent police brief in the *Williston Herald*. Arrested for gross sexual imposition a month after I'd interviewed him on a run to deliver sand to a frack in his semi. The prosecutor dropped the charges the following year, but I always remembered seeing the usually cheerful Cali dragging through the Cenex gas station in Watford City to meet me at a booth and explain, his face grayed in shame. "My life's in ruins," he said, looking out into the murk of evening, though he insisted he was innocent. I stared across the fluorescent expanse of that gas station as *Law and Order* played on TV, racked by the same unease as when I had glimpsed those filter socks sunning on the cement. Decay, all around us. I ran into former pastor Jay Reinke over dollar beers at Williston Brewing Company and recounted this episode, unsure of what to think. Jay had worked with men who had backgrounds that much of society considered unforgivable, and he reminded me that a person was more than the emblem of some horrible allegation. I was coming to accept that disappointment was an invariable thread of the Bakken story.

Through all of these trials, Danny conducted himself with as much honor as he could manage. He went back to an old employer that assigned him to pull saltwater from Continental Resources' oil wells. It was one of the best jobs in the oilfield in those days, a steady seventy hours a week. The company furnished him with an apartment in the eastern oilfield community of Stanley. His new home was serviceable and generic, like the old place on the Canadian border, but I have already shared my theory that there is comfort in the generic. Beige carpet, black chairs and couch, a dining room table with mats that had pictures of pears and apples and grapes. Outside, a banner blared: RENT THE BIGGEST UNITS! NEW SPACIOUS TWO/THREE/FOUR BEDROOMS READY EXTENDED TWO-CAR GARAGES/CALL NOW.

Danny began attending a men's church group, where they abided by the Proverbs verse "As iron sharpens iron, so one man sharpens another." His chest pains were returning, even if he wasn't hauling oil anymore. Saltwater carried a tinge of oil and similar chemical fumes. The company sent him and the others to a standard oil safety training course, and Danny heard the instructor go beyond the usual warnings of hydrogen sulfide to talk about the dangers of benzene as a carcinogen. But he accepted that danger was the fate he had assigned himself. His old friends from the Outer Banks had gotten out a long time ago; many southerners slunk home at the first snowfall. He had outlasted nearly everybody he knew.

The ice thawed. Danny moved to a safer truck. He began to harbor a delicate optimism, dedicating the forty-five-minute wait for the saltwater to load on each trip toward self-improvement. He put himself on a rigorous reading schedule. Danny read *Confessions of an Economic Hitman* ("shocking but true," he concluded); *The Intelligent Investor*, the 1949 classic written by the man who mentored Warren Buffett; and *Crazy Love: Overwhelmed by a Relentless God*. He timed his books to accommodate his mental state, reading more intellectual works in the morning, when his mind was fresh, and moving to Western and mystery novels as the day wore on and he grew tired. So in this way he was a cog in the operations of Continental Resources, a pioneer of the Bakken's oil development. The company's chief executive, Harold Hamm, remained bullish about North Dakota's future. He was coming from Oklahoma City to the biannual petroleum conference in Bismarck to cheer the prospects for oil in these difficult times and introduce a man he believed would lead—no, *return!*—America and the fossil fuel industry to greatness.

That man was Donald J. Trump.

This Is Your Treasure

I left North Dakota a few days after that meeting with Danny at the Pilot, where he bid me goodbye with an air of hopelessness before resuming his nap in the semi—four in the afternoon and there was nothing to do but sleep. It was January 2016, and my departure had been planned long in advance, but world events made this timing fortuitous. Oil prices fell below $27 a barrel to a thirteen-year low. Two happenings in the oilfield seemed a more symbolic denouement of an era.

The Williston Brewing Company had quietly raised the price of beers back to the usual amount, in what I took as a sign of surrender. Owner Marcus Jundt concluded that Williston had too many restaurants, too many gas stations, too many hotels, too many apartment buildings: "It's overbuilt." He had loved being a part of a historic oil rush, but wasn't sure his financial returns had justified the risk. "I am married to Williston. . . . I can't pick up my buildings and leave. I wish I could but I can't," he said.

Then Williston moved to ban the town's two strip clubs, Heartbreakers and Whispers, from operating downtown over concerns that they had had too many police calls over the years. People crowded city hall for a hearing, much as they had done over the debate about shuttering man camps. A man in a Harley-Davidson cap rose to address the commissioners. I recognized him as a fellow I'd interviewed more than three years earlier, during my first visit to the oilfield. At the time, he'd said his wife had run off with one of the out-of-state oil workers she'd met at DK's Lounge & Casino, somebody who told her she was the most beautiful woman

302

he had ever seen. Now the man in the Harley-Davidson cap urged officials to look at police calls to DK's if they were so concerned about safety. But the commissioners had made up their minds, and ousting adult entertainment sent the message they wanted: the wild times were over.

There were a couple of ways out of the oilfield, and mine was going east on Interstate 94 all afternoon, passing towers of pipes stacked by the highway in preparation for building the Dakota Access Pipeline. Take Exit 351 to downtown Fargo: six hours from the oilfield and across the state, another world away. I usually stopped there for the night on the way back to Minneapolis. I went to my usual Howard Johnson but found it closed down, the furniture in disarray, and was struck with the sense that a great deal of time must have passed. I drove a few more miles down Broadway to the Hotel Donaldson, drooping with exhaustion, and walked into the café downstairs. All the people, their chatter—it seemed as though I was looking at them through a window. The lights and the colors seemed too bright, and I found myself grasping for that old oilfield palette: the neon of a truck stop sign, the burnt-orange of a scoria tract with beige and olive tanks, the lusterless array of trailers and tanks and chain-link and junk. I used to think I was back in the *real world* by the time I reached Fargo, but it struck me that the Bakken was more real than any place I'd been. The mirage was everywhere else.

I returned twice more that spring. Thousands came to the Bismarck Civic Center, three hours southeast of the oilfield's core, to attend the industry's annual petroleum conference. The laborers' union that would be building Dakota Access hung up a bright orange tent and cooked burgers and handed out drinks from coolers. Inside, the mood was surprisingly hopeful as a parade of oil leaders took the stage. The American shale industry had refused to surrender in this standoff with OPEC, learning to produce oil at far, far lower costs, and nowhere had the war been harder fought than North Dakota.

"One of my favorite themes is to connect rednecks and roughnecks, so I often use the NASCAR theme to describe what you're going through," began Lynn Helms, the director of the Department of Mineral Resources. As pictures of race cars beamed from the screens on either side of him, he explained it like this: Take a five-speed shifter and replace the gears in the transmission with oil prices and you get a sense of what happened in the industry. Producers were stuck in neutral as oil prices fell, and at the beginning of the year, when they hit their lowest point, the race car shifted into reverse. He toggled between two screens showing the placement of drilling rigs before the oil crash and after. The latter had a lot of white space.

"That's a NASCAR wreck by anybody's stretch of the imagination," said Lynn. But now, he believed, the race car had shifted into neutral, and a big flag signaled a restart. Crews were recovering more oil from the wells. Rigs had grown more efficient. Flaring was down. Lately the oil industry worried about how to win back its workforce, given that so many employees had lost confidence that it was a place to make a lucrative, stable career. "They packed their bags and many of them have gone home," he said. The industry foresaw sixty-five thousand wells that needed to be drilled in the coming decades, and we had developed only a fifth of that so far. "It is a long, long time before we get the checkered flag." Months later, the US Geological Survey announced that the largest continuous oil deposit it had ever assessed was in west Texas. Known as the Wolfcamp shale, it was three times the size of the Bakken.

⋮ ⋮ ⋮

It was about the time that Nevin told me the rig was going to stack that I noticed talk of the presidential campaign blaring on Fox News in his trailer. A Republican candidate debate had come on as we talked about drilling. While I religiously followed the moves of OPEC on my phone, sporadic bits of Fox News in a rig trailer were just about the only glimpse of national news I got during my time in the Bakken. Nevin told me he favored Ben Carson at the time. "I don't care if it's a female president, I don't care if it's a black president . . . get in there and fix something." But one political truism held: everybody disliked Obama. I even visited one rig (not Nevin's) where they had toilet paper adorned with Obama's face. People in North Dakota didn't believe he supported the oil industry or appreciated the sacrifices they were making out here.

Back in Minneapolis, I had several occasions to cover rallies by Bernie Sanders, and it was jarring to listen to populist left-wing rhetoric after spending so much time in a free-market world. Fifteen-dollar minimum wage—we had that through the private sector in the Bakken. Eliminating college debt—the Bakken allowed young people with no college education to excel in high-paying careers and others with college loans to pay them off. An end to mass incarceration—the oilfield had given new chances to ex-cons. Rebuilding the middle class—it had employed thousands of struggling people. But this grand experiment in curing America's ills with private enterprise had lost much of its grandeur, the future still so deeply uncertain.

So I was eager to hear what Donald Trump would say, not least because on one early reporting excursion, well before his presidential run, I wrote in my notebook that the workers here were making America great again. The day after Lynn's speech at the oil conference in Bismarck, thousands of people waited hours to get into the stadium where the Republican candidate was scheduled to speak. They bought boxes of popcorn and donned red hats that said MAKE THE BAKKEN GREAT AGAIN. Continental Resources CEO Harold Hamm took the stage around two in the afternoon. The audience applauded when he mentioned Trump. "And North Dakota just put him over the edge!" More cheering and whistling. He wished he could report that oil prices were better than $50 a barrel, but that was not so bad, either. "It's going back, folks! It's going back!" He said Trump had asked him about the energy renaissance in North Dakota the first time they met. "And I kept telling him about the giant field that we had . . . and what it could do to power America back to greatness."

Minutes later, the crowd jumped to its feet. "Trump! Trump! Trump! Trump! Trump! Trump!" The candidate, in a dark suit, walked up the steps and into the glare of the light. He was everything the Bakken story embodied: a master of media hype, champion of deregulation, alleged con artist, condemner of fake news, declarer of bankruptcy, promoter of the disillusioned white middle American, symbol of male dominance, outcast, capitalist, avower of made-in-America glory, friend of Big Oil, teacher of get-rich-quick schemes, hustler, underdog, straight talker, the answer.

"North Dakota brought us over the line, folks!" Trump praised North Dakota for showing how energy exploration creates shared prosperity. "You've had a downturn but we did hit $50 today. I will take credit for that! Harold, I want 10 percent—at *least* 10 percent! . . . We will accomplish a complete American energy independence—complete!" The crowd roared. "Imagine a world in which our foes and the oil cartels can no longer use energy as a weapon!"

Trump claimed that Obama had done everything he could to keep us dependent on others. He had rejected the Keystone Pipeline. Every move Obama made blocked production of oil and gas; bureaucrats controlled the industry. "No way. No way. These actions have denied millions of Americans access to the energy sitting right under our feet that we didn't even know we had five years ago and ten years ago. This is your treasure! You, the American people, are entitled to share in the riches!" Obama had weakened national security by keeping us reliant on foreign energy. "Not going to be for long, folks! Not going to be for long! . . . America first, folks! America first! Make America great again!"

It was a confounding speech, given that the world was awash in oil and that the industry's downturn stemmed from producing *too* much of it. Still, Trump vowed to repeal policies that restricted energy production. "We're going to keep our jobs here and we're going to bring jobs back," he said. The oil and gas industry would create a resurgence in American manufacturing with millions of high-paying jobs. *"Manufacturing!"* He dragged out the word. Everywhere he went, he saw collapsing towns that had once been vibrant with factories. "We're going to put America back to work!" Some leaders of the Three Affiliated Tribes, who sat in the front row, were miffed that Trump had rejected an invitation to meet with them or even acknowledge their role in producing the Bakken's oil. But tribal oil executive Dave Williams was excited, at least, that he'd gotten to network with executives from Whiting Petroleum and Hess at the conference. The day before Trump's speech, someone had come up to the Missouri River Resources booth to ask if they were drilling more wells. "Hell yeah!" Dave told him. "Oh, hell yeah!" The tribal government would approve another loan for the project.

·:· ·:· ·:·

Gregg Thompson predicted the oilfield towns would become full "when all the coastal cities are destroyed in a Trump-driven nuclear war and the survivors have to migrate to middle America!" Months after the "Fracking Hell" episode of *Underworld, Inc.* aired, an image of Gregg dressed in a furry hat and sunglasses, hugging a cat, appeared in a series of photos about North Dakota on Slate.com. He was pleased that the caption referred to him as a YouTube celebrity. "If you've been called a YouTube celebrity by Slate.com," Gregg said, "it's official." Yet being a video star was not especially lucrative, and Gregg wished he could have his old job back at Walmart. He had gone back to work at the sign shop in Olympia, Washington, but was laid off again, and his sex offender status made it difficult to find work a decade after leaving prison. He enrolled in Medicaid and contemplated whether he would have to scrape out a life on the streets. Soon Gregg found a job working at a recreational pot producer (marijuana was legal in Washington State).

Danny was desperate to see Trump elected—a man who spoke a language that he could understand, a president who would revive the oil industry (by the following year, Trump's second-highest approval ratings would be in North Dakota). He would go on to have his most successful year in North Dakota, making $100,000 transporting saltwater from oil wells. Danny attributed this to the industry's move from the frenzy of boom to bust to normal. Businesses had to be run well these days. He was saving and investing much of his income, as he had set out to do, and if he wasn't entirely happy, he was at least living with faith and purpose. Danny had come here as exactly the sort of freewheeling southerner whom the northerners despised, and as the years passed he evolved into just the sort of transplant the oilfield coveted: a disciplined professional whose wife had finally joined him. The couple even signed an apartment lease at the Bluffs of Williston, a higher-end development whose owners from Minneapolis had seen occupancy improve after being forced to renegotiate their bank loans during the worst of the slump.

The tattooed biker who'd talked Danny into coming here all those years earlier called him up from North Carolina—he'd long since flamed out of the oilfield—asking if it was worth returning to the Bakken. But Danny dissuaded him. "It's just North Dakota now," he said. No longer a destination for fly-by-night schemes. Back in the oilfield, everyone was abuzz over the Dakota Access Pipeline: the final crown of this civilization that had risen so defiantly from the cinders of the frontier, advancing rod by rod, mile by mile, to carry the fruits of its production to the rest of the nation. "The more low-key they can keep everything, the easier we can sneak it through," a pipeliner at a bar in Watford City told me, taking a hit of apple-flavored Skoal. The pipeliner, from Pennsylvania, had just been working to clear the right-of-way over a twenty-mile stretch in Mandaree on the Indian reservation.

They had been cutting the farmers' fences and laying out mats over the wetlands so they could run the equipment through swamps and streams. He had been excited to work out of the badlands, and I became intrigued when he mentioned a place by the War Pony scoria pit. I remembered driving there the summer before with the tribal ranch manager, Ted Siers, when he was in talks with the pipeline company. The setting was so pristine that it was jarring to even see a few pipeline warning poles; envisioning a thirty-six-inch leviathan like Dakota Access was unfathomable. We were standing on the yellow-beige grass looking onto land that rambled and sloped down to what I thought was a road but turned out to be the Little Missouri, flat and still and muddy, unspooling through the valley where the buttes dozed under the sun. The ranch manager had tried to convince them to at least build it west of a power line to avoid more sensitive vegetation. *You don't see the beauty of the badlands?* The men from Texas claimed they could restore the terrain to its natural state, but the ranch manager didn't believe them, and wondered what would happen if a pipeline spilled oil in the waterway.

At the bar, the Pennsylvanian pipeliner sipping a can of Busch was saying they put crews in the badlands early on because they needed longer to hack through the rough terrain. "This pipeline is the biggest thing that happened in a while," the Pennsylvanian said. His friend on the pipeline walked in, still mad that his girlfriend had picked a fight. "I'm like, 'Okay, go find another guy that brings home $3,000 a week.'" The friend studied the bar. "I should get a shot of Crown," he said, pushing his hair back. He was bound for Bemidji, Minnesota, and needed a buzz for the seven-hour drive east.

The pipeline would traverse the most idyllic part of the Hartel family's ranch, acreage that had been untouched as long as they'd owned it. The Hartels couldn't convince Dakota Access to circumvent their land. The company flew in a big man from Texas to negotiate and they reached an agreement after many meetings, slightly changing the route to avoid the fragile, sandy soils and cross over the corn crop. The Hartels tried to raise the price of the easement so high that it would scare off Dakota Access, and were surprised that the company agreed to pay it.

I drove out to the ranch, turning past a pyramid of hay bales adorned with a sign that said, GOD BLESS AMERICA! AGAIN. LeMoine was near his green tractor, wearing a white cowboy hat and a blue and white checkered shirt. The snow had melted since our last meeting, and birds chirped in the June sun. He was preparing to cut the hay. "You've got to go in with the attitude with these pipelines that they're out to cheat and lie and take advantage of you," LeMoine said. "But it's not going too bad." We joined Kyle and drove past the feedlot toward the pipeline. I was startled when it came into view: a great sea-green colossus rolling through the

hills on a dirt clearing, turning ninety degrees to meet another
stretch of pipeline curving down a slope from the opposite direction. It looked extraordinary in these open fields, the industrial
green metal clashing with the green of nature. Our trio sat quietly,
watching where the pipeline vanished in the curves of the grassland. To see the ground torn up like this—LeMoine could scarcely
bear it.

"If you ignore the pipeline, it looks like the land has been here
for thousands of years," Kyle said. He wondered why the state
hadn't helped negotiate a route that avoided more of the pristine
land. This stretch of pipe was supposed to be underground by the
week's end.

Ever the entrepreneurs, Kyle and his brother started a company to reclaim land after pipelines went in the ground. Kyle
couldn't do much until he retired from the federal government, so
his brother was taking the lead: sitting down with ranchers, draft-
ing a custom reseeding plan, and getting the pipeline company to
pay for it. They were investing in drones that would monitor the
land for weed infestations and settling of soil.

We saw all the standard oilfield junk in the distance, tanks and
trailers askew. The Hartels still resented the way outsiders had
abandoned their things for other people to clean up. The community was less trusting, more protective of its interests. But Kyle observed that most of the locals were financially better off from the
oil. It heartened him to see his church overflowing with young
families with children after so many years of struggle and decline.

We drove back near LeMoine's house and stood amid the smell
of soil and livestock that harkened back to his upbringing cleaning the barn and milking cows. He would never tire of this life. A
rancher feeds his cows before he feeds himself, and he checks on
his heifers in the middle of the night, when he'd rather sleep. He
pulls a calf out of an ornery cow and gives the newborn mouth-to-
mouth resuscitation—not because he thinks of the dollars in the
fall but because he thinks, *This is a life*. He believes the land came
from God and that he is the steward, and he expects the generations that come after to carry on his ways.

The wife of Kyle's son would give birth to a daughter in several months. The ranch would bear a sixth generation that would know many years after LeMoine's time whether the grassland above the Dakota Access Pipeline would ever be the same. The company "can't get it back like they think they can," LeMoine predicted. We stood there in the glow of summer's first day, listening to the semis rumbling less than a mile down the road. The rush of wind and tankers and tires beamed over the fields like a song.

Acknowledgments

This project would not have been possible without the support of my editors at the *Minneapolis Star Tribune*, who were exceptionally generous in granting me time off to explore this topic. I want to thank editors at the *Awl* and *Atlantic* for publishing stories I wrote during the oil boom, and my agent, Andrew Stuart, for suggesting that I expand my early reporting into a book. Thanks to Public Affairs for giving me the opportunity to write this book, and the team that helped pull it all together: editor Clive Priddle, assistant editors Jane Robbins Mize and Athena Bryan, production editor Melissa Veronesi, publicist Kristina Fazzalaro, and copy editor Sue Warga.

I had the support of extraordinary friends who visited me out in western North Dakota, especially Erik, who accompanied me on reporting excursions at the Wild Bison truck stop and the 4 Mile Bar and was encouraging even at the most speculative stages of this project. Raad, I can't believe you agreed to drive across North Dakota with me on a madcap adventure and debate South Asian literature at DK's. Mari and Chao came out to see me and go mountain biking in Theodore Roosevelt National Park, arranging a much-needed vacation from nonstop work—our times in the badlands are some of my happiest memories of North Dakota. David was kind enough to host a celebration for me when I needed a trip back to Minneapolis the most. Justin gave me a spare room as I went back and forth and struggled to find housing after returning from the oilfield. Max and Lisa believed in me when nobody else did, read drafts, and provided unconditional support.

Thanks to my North Dakota friends and sources who shared their stories and in some cases risked their careers to speak with me.

My family has been the biggest source of support and encouragement throughout: my parents and my sister, Erika. I am especially indebted to my aunt Lore, who helped me explore my Norwegian roots in Minnesota. The opportunity to learn about my great-grandmother Clara and connect with Omar, Frank, and Lynn was unforgettable, and I often thought of them when I sat at the kitchen tables of the Scandinavian American farmers of North Dakota.

Notes

My reporting on the ground mainly covers the span between two significant months in the world's history of oil: June 2014 to January 2016. I relied on interviews and observations for much of my reporting, but have also made use of the sources outlined below.

Introduction

3   **residents built too many towns:** Elwyn Robinson, "The Themes of North Dakota History," address delivered at University of North Dakota, November 6, 1958.

5   **historian Elwyn Robinson claimed:** Ibid.

I Should Be Dead

11   **Highway 85 was the most dangerous:** "Stats Show Oil Patch Highway Is Most Dangerous in the State," Associated Press, February 23, 2015.

11   **A truck driver started backing up:** David Rupkalvis and Jerry Burnes, "3 Killed, 5 Injured in Series of Rural Crashes," *Williston Herald*, June 8, 2013.

11   **The driver of a Chevy Silverado:** "Twenty-Three-Year-Old Man Dies in Crash on Highway 85 in N.D.," Associated Press, December 2, 2014.

11   **Two teenagers died:** Neal Shipman, "Two Watford City Teens Killed, One Injured in Collision with Semi," *McKenzie County Farmer*, March 13, 2013.

11   **The mayor of Watford City:** Lauren Donovan, "Mayor Wonders When DOT Will Take the Blame for Accidents," *Bismarck Tribune*, March 6, 2013.

11   **A semi hit a Ford truck:** "2 People Killed Western N.D. Crash," Valley News Live, September 14, 2015.

11   **A man from Wisconsin:** "Highway Patrol identifies Wisconsin Man Who Died in 3-Vehicle Crash in N.D. Oil Patch," Associated Press, December 11, 2014.

11   **One icy evening:** "2 Alabama Men Among 3 Killed in North Dakota Wreck," Associated Press, December 18, 2014.

Tales at the Water Depot

16   **it took twenty-three hundred truckloads:** Transaction III: North Dakota's Statewide Strategic Transportation Plan, Department of Transportation.

16   **an average of one to five million gallons:** "Water Consumption in the Bakken," Energy and Environmental Research Center, North Dakota State University, www.undeerc.org/Bakken/Water-Consumption-in -the-Bakken.aspx.

19   **Black and gold balloons:** Description of the celebration was derived from Deborah Sontag, "Where Oil and Politics Mix," *New York Times*, November 23, 2014, and "Oil Industry Says Thanks to N.D., Celebrates Million-Barrel Milestone," *Prairie Business Magazine*, June 26, 2014.

Beyond the Eyes of Roosevelt

20   **They had to close the span:** Lauren Donovan, "Long X Bridge on High- way 85 May Be Replaced," *Bismarck Tribune*, August 3, 2015.

20   **where explorer Meriwether Lewis:** "Lewis and Clark Timeline 1805," National Park Service, www.nps.gov/jeff/learn/historyculture/lewis -and-clark-timeline-1805.htm.

20   **McKenzie County still had only 6,360 people:** Neal Shipman, "Mc- Kenzie County Is Fastest Growing County in Nation," *McKenzie County Farmer*, May 4, 2015.

22   **"Where do we go?":** "Scary: Incredible Up-Close Footage of Massive Tornado in North Dakota," YouTube, posted by Euronews, May 27, 2014, www.youtube.com/watch?v=bSKwC8Zl6wI.

22   **The twister hurt nine people:** Josh Wood, "Rare North Dakota Tornado Hits 120 mph," Associated Press, May 27, 2014.

27   **"There is not a single thing":** video of Governor's Pipeline Summit, June 14, 2012.

27   **busiest areas still trucked:** Amy Dalrymple, "Pipelines in the Bakken: Expansion Critical, but Landowners Grow Weary," Forum News Ser- vice, November 4, 2012.

28   **considered an especially dangerous intersection:** Amy Robinson, "U.S. Highway 85 Is the Deadliest Highway in State," *McKenzie County Farmer*, February 24, 2015.

28   **a pair of twenty-year-olds:** "Williston Man Killed in Two-Vehicle Crash near Alexander in Western N.D.," Forum News Service, December 8, 2014.

28   **The tanks of oil waste:** The description of the explosion was derived from Kathleen J. Bryan in "Lightning Strikes Oilfield Site," *Dickinson Press*, July 8, 2014. Additional information came from interviews with several county officials, including McKenzie County landfill manager Rich Schreiber and a summary report from the state health department.

The Wild Bison

32   **staggered to a nearby bar:** Lauren Donovan, "Homeless in a Dumpster," *Bismarck Tribune*, February 4, 2014.

34   **painted the 13,500-square-foot building:** Kate Ruggles, "Wild Bison Travel Center Opens Near Alexander," *McKenzie County Farmer*, August 25, 2013.

Williston Brewing Company

42   **Connecticut hedge fund forced his ouster:** "Mill Road Offers $27.9 Million for Kona Grill," *Dealbook* blog, *New York Times*, May 19, 2009.

42   **book about Williston's attractions:** Iver Aafedt Marjerison, *The Boomtown Bucket List: 100 Ways to Unlock the Magic of Williston, North Dakota* (CreateSpace Independent Publishing Platform, 2015).

42   **Pipeline camp diets:** Dermot Cole, *Amazing Pipeline Stories: How Building the Trans-Alaska Pipeline Transformed Life in America's Last Frontier* (Fairbanks: Epicenter Press, 1997), 91–97.

45   **historian H. W. Brands:** H. W. Brands, *Age of Gold: The California Gold Rush and the New American Dream* (New York: Anchor Books, 2003), 245.

47   **"Do you have what it takes":** Richard Rubin, "Not Far from Forsaken," *New York Times*, August 9, 2006.

49   **Rents were higher than those in Manhattan:** Jerry Burnes, "Williston Rent Highest in Nation," *Williston Herald*, February 15, 2014.

49   **erected housing at the fastest rate in the country:** "N.D. Tops Census Bureau's List of Fastest Housing Development Rates," *Dickinson Press*, May 22, 2014.

50   **"Marcus Jundt has brought more to Williston":** Jim Powers, letter to the editor, *Williston Herald*, June 6, 2014.

50   **sixty thousand residents by the end of the decade:** Ernest Scheyder, "Sewage Flow Becomes Williston's Oil Bust Indicator," Reuters, August 6, 2015.

50   **timeline was later revised to 2050:** Renée Jean, "Helms Says $125 Billion Invested in Bakken," *Williston Herald*, September 15, 2017.

51   **He also fussed that the city:** Eric Killelea, "Much Ado About a Banner," *Williston Herald*, April 19, 2014.

51   **"Marcus was a little over the top":** Eric Killelea, "Mayor Howard Klug," *Williston Herald*, June 11, 2014.

Great American Scam

The description of the case mainly comes from *SEC v. North Dakota Developments LLC, Robert L. Gavin, and Daniel J. Hogan, et al.*, US District Court in North Dakota, 2015.

54 **The *South China Morning Post*:** Richard Warren, "Hong Kong Investors Buy Hotels to Profit from Oil Boom in U.S. Midwest," *South China Morning Post*, October 2, 2013.

54 **The *Economist* wrote:** "There's Gold in Them There Wells," *Economist*, December 21, 2013.

54 ***Forbes* quoted Hogan:** "Will America's Shale Boomtowns Bust? A Report from the Heart of North Dakota's Fracking Country," *Forbes*, February 22, 2015.

54 **A columnist for London's *Daily Telegraph*:** Ed Cumming, "Fracking Rush Fuels a Property Boom," *Telegraph*, March 18, 2014.

55 **Hogan even gave $500:** Eric Killelea, "Big Dollars Flow into Mayoral Race," *Williston Herald*, May 17, 2014.

55 **CNBC anchor Brian Sullivan:** Brian Sullivan, "How the Oil Plunge Affects One North Dakota Boomtown," video on CNBC.com, December 1, 2014.

57 **Complaints from English investors:** Tony Hetherington, "Property Horizons Offers Full Refund," *Financial Mail on Sunday*, May 24, 2014.

58 **the *Home Journal* reported:** "State of Society of California," *Home Journal*, September 1, 1849.

58 **E. T. Barnette sailed north:** "John Labbe 'Johnny' McGinn," Alaska Mining Hall of Fame, http://alaskamininghalloffame.org/inductees /mcginn_print.php.

59 **A band of vigilantes:** Catherine Holder Spude, *Saloons, Prostitutes, and Temperance in Alaska Territory* (Norman: University of Oklahoma Press, 2015), 29–32, 35.

59 **Alexander McKenzie traveled:** "Alaskan District Judge Noyes Awakens Wrath of Mine-Owners at Nome by Astonishing Acts," *San Francisco Call*, August 31, 1900; "A Tough Frontier Sheriff," *Minot Daily News*, November 1, 2016.

Streetlights

65 **and by 1999:** Leslie Brooks Suzukamo, "Bust to Bounty," *Pioneer Press*, December 8, 2007.

67 **approaching record levels:** "U.S. Oil Drillers Add Rigs for Second Week in a Row: Baker Hughes," Reuters, June 10, 2016.

67 **Whiting planned to accelerate:** Howard Pankratz, "$6B Tie Up of Whiting, Kodiak Creates Bakken Power Play, Companies Say," *Denver Post*, July 14, 2014.

70 **A flare had recently scorched forty-five hundred acres:** Maxine Herr, "Flare Appears to Be Cause of Grassland Fire," *Petroleum News Bakken*, April 19, 2015.

A Fugitive at the Border

75 **up to $100,000 of his medical expenses:** "Prisoner's Medical Bills May Reach $100,000," *Crosby Journal*, December 17, 2014.

75 **eight times saltier than the ocean:** Lisa Song, "'Saltwater' from North Dakota Fracking Spill Is Not What's Found in the Ocean," *InsideClimate News*, July 16, 2014.

77 **fumed that they were tinted orange and hot:** Lauren Donovan, "Potentially Radioactive Material Spilling out of Trailers near Watford City," *Bismarck Tribune*, February 22, 2014.

78 **he pleaded guilty in 1993:** SEC news digests, September 6, 1991, and September 20, 1993.

78 **ripping out the wires of the Taser probes:** Joseph Law, "Man Caught by Deputies After Vehicle and Foot Chase," *Rexburg Standard Journal*, July 2, 2012.

79 **the feds learned he was hiding:** The account of the fugitive's escape was derived from Megan Cassidy, "Natrona County Sheriff's Office Continues Search for Escapee," *Casper Star-Tribune*, September 3, 2013.

79 **Their target:** Joshua Wolfson, "Authorities Search for Prisoner After Escape near Independence Rock," *Casper Star-Tribune*, September 1, 2013.

79 **disheveled and unshaven:** Kyle Roerink, "Wyoming Fugitive Spotted near Rawlins, Wamsutter; Still Loose," *Casper Star-Tribune*, September 11, 2013.

79 **authorities found more:** John D. Taylor, "Filter Socks Found Near Crosby," *Crosby Journal*, April 30, 2014.

80 **He'd accidentally shot somebody:** Jenny Michael, "Glen Ullin Man Faces Felony Charge for Shooting Gun Through Floor," *Bismarck Tribune*, August 13, 2012.

82 **"We've been hosed":** John D. Taylor, "Filter Sock Fine Negotiated Down from $800,000," *Crosby Journal*, reprinted in *Golden Valley News*, December 4, 2014.

The Sheer Emptiness of It

95 **The big to-do in Lignite:** Patrick Springer, "N.D. Water Officials See Results from Crackdown on Illegal Water Sales," Forum News Service, July 6, 2015.

Nobody Lives Here

103 **it took three trucks to deliver the sixty-two tons of machinery:** "County Is Home to the World's Largest Trash Compactor," *McKenzie County Farmer*, September 16, 2015.

Empire of Junk

122 **40 percent of elementary students were homeless:** Amy Robinson, "40 Percent of Watford Elementary Students Considered 'Homeless,'" *McKenzie County Farmer*, October 7, 2014.

Capitalism Is Legal

Description of leasing activity on the reservation was largely derived from the cases of *Ramona Two Shields and Mary Louise Wilson v. the United States of America*, US Court of Federal Claims, February 2013, Washington, D.C., and *Ramona Two Shields, et al. v. Spencer Wilkinson Jr., et al.*, US District Court, North Dakota, November 2012. The following articles also informed my account: Sierra Crane-Murdoch, "The Other Bakken Boom: America's Biggest Oil Rush Brings Tribal Conflict," *High Country News*, April 23, 2012; Abrahm Lustgarten, "Land Grab Cheats North Dakota Tribe out of $1 Billion, Suits Allege," *ProPublica*, February 23, 2013; and Jack Nicas, "Shale-Oil Boom Divides North Dakota Reservation," *Wall Street Journal*, February 28, 2013.

137   **The miners attacked them:** Description of exploitation of Native Americans during the California Gold Rush is mainly credited to Benjamin Madley, *An American Genocide: The United States and the California Indian Catastrophe, 1846–1873* (New Haven: Yale University Press, 2016), Kindle ed., ch. 6, "Rise of the Killing Machine: Militias and Vigilantes, April 1850–December 1854."

A Great Steaming Pile of Money

146   **"during an economic development summit in 2013":** CD of Indigenous Nations Economic Development Summit, New Town, November 20, 2013.

Peyton Place on the Plains

Descriptions of the case were derived from *USA v. Loren Toelle, Stanley Toelle*, US District Court, Idaho, February 2016.

175   **the case enlisted:** press release, "Seven Arrested for Multi-State Drug Trafficking and Money Laundering Ring," US Attorney's Office, District of Idaho, February 5, 2016.

176   **"You seem very intelligent":** Description of sentencing was derived from Thomas Clouse, "Former Las Vegas Stripper Gets over 17 Years for Leading Drug Ring That Ensnared Family and CdA Physician," *Spokesman-Review*, May 2, 2017.

Deal Junkies

Descriptions of the case were derived from *SEC v. Stifel, Nicolaus & Co. Inc. and David W. Noack*, US District Court, Wisconsin, 2011, particularly the admitted facts in the final judgment on December 6, 2016, along with Charles Duhigg and Carter Dougherty, "From Midwest to MTA, Pain from Global Gamble," *New York Times*, November 1, 2008.

180 **A book called *The Looting of America*:** Les Leopold, *The Looting of America: How Wall Street's Game of Fantasy Finance Destroyed Our Jobs, Pensions and Prosperity—and What We Can Do About It* (White River Junction, VT: Chelsea Green Publishing, 2009), Kindle ed., ch. 1, "The Hooking of Whitefish Bay."

Going to War

185 **Former CIA director General David Petraeus:** Eric Killelea, "Wardner: Petraeus Called Oil Patch a 'War Zone,'" *Williston Herald*, September 26, 2014.

185 **Halliburton announced it was hiring eleven thousand:** Drew Sandholm, "Halliburton to Hire 11,000 in 2011," CNBC.com, August 24, 2011.

The Derrick Goes Sideways

189 **Bloomberg News headline said:** Tom Randall, "Oil Warning: The Crash Could Be the Worst in More Than 45 Years," Bloomberg, July 23, 2015.

192 **a war veteran had driven from Tennessee:** James Osborne, "Drop in Oil Prices Leaves Roughnecks at Loose Ends," *Dallas Morning News*, February 17, 2015.

193 **Whiting was preparing to buy Kodiak:** Laura Lorenzetti, "Whiting Becomes Largest Bakken Shale Producer with $6 Billion Kodiak Purchase," *Fortune*, July 14, 2014.

$100 Oil to $1 Beer

206 **Many miners in America's nineteenth-century:** The statement on miners subsisting on beans, sourdough, and pork, as well as details from the Klondike Gold Rush in this paragraph, were derived from Ann Chandonnet, *Gold Rush Grub: From Turpentine Stew to Hoochinoo* (Fairbanks: University of Alaska Press, 2005) 49, 54, 147.

206 **Chinese miners:** Andrew F. Smith, *Eating History: 30 Turning Points in the Making of American Cuisine* (New York: Columbia University Press, 2009), 47.

206 **Patrons savored French cuisine:** "San Francisco's Culinary History: Part 1 of 12," Table Agent, https://tableagent.com/article/san-franciscos-culinary-history-part-1-of-12.

207 **briefly shut down:** Melissa Krause, "Hula Grill Hullabaloo," *Williston Herald*, October 13, 2015.

211 **in the Houston area:** Nicholas Upton, "Cheap Oil Ripples Through the Oil Patch," *Franchise Times*, Spring/Summer 2016.

211 **deal worth about $20 million:** Katherine Feser, "Casa Olé Parent Getting a New Owner," *Houston Chronicle*, March 18, 2014.

212 **the president had attended a fundraiser:** Paul Walsh, "Former Pillsbury Estate to Be Auctioned," *Minneapolis Star Tribune*, October 28, 2009.

Nat Geo's in Town

214 **A New York *Daily News* article:** Dermot Cole, *Amazing Pipeline Stories: How Building the Trans-Alaska Pipeline Transformed Life in America's Last Frontier* (Fairbanks: Epicenter Press, 1997), 25.

218 **Authorities claimed that Gregg:** Pre-sentence investigation identification, Washington Department of Corrections, July 25, 2002.

218 **the *Williston Herald* listed:** Jenna Ebersole, "Number of Sex Offenders on the Rise," *Williston Herald*, October 30, 2012.

223 **New York subway billboards:** Ernest Scheyder, "Snow-Capped Peaks of 'Blood & Oil' Get Panned by North Dakotans," Reuters, September 28, 2015.

Fracking Hell

230 **"Fracking Hell" enraged the residents of Williston:** Elizabeth Hackenberg, "Local Uproar over Nat Geographic's 'Fracking Hell': Bar Regulars Say Depictions of Violence Fabricated," *Williston Herald*, October 17, 2015.

231 **"The Gold Rush was one big O.J. trial":** David Germain, "Mother Lode of Lore Mined by Klondike Centennials," Associated Press, August 3, 1997.

231 **an article ran in the *Pioneer All-Alaska Weekly*:** Dermot Cole, *Amazing Pipeline Stories: How Building the Trans-Alaska Pipeline Transformed Life in America's Last Frontier* (Fairbanks: Epicenter Press, 1997).

231 **The *Williston Herald*'s crime reporter:** Elizabeth Hackenberg, "Was Fracking Hell Fake?," *Williston Herald*, December 11, 2015.

Wasteland

240 **A sampling of public comments:** Public comments received by North Dakota Department of Health, TENORM rule changes, early 2015.

240 **had risen from 185 to 435:** Jeff Bader, North Dakota Geological Survey, presentation at Williston Basin Petroleum Conference, Bismarck, May 25, 2016.

241 **Then a pipeline:** Amy Dalrymple, "Source of Divide County Pipeline Leak Not Detected for Days," Forum News Service, August 11, 2015.

The Perils at Twenty Feet

249 **The first death happened:** Descriptions of worker fatalities and risks were derived from Emily Guerin, "'Senseless Exposures': How Money and Federal Rules Endanger Oilfield Workers," *Inside Energy*, February 29, 2016, and the report "Suspected Inhalation Fatalities Involving Workers During Manual Tank Gauging, Sampling, and Fluid Transfer Operations on Oil and Gas Well Sites, 2010–2014," website of the Centers for Disease Control and Prevention, www.cdc.gov/mmwr/volumes/65/wr/mm6501a2.htm.

250 **OSHA researchers found:** Todd Jordan, director of OSHA health response team, "Hydrocarbon Exposures During Tank Gauging and Sampling Operations," presentation at National Occupational Research Agenda oil and gas sector council meeting, March 19, 2015.

250 **issued a hazard alert:** "Health and Safety Risks for Workers Involved in Manual Tank Gauging and Sampling at Oil and Gas Extraction Sites," NIOHS-OSHA hazard alert, 2016.

251 **"In an era of rising economic challenges":** public comments submitted to Bureau of Land Management on FR Doc #2015-24008.

251 **Remote oil measurement technology:** Guerin, "'Senseless Exposures': How Money and Federal Rules Endanger Oilfield Workers."

251 **the agency moved to *allow* automated systems:** Mike Soraghan, "BLM Overhauls Measurement Rules, OKs Automatic Tank Gauging," *E & E News*, October 17, 2016.

Pipelining Blues

257 **a hearing to restrict the waste of natural gas:** North Dakota Industrial Commission hearing, April 22, 2014.

258 **granted exemptions for more than a hundred oil wells:** "North Dakota Industrial Commission Grants Flaring Exemption," Forum News Service, April 21, 2015.

You Chose Oil over Us

264 **former North Dakota executive settled:** Press release, "SEC Charges Sales Executive in North Dakota for Enabling Financial Fraud," February 6, 2015.

270 **a blog post on the liberal *Daily Kos* website:** Sharon Wilson, "Fracking Earthquakes and Industry's Deadbeat Dad Problem," *Daily Kos*, December 28, 2013.

271 **flush with contributions from oil companies:** Ernest Scheyder, "Race for North Dakota's Agriculture Commissioner Is All About Oil," Reuters, July 22, 2014.

271 **but the pioneer claimed prospecting for gold:** Richard Dillon, *Fool's Gold: The Decline and Fall of Captain John Sutter of California* (Sanger, CA: Write Thought, 1967), Kindle ed., ch. 19, "The Patriarch."

Exodus

272 **one of the principals, John Sessions:** Renée Jean, "Williston Housing Development to Open in Style," *Williston Herald*, May 28, 2015.

278 **Mark Twain wrote of the California Gold Rush:** Mark Twain, *Roughing It* (Hartford, CT: American Publishing Company, 1872), ch. 57.

280 **"We're housing one percent":** Jessica Holdman, "Companies Make Temporary Housing a Permanent Business," *Bismarck Tribune*, August 11, 2012.

284 **Target Logistics Sued:** *Target Logistics Management LLC and Lodging Solutions–Williston LLC v. City of Williston*, US District Court, North Dakota, April 2016.

284 **researchers at North Dakota State University:** Nancy Hodur and Dean Bangsund, "Assessment of the Oil and Gas Industry Workforce," North Dakota State University, May 2016.

Bile of the Subterranean

The description of the pipeline breach, beyond the recollection of Joanne Njos, was mainly derived from *North Dakota Industrial Commission v. Summit/Meadowlark*, June 2015; North Dakota Department of Health's lengthy "Oil Field Environmental Incident Summary"; press releases issued by Summit about its cleanup methods; and an interview with the health department's water quality director, Kurt Rockeman.

287 **used a surfing metaphor:** Bill Loveless, "Dude! Oil Industry in 'Hang 10' Mode on Low Oil Prices," *USA Today*, September 21, 2016.

290 **The company had installed:** Amy Dalrymple, "Pipeline Company Didn't Use Remote Sensors Before Leak," Forum News Service, March 1, 2015.

290 **Struggling with a shortage:** Amy Dalrymple, "No State Inspection During Installation of N.D. Pipeline That Spilled 3 Million Gallons of Saltwater," Forum News Service, January 27, 2015.

291 **Lawmakers approved:** Zahra Hirji, "Lawmakers Move to Regulate Pipelines, After a Record Spill in a Drilling Boom," *InsideClimate News*, March 11, 2015.

291 **The university's study:** "Liquids Gathering Pipelines: A Comprehensive Analysis," Energy and Environmental Research Center, North Dakota State University, December 2015.

292 **proposed fining Summit $2.4 million:** James MacPherson, "State Waffling on Fine for Blacktail Creek," Associated Press, December 15, 2015.

293 **7,584 gallons of brine:** Amy Dalrymple, "Year After N.D.'s Worst Pipeline Spill, Same System Leaks Again," Forum News Service, January 8, 2016.

Frigid Despair

296 **a man hit a woman:** "Man Guilty on All Counts in Beating, Assault," *Williston Herald*, March 31, 2017.

298 **They'd come to arrest a man:** Elizabeth Hackenberg, "Man Arrested in Bomb Scare Appears in Court, Bond Set at $30,000," *Williston Herald*, December 10, 2015.

Xavier Dussaq

MAYA RAO is a staff writer in the Washington, DC, bureau of the *Minneapolis Star Tribune*, and her work has appeared in *The Atlantic, Awl, Philadelphia Inquirer, Longreads,* and more.

PublicAffairs is a publishing house founded in 1997. It is a tribute to the standards, values, and flair of three persons who have served as mentors to countless reporters, writers, editors, and book people of all kinds, including me.

I. F. Stone, proprietor of *I. F. Stone's Weekly*, combined a commitment to the First Amendment with entrepreneurial zeal and reporting skill and became one of the great independent journalists in American history. At the age of eighty, Izzy published *The Trial of Socrates*, which was a national bestseller. He wrote the book after he taught himself ancient Greek.

Benjamin C. Bradlee was for nearly thirty years the charismatic editorial leader of *The Washington Post*. It was Ben who gave the *Post* the range and courage to pursue such historic issues as Watergate. He supported his reporters with a tenacity that made them fearless and it is no accident that so many became authors of influential, best-selling books.

Robert L. Bernstein, the chief executive of Random House for more than a quarter century, guided one of the nation's premier publishing houses. Bob was personally responsible for many books of political dissent and argument that challenged tyranny around the globe. He is also the founder and longtime chair of Human Rights Watch, one of the most respected human rights organizations in the world.

· · ·

For fifty years, the banner of Public Affairs Press was carried by its owner Morris B. Schnapper, who published Gandhi, Nasser, Toynbee, Truman, and about 1,500 other authors. In 1983, Schnapper was described by *The Washington Post* as "a redoubtable gadfly." His legacy will endure in the books to come.

Peter Osnos, *Founder*